D1789319

GLOBAL SECURITY WATCH

THE MAGHREB

GLOBAL SECURITY WATCH

THE MAGHREB

Algeria, Libya, Morocco, and Tunisia

Yahia H. Zoubir and Louisa Dris-Aït-Hamadouche

 PRAEGER

AN IMPRINT OF ABC-CLIO, LLC
Santa Barbara, California • Denver, Colorado • Oxford, England

Library of Congress Cataloging-in-Publication Data

Zoubir, Yahia H.
    Global security watch—the Maghreb : Algeria, Libya, Morocco, and Tunisia/Yahia H.
Zoubir and Louisa Dris-Aït-Hamadouche.
        pages cm. — (Global security watch)
    Includes index.
    ISBN 978-0-313-39377-8 (hardcopy : alk. paper) — ISBN 978-0-313-39378-5 (ebook)
1. Africa, North—Strategic aspects.   2. Africa, North—Foreign relations.   3. Africa,
North—Politics and government—21st century.   4. Security, International—Africa,
North.   I. Dris-Aït-Hamadouche, Louisa, author.   II. Title.   III. Title: Maghreb.
    DT205.Z68 2013
    355'.033061—dc23   2012049191

ISBN: 978-0-313-39377-8
EISBN: 978-0-313-39378-5

17   16   15   14   13   1   2   3   4   5

This book is also available on the World Wide Web as an eBook.
Visit www.abc-clio.com for details.

Praeger
An Imprint of ABC-CLIO, LLC

ABC-CLIO, LLC
130 Cremona Drive, P.O. Box 1911
Santa Barbara, California 93116-1911

This book is printed on acid-free paper ∞

Manufactured in the United States of America

To the memory of my mother who is always present in my heart; to my father who has provided indefectible support and encouragement; to Cherif, the love of my life, for his unwavering support and to my two angels, Hani and Chahine.

—LDAH

To the memory of my mother (1933–1978); to my wife Cynthia and my children, Nadia, Jamel, and Malek, whose love and support have helped me endure the long working hours. With sincere thanks to my son-in-law, Sam Herring for his help with the editing of some of the chapters. To my youngest sister Dalila, who deserves a much better life.

—YHZ

Contents

Acknowledgments

Yahia Zoubir would like to thank Alicia Merritt, Acquisitions Editor, Reference with whom he had worked in the early 1990s on a book on Western Sahara for Praeger, for suggesting the writing of this book. He would also like to thank the officials who were willing to share information with him on some aspects of security in the Maghreb. The authors would like to thank Steve Catalano, Senior Editor, Military History and Security Issues Praeger Publishers ABC-CLIO for his constructive input. They would also like to thank Sasikala Rajesh, Project Manager, for the editorial talents she contributed to improve the quality of the manuscript.

Introduction

The question of security in the Maghreb region is no easy task because of the difficulty in obtaining information from security officials in the region who are always suspicious about discussing what they believe is sensitive information. This is probably the explanation as to why there has never been any work devoted to this subject in any language. Some scholars, such as Anthony Cordesman, have approached the subject from the military balance prevailing in the region. They have offered statistics on the armed forces and the equipment they have acquired from different sources. The websites of the different ministries of defense in those countries offer some indications as to the weaponry in the possession but have no publication on the security doctrines, at least not in any comprehensive perspective. There is little on the overall considerations regarding the Maghreb perceptions of security and the factors that the policy makers believe to be of the highest importance to their national defense. There are no public "White Papers" or "Security Strategy" publications. The few interviews we have conducted with officials give us a limited glimpse of only the security doctrines; we can only infer from public statements. There are also no reliable sources as to how security decisions are made or who makes them even if there is some indication as to who is in charge of security matters. Some well-informed journalists have reported on how some specific security issues are viewed by security officials; we have exploited some of them in the chapters in this book. We have done the same with well-researched academic articles, which we have cited whenever appropriate.

In this book, we have sought to look at security from its different angles which include, inter alia, human security, and those critical issues and threats that have affected the stability of the incumbent regimes. The uprisings, which have erupted cyclically, especially since 2010, inform on the strengths and the weaknesses of security in the Maghreb region, which today have intensified the threats, perceived or real, confronted by the regimes. As will appear in this work, the Maghreb regimes have faced a security dilemma, which has resulted in recent years in an arms race that has been conducted to the detriment of socioeconomic development whose failure is in fact at the root of many of the problems threatening the security and stability of the incumbent regimes, as well as the sovereignty of the states in the area. The region has also suffered from a lack of collective security; because of the suspicions prevalent among the neighbors, the establishment of a Maghreb security has been impossible to materialize. Those suspicions have also thwarted the construction of an integrated Maghreb, which could potentially promote growth and prosperity. Indeed, in spite of the rhetoric regarding the necessity of creating a united Maghreb, the states that make it up have failed to implement the project laid out in the Arab Maghreb Union (UMA) founded in February 1989. The UMA has been dormant since 1994 because the regimes have failed to resolve the question of Western Sahara, the former Spanish colony. Relations between Algeria and Morocco have been strained due to their contrasting positions and interests vis-à-vis this protracted conflict. Although external and geopolitical factors account for this lack of resolution of the conflict, the policy makers have been entrenched in their respective positions without succeeding in enunciating a formula that would allow for a resolution that would overcome the ideological and political postures that surround this conflict. The dispute is not the only factor impeding the erection of a united Maghreb; however, it remains a major obstacle because it is one of the primary reasons for the arms race between Algeria and Morocco. The lack of trust has prevented the brotherly neighbors from looking beyond narrow national interests and moving toward an economic integration that would certainly benefit their regional and domestic development. Their zero-sum game vision with respect to security has hindered the prospect for greater cooperation, let alone, a security community; as shall be seen, though cooperation exists in some functional areas, it remains quite limited and always full of suspicions. There is consensus among Maghreb specialists that regional integration would bring economic benefits to all the countries; yet, the Maghreb states are reluctant to abandon old schemes and raise the region to higher levels of development that would help them reduce their dependency on outside actors, such as the European Union. Rather than face external powers with a common strategy, they have sought to negotiate individually with more powerful actors without altering their dependent relations.

The chapters in this book will seek to elucidate some of the problems that have hindered the construction of a united Maghreb and the development of collective security. We have divided the book into seven chapters.

We have invited Cherif Dris to write the first chapter to provide a historical analysis of the evolution of the Maghreb states and the way in which they have conceived their security within the framework of the postcolonial state-building. The chapter deals with civilian-military relations in each of the Maghreb states. Although the UMA is made up of five members, we have focused on four states and have included Mauritania only in Chapter Six, which pertains to the security in the Sahel. This is justified by the specificities of that country and also because Mauritania is affected more directly by developments in the Sahel and the security agreement it has entered with Algeria than with a similar process of state-building. Chapter One traces the different trajectories, which the Maghreb elites have set in place in the construction of the postcolonial state in which the security/military apparatus has played a considerable role. In spite of their differences, the Maghreb elites have equated the security of the state with the security of the authoritarian regime. The security doctrines of each state inform on the structural violence of the Maghreb authoritarian states. The chapter also analyzes the emergence of terrorism and other threats and how they have impacted the Maghreb states' defense doctrines.

Chapter Two focuses on the way the Maghreb regimes have managed the structural violence inherent to the process of state-building as it has been conceived. The incumbent regimes have responded differently to the cyclical riots that have threatened their power and upset the social contract between society and the state that they have established after independence. The chapter reviews the various domestic threats, including terrorism and radical Islamism, which have shaken the sociopolitical postcolonial consensus. We provide an enumeration of the terrorist attacks in order to shed light on the severity of societal grievances against the incumbent regimes and how the latter have addressed them.

Chapter Three focuses on human security and the concomitant deficiencies in the processes of economic development, which have resulted in violence against the regimes in place. The chapter highlights some of the major shortcomings that have undermined the solidity of the states, namely, corruption, violations of human rights, environmental challenges, and bad governance. The incumbent regimes have introduced reforms, but they have been insufficient to address the fundamental needs of society at large. In fact, these insufficiencies account for the uprisings that have undermined the durability of the authoritarian states. Maghreb societies have endured authoritarianism without consequential development, which would have fortified the social contract between the rulers and the ruled. In other words, societies are no longer content with "development first, democracy later," especially because neither genuine development nor democracy has materialized.

Chapter Four focuses on intra-Maghreb relations, unraveling the root causes of the rivalries that have opposed the Maghreb states and strained their relations. The self-perceptions and perceptions of the neighbors have poisoned bilateral relations between Algeria and Morocco, Algeria and Libya, Libya and Tunisia, and Libya and Morocco. Border disputes have been a major bone of contention that the states have had to resolve through negotiation or through armed conflict as was the case between Algeria and Morocco in 1963. The conflict in Western Sahara resulted in a devastating war (1976–1991) between Algerian-backed

Sahrawis and Moroccan forces and has exacerbated tensions between Algeria and Morocco to this day. The chapter also looks at the Maghreb alignments with and dependence on external powers. It will also analyze the Maghreb states' reactions to the civil war in Libya and the absence of a common response.

Chapter Five analyzes the conflict in Western Sahara and the repercussions that the dispute between Sahrawis and Moroccans has had on Algerian-Moroccan relations. Although the dispute is between Sahrawis and Moroccans, the chapter focuses on the divergent positions between Algeria, which supports the Sahrawi cause, and Morocco, which claims the territory as its own, no matter the nonrecognition of its sovereignty over it by the international community. The struggle for hegemony between Algeria and Morocco and their competing interests is analyzed from a historical perspective, which sheds light on the causes of their hostility toward each other, their claim to brotherhood notwithstanding. The chapter also provides a review of the measures, such as the construction of the walls, to secure the occupation of the disputed territory. It will also highlight the exploitation of the territory's rich resources to increase Morocco's assets. An evaluation of the arms race between Algeria and Morocco is undertaken in this chapter to underline the adverse consequences of the conflict on the bilateral relations between Algeria and Morocco.

Chapter Six provides a comprehensive analysis of the security in the Sahara-Sahel region and the national approaches to the old and new threats they have faced in recent years, namely, terrorism, drug trafficking, and illegal migration, among others. We analyze the antiterrorist legislations enacted not only by the Maghreb states but also by the Sahel states, which share the same concerns. Not only have the Sahara-Sahel countries adopted new legislations, but they have also undertaken a variety of approaches, such as economic diplomacy (Morocco toward the Sahel states) and collective security (Algeria with the Sahel states). The chapter also provides a perspective on recent developments, including the Tuareg question, which has destabilized northern Mali, as well as the alliance between Tuareg factions and terrorist groups. The situation in northern Mali, which has been exacerbated by the civil war in Libya, coupled with other threats, has affected not only the security of the entire Sahel-Sahara region, but it is now also perceived rightly or wrongly as a real threat by outside powers, such as the United States and the European Union. The chapter reviews the various security arrangements that the states have taken collectively to face the new threats.

The final chapter informs on the roles of external powers regarding Maghreb security. It highlights the geopolitical dimension of the Maghreb in international relations and the security-military ties between the Maghreb states and outside powers. The chapter provides an in-depth analysis of U.S. security–military relations with each of the Maghreb states. It then focuses on the European Union's perceived threats emanating from the Maghreb and how it has addressed them. Although China is not a big player in the Maghreb, it, too, has seen its interests affected by security issues in the Maghreb and thus pays greater attention to developments there, most notably since the fall of the Qaddafi regime. Russia's role in the region as an arms supplier is far from negligible; thus, it is reviewed thoroughly in the chapter. In fact, the chapter provides a comprehensive examination of the arms sales by outside powers and how this has found fertile grounds in the Maghreb due to the regional arms race.

In our conclusion, we provide a brief perspective on Maghreb security and propose a few scenarios as to the future of security in the Maghreb and whether it can be achieved without an integrated market.

PART I

Internal Security

CHAPTER 1

Historical and Current Overview of the Security Issue in the Maghreb

Cherif Dris

The main objective of this chapter is to provide a general overview of the security equation in the Maghreb region. Many aspects of the security doctrines in this geopolitical area could not be explained if the historical background, especially in the realm of civilian-military relations, were not taken into account.

SECURITY AT THE HEART OF NORTH AFRICAN STATE-BUILDING: THE WEIGHT OF DECOLONIZATION

After 23 years of autocratic rule, Tunisians overthrew President Zine al Abidine Ben Ali resulting in the collapse of one of the most repressive regimes in the Arab world. A month later, Egyptian President Hosni Mubarak faced the same fate; no one had been able to foresee the scale and capacity to which the Egyptian masses were able to mobilize. In Libya, during October 2011, after six months of fierce rebellion, backed by NATO, which provided military air support to the opposition rebels, Muammar Qaddafi was assassinated ending 42 years of personal rule.

At the onset, it is important to put into perspective the theory that emphasized the resilience of authoritarian regimes and the one that focused on the weakness of the Maghrebi states. Since their respective independences, the Maghrebi regimes have faced crises and tensions that emboldened their rule and strengthened their authoritarian resilience. The ruling elites in the Maghreb have been quite astute and successful in regenerating the authoritarian model of government[1] through a multitude of processes and patterns: redistribution of the oil rent, formal organization of elections (electoral authoritarianism), and the appointment to governmental positions of some opposition figures.[2] The Algerian experience following the events of October 1988 shed light on the capacity of an authoritarian regime to resist changes and develop mechanisms that allowed it to survive despite the projections of some analysts who predicted the fall of the regime. The ruling elites conceded some opening up of policies by legalizing opposition parties and allowing the creation of new ones. However, all of these measures were meant to perpetuate the status quo. The outbreak of terrorism in the early 1990s aided the reinforcement of the authoritarian nature of the Algerian regime notwithstanding the fact that terrorist violence redoubled in ferocity leading some to foretell the advent of a fundamentalist state in Algeria.[3] The question was not whether the regime was about to fall but how soon it would.

While Algeria was struggling against terrorist groups, the much-feared spillover effect on other Maghreb countries did not occur. Many reasons explain why the geographic scope of the terrorist threat was limited to the Algerian territory. In order to understand this, two countries deserve our attention. First, Algeria's neighbors managed the Islamist phenomenon by pursuing a more repressive strategy as was the case in Tunisia and Libya. While Algerian authorities displayed great flexibility by allowing the existence of Islamist parties, Tunisian and Libyan authorities were unyielding on this issue. Libya did not allow the existence of any party, let alone an Islamist party, whereas Tunisia was steadfast in its opposition to Islamist parties. Second, another way to thwart the Islamist threat was to dilute the religious referent and use it as one of the main components of political legitimacy or political identity; the Moroccan monarchy opted for this strategy, which was instrumental in neutralizing the Islamists.[4] The ability of the Maghrebi governments to resist crises and revolts gave some credit to the thesis of the non-applicability of democratic transitions in the Arab sociopolitical contexts. However, the political and social uprisings in Tunisia, Egypt, and Libya and the social unrest that broke out in Algeria and Morocco debunk this thesis.[5] Implicitly, those ongoing changes call into question the relevance of the theory of resilience of the Maghreb states. Are Maghrebi regimes still resilient to change? Before answering this question, it is important to reassess the role of history, that is, the role of decolonization in the building process of the Maghrebi states.

Different Trajectories, a Common Objective: Strong Regimes

No one can dispute the weight of history in the state-building process, particularly in the Third World context to which the Maghreb countries are no exception. However, the weight of decolonization in the formation of the Maghrebi states cannot be overestimated. The following cases need to be analyzed.

The first case concerns Tunisia and Morocco, which experienced a different type of colonization from that of Algeria. The two were designed as French protectorates, a legal and political status that gave Tunisians and Moroccans some political and social rights. In contrast, Algeria was a French colony in the fullest meaning of the term; in fact, Algeria became a French department like any other in France. The difference in status accounts for the difference of trajectories that the Maghreb countries have pursued. Moroccans and Tunisians were granted independence without armed struggle, whereas Algerians waged a brutal war of independence.[6] The Libyan case has some similarities with those of Tunisia and Morocco, but it is closer to Algeria since Libyans waged an armed struggle under the leadership of Omar Al Mokhtar against the Italian occupation.

However, beyond this difference, the trajectories of these countries share a common denominator: the exaltation of violence as a key element of political practice. The elites who took the reins of power after independence were mostly in favor of a model of a centralized and unified state. The fear that their country might sink into a new form of violence and division was justified in the eyes of the elites of the establishment, fearing an authoritarian state in which only one party would be allowed to operate in the political arena. Yet, the ruling elites in Maghrebi countries relied either upon the armed forces or different security apparatuses, in order to tighten control over their societies. As shall be seen, the Tunisian and Libyan regimes were intent on setting up security systems that guaranteed total penetration of society. Thus, the state that emerged out of the decolonization process can be designated under the category of a "security state," especially in Tunisia and Libya, since the police and the militia seized power; however, in Algeria, the Armed Forces, who played a key role in the war for independence, became politicized and thus played an important role in politics.[7]

Regardless, it would be misleading to contend that there exists some uniformity concerning the shape of the Maghrebi states. Although in Algeria the army has been considered a pillar of the regime[8]—it still remains but not as a *primus inter pares*— in Tunisia, Morocco, and Libya, the system is quite different. The ruling elites in these three countries share as a common denominator a fear of the armed forces and the possibility that they might seize control of the political process. They deliberately marginalized the military while giving more importance to other security apparatuses, namely, the intelligence services, the police, and the Kata'ib (brigades) as was the case in Libya under Qaddafi's rule. Tunisia and Libya deserve closer scrutiny. On assuming office, after he orchestrated a medical coup d'état against President Habib Bourguiba, General Zine Al Abidine Ben Ali gradually marginalized the army because he was convinced that the stronger the military institution remained the greater were its chances of threatening his regime. His strategy was based on the premise that the police must constitute the core of the Tunisian security system. In so doing, Ben Ali was assured of the loyalty of the security apparatus that had gained more power than the army.

In Libya, Colonel Qaddafi was wary of any role that may give the armed forces any leverage enabling them to threaten the survival of the regime. Like

Ben Ali, Qaddafi did not trust the military and relied instead on the Kata'ib (brigades where members are recruited from inside the tribes that pledged allegiance to Qaddafi) despite the fact that the overthrow of King Sanussi in 1969 was made possible due to the actions of the military. The Libyan case is the perfect illustration of the prevalence of the traditional culture in which the sense of loyalty to the state was absent and in which the fundamental political practices rested upon a certain vision of the tribe as the key unit to which allegiance was owed. The Jamahiriya was a collection of tribes in which Qaddafi's tribe, al-Qaddadfah, sat at the center of the decision-making process, playing a mediating role among the other tribes.[9] Accordingly, the role of the Libyan army in the security apparatus was marginal compared to other security agencies and structures like the Kata'ib. The revolt of February 2011 had demonstrated clearly the weakness of the security apparatus set up by the Qaddafi regime. While the Kata'ib, which had among their midst some mercenaries recruited from neighboring African countries, were vested with the mission to contain the rebellion, the regular army refused to take part in this mission and decided instead to join the opposition. If anything, the defection of the regular army shed light on the limits of the security state as conceived by Qaddafi. A similar scenario occurred during the revolt when the military refused to execute President Ben Ali's order to disperse the protesters by force.

The scene in Algeria was quite different. As a former French colony, the weight of decolonization in the state-building process was considerable. This could already be seen in the pre-independence founding texts of the Algerian state, namely, the August 1956 Charter of the Soummam. In this document, the leaders of the national liberation movement emphasized the necessity of building a strong democratic state based on some Islamic principles. However, the June 1962 Charter of Tripoli envisioned an independent Algeria ruled by a single party, the National Liberation Front (FLN), whose economic program would be based on socialism. This charter, which has not been accepted by all the political elites, has been imposed by a small group who were aware of the necessity of building a strong state endowed with heavy security structures on which the regime can rely to exert full control over society. The military coup of 1965 was a turning point in the history of the new state; it marked the birth of a regime whose backbone would be the military, which exerted control over all aspects of political, economic, and social life. The Military Security, in particular, was endowed with a political role that enjoyed a quasi-autonomous role within the military institution.[10] Since then, the military and the security apparatus imposed a political order in which participation to the political process has rested on co-optation and political patronage. Although the political process was closed, the ruling elites imposed a system of political recruitment centered on patronage, nepotism, and regionalism.[11] The situation did not change with the coming to power of Colonel Chadli Bendjedid in 1979. While many expected the designation of either Mohamed Salah Yahiaoui or Abdelaziz Bouteflika, the army opted for the highest ranked and most experienced among them, that is, Bendjedid. Less charismatic than his predecessor, Bendjedid understood nonetheless that his room for maneuver should be enlarged so that he would be able to reshape the decision-making process through the strengthening of the role of the Sécurité Militaire (intelligence services). He also sought new alliances with the commanders of some military regions so that he could counterbalance the power of the eastern region. However, unlike Boumediene, Bendjedid was unable to exert full control over the military and the intelligence services. Nor were those who eventually succeeded him, especially in the aftermath of the armed Islamist uprising. The security situation since the 1990s has given the military and the security services the role of violence managers, and the opportunity to tighten control over the decision-making process, thus reinforcing the authoritarian character of the regime. With the accession of Abdelaziz Bouteflika to power in 1999, the situation has not changed significantly despite the fact that Bouteflika succeeded in marginalizing the role of the military through greater reliance on the intelligence services. In other words, Bouteflika succeeded in reshaping the structure of the decision-making process by marginalizing some traditional clients without changing the true nature of the regime.[12]

These cases shed light on the characteristics of the Maghreb regimes as a political construction where the weight of colonization weighs heavily. More importantly, Maghrebi political regimes mirror a social reality in which traditional culture, tribalism, and regionalism persist. Hence, it would be difficult to analyze authoritarianism in those countries without taking into account those factors. Any analysis that tries to project Western models in studying the realities of the Maghreb would indeed be deficient.

In analyzing the emergence of authoritarianism in the Maghreb and the persistence of the ruling elites to blend national security with the security of the regime, greater emphasis should be put on civilian-military relations: how the military elites manage their relations with the political elites and how they perceive their role in the state-building process. Furthermore, the management of public affairs merits reflection in this chapter.

THE MILITARY AND NATIONAL SECURITY: CIVILIAN-MILITARY RELATIONS IN THE CONTEMPORARY MAGHREB

Are the overwhelming roles of the armed forces and the different security agencies in the public affairs of the Maghreb nations the inevitable corollary of the security state that emerged in postindependence? The works that addressed this issue have all highlighted the role of the army and its influence over the security policies of the Maghreb countries. With the exception of Morocco, where the king exerts great influence over the military (barring the failed military coups of General Oufkir in 1972, Medbouh in 1978, and Colonel Dlimi in 1983), the configurations of civilian-military relations in the Maghreb region are not symmetrical.

In this section we will examine the civilian-military schemes in four Maghrebi countries.

Algeria: The Military as Custodian of the State

In Algeria the military's role in defining security policy is far from negligible. Since gaining independence in 1962, the defense and security policy has always been an exclusive prerogative of the military institution. Could there have been any other outcome in a country where the ruling elites were mainly constituted of officers of the National Army of Liberation (ALN), which later became the National People's Army (ANP)? The control that the ANP exerts over the security apparatus should be analyzed against a background of a process initiated during the war of liberation.[13] At that time, there were two contending visions over what form the independent Algerian state should take. This first vision, put together by Abane Ramdane and Hocine Aït Ahmed, insisted on the subordination of the military to civilian control. The Soummam Platform of 1956 highlighted this principle. The second vision rejected this proposal, arguing that the struggle for independence should not impose the supremacy of politics as long as the military struggle is closely linked to political resistance. Both as military officers and political leaders, Abdelhafid Boussouf, Krim Belkacem, Lakhdar Ben Tobal, and Houari Boumediene rejected the vision of Aït Ahmed and Abane. It is no exaggeration to posit that during the seven years of military struggle against French colonial forces, personal conflict and leadership rivalry were among the key factors that structured the actions of the Algerian national movement. In fact, beyond the rivalry of leadership, there were at that time two visions about the future of the Algerian independent state. In the aftermath of independence, the second option prevailed; the army of the frontiers (i.e., ALN, whose troops were based in Morocco and Tunisia), led by Colonel Houari Boumediene, imposed a major political change through a coup against the Provisional Government of the Algerian Republic (GPRA), proclaimed in September 1958, paving the way for Ahmed Ben Bella to become the first president of the newly independent state.[14] In 1965, however, Boumediene deposed President Ben Bella after a military coup. This political order in which the military plays a preponderant role has remained in place since 1962. Indeed, under Boumediene's rule, more than half the members of the Council of the Revolution served in the ALN. Colonel Boumediene had merely executed the conception developed by the Oujda Clan and the founders of the MALG (the predecessor of the Algerian intelligence services) who firmly believed that the military must have supremacy over politics, thus marginalizing the FLN.[15]

Boumediene's successor, Colonel Chadli Bendedid, was no exception to this pattern. As a high-ranking military officer, Bendjedid was cognizant of the fact that he should reinforce presidential powers while ensuring the cohesion within the military. However, at the same time, he was more anxious to reduce the influence of the intelligence services over the decision-making process than restructuring the military institution. In 1987, not only did he decide to reorganize and restructure the Algerian military, but also to break down the intelligence services into different departments; this was the pillar of his strategy. The rationale for this strategy was to reduce the weight of the military security in the management of public affairs. This strategy failed in October 1988 and compelled him to initiate political and economic reforms. In January 1992, the High Security Council, made up of senior military officers and civilians, made the decision to interrupt the electoral process after the sweeping victory of the Islamic Salvation Front (FIS) in the first round of the legislative elections held in December 1991. The military hierarchy also forced President Bendjedid to resign. This resulted in the succession of events followed by a cycle of violence and political instability that caused the death of more than 120,000 people.[16]

The consequence of the interruption of the electoral process and the upsurge of violence resulted in the restructuration of civilian-military relations. The military and the security services gained the upper hand in deciding the direction and the strategy regarding the management of the political crisis. The formation of the High Council of State following the assassination of President Mohamed Boudiaf is a clear confirmation of the shift that occurred in the Algerian civilian-military equation. More importantly, the introduction of emergency law in February 1992 gave the military a supremacy over the other structures of government, namely, the parliament and the judiciary. In addition to exerting tight control over the management of the counterterrorism strategy, the military establishment, represented by the regular armed forces and the intelligence ervices, played an instrumental role in shaping the political landscape following the appointment of retired general Liamine Zeroual as president of state in October 1994 (elected president in November 1995). In the 1990s the balance of power inside the military establishment tilted in favor of the chairman of the chiefs-of-staff, Lieutenant-General Mohamed Lamari,[17] who took the leadership of the counterterrorism strategy—a role that had been held hitherto by the intelligence services. The rise of Mohammed Lamari to the highest rank within the military establishment represented a qualitative evolution in terms of the balance of power inside the regime, as he became, until his resignation in 2004, one of the most influential decision makers—a role that enabled him to impose a particular vision regarding the management of public affairs.

Beyond this qualitative shift, one should never lose sight of the fact that the military has always preserved an *esprit de corps* regardless of the disagreements that have divided the key leaders. Furthermore, the military institution in

Algeria holds power but has always preferred to give civilians the responsibility of managing public affairs.[18]

The coming to power of Abdelaziz Bouteflika in April 1999 did not induce any major transformation in the civilian-military relations order, in place since 1962. Like his predecessors, Bouteflika was appointed by the military hierarchy and then elected as a result of universal suffrage, after the withdrawal of the six other contenders for the presidency. Bouteflika, the foreign minister from 1963 to 1978, had sought to lessen the weight of the army in politics because he was convinced that as long as he remained indebted to the military for his election he would be unable to impose his own style of management of public affairs. Thus, he strove to transform the presidential institution into the pillar of the decision-making process and protect presidential power from contending influences.

Bouteflika's obsession to gain independence from those who helped him come to power led him to pursue a strategy aimed at marginalizing the most influential officers in the military hierarchy, namely, General-Major Mohamed Lamari. His reelection in 2004 widened his room for maneuver. One of the tangible indications was his successful introduction of amendments to the constitution in November 2008—the most consequential being the revision that allowed him to run for a third mandate (the 1996 constitution limited presidential mandates to two terms). Has he succeeded, where his predecessors failed, in exerting total control over the armed forces and the other security agencies?

Some analysts purport that Bouteflika would have never been reelected in 2004 and 2009 without the support of intelligence services.[19] Bouteflika's strategy of minimizing the influence of the military institution compelled him to rely on the intelligence services. However, reducing the influence of the military does not translate into total emancipation from the intelligence services. The alliance forged between the secret services and the presidential clan has certainly helped to restructure the configuration of the balance of power inside the Algerian regime favoring the presidential institution and minimizing the influence of the army. Yet, the shift in the relations of power has not translated into a civilianization of the regime. However, one can raise the question as to whether the Arab revolts may prompt the long-hoped-for civilianization of the regime.

Morocco: The King as Commander of the Faithful and Supreme Commander of the Armed Forces

Morocco's case is unique in many ways, at least in the Maghreb, because the military has not ever played a major role in the political system. The reason lies primarily in the monarchical nature of the regime that has always been suspicious of the armed forces. However, this minimal role also derives from the historical process that led Morocco to independence. Unlike Algeria, Morocco obtained its independence without waging a war of liberation against the French. Morocco had a different status as a protectorate of France; it was thus not a colony in the full sense of the word. Moroccans did not have to resort to war to obtain their country's independence and build a state. Therefore, gaining independence without waging a war deprived the military from drawing any legitimacy that could be used to justify interference in the political debate. In Algeria, the military was able to shape the political landscape, whereas in Morocco the monarchy closely assumed this mission. Since Morocco is an absolute monarchy, the king has not only reigned, but he has also governed the kingdom. Thus, the armed forces fell under his authority. As supreme commander of the Royal Armed Forces (RAF), the king is responsible for the defense and security policies with the armed forces playing a mere supporting role. For instance, when the monarchy decided to include the annexation of the territory of Western Sahara in the national security agenda, the armed forces did not challenge this decision as long as this annexation allowed Morocco to confirm its regional leadership in North Africa.

The monarchy has since the early years of independence charted the course that the Royal Armed Forces should take: preserving the independence and territorial integrity of Morocco, the traditional objectives of a newly independent state, which considered the borders drawn by the former colonial power, France, as contrary to Morocco's interests. Indeed, while the Organization of African Unity maintained the inviolability of the borders inherited from the colonial era, the Moroccan monarchy claimed its right to stretch these borders to the territories it considered to be part of greater Morocco, which extend from Tangier to the Senegal River. Henceforth, the mission devoted to the Royal Armed Forces could not but be limited to recovering those territories. Furthermore, Morocco's national security conception has also been founded on the conviction that Algeria has always sought to impose its leadership in the region by opposing, through different means, the right of the monarchy to assert the kingdom's integrity over the territories that were under Spain's occupation. In October 1963, Algerian and Moroccan troops waged a short border war—the Sand War—and set off a long-lasting strained relationship between the two countries, which are considered to be the engine of Maghreb integration.

Countering the Algerian military model was a strategy intelligently designed by former King Hassan II to assert his domination over the Moroccan Armed Forces who shared the same ambition of recovering what they considered to be Moroccan territories; such alignment with the monarchy would have allowed them to play a political role in the political system. The turning point in the relations between the monarchy and the RAF came in 1975 with the Western Sahara conflict. When the Moroccan national security doctrine was elaborated, Hassan II insisted on putting the RAF on the frontline of the war that he declared against the Polisario Front, the Sahrawi independence movement that emerged in 1973 to liberate the former Spanish colony. Such direction was dictated by the fact that most of the king's fear had evolved from the failed coup attempt orchestrated in 1972 by General Oufkir. Therefore, the Western Sahara issue offered Hassan II an unexpected leverage that allowed him to neutralize the RAF thus denying them any political role. The death of King Hassan II in July 1999 and the accession to the throne of his son Mohammed VI did not dispel the mistrust that the monarchy has nourished against the military. Mohammed VI was resolute in preventing the RAF and the different security agencies having any influence over the monarchy's affairs. In order to demonstrate his ability to rule, Mohammed VI made the bold decision to fire Driss Basri, King Hassan II's powerful minister of the interior. This was Mohammed VI's way to send a strong signal expressing the will of the monarchy to preserve the order prevailing since the country's independence; in no way would power in Morocco fall under the control of the armed forces. The king sought also to limit the missions of the security agencies and the armed forces so that he could exert undisputed control over the country. This situation is not likely to change in spite of the political reforms that the king introduced in July 2011 in the aftermath of the Arab Spring. The place of the RAF in the Moroccan political system will remain unchanged, that is, one of a minor actor with the specific role of protecting the sovereignty of the kingdom, as defined by the monarchy. Hence, the probability that the armed forces will impose their vision regarding Morocco's defense policy is limited. As worked out in the earlier years of independence, the civilian-military relations scheme has limited the capacity of the RAF and the security services in defining the security and defense priorities of Morocco. According to the Moroccan Constitution, the king, as supreme commander of the armed forces, is in charge of the defense policy. This responsibility also includes the conception of military operations, a mission usually devoted to professionals.[20] Moroccan scholar Abdallah Saaf has pointed out the total subordination of the RAF to the king: "The administration of national defense as it currently exists in Morocco is not a framework within which one can identify the direction of defense policy, the evolution of the military, the study of real and potential threats, enemies and dangers or the division of security responsibilities among different institutions. The administration is only responsible for administrative issues. It is a kind of mediator between the government and parliament on matters of budget, legislation and regulations relating to the common life of the military."[21]

Beyond the monarchy's will to maintain total control over the military institutions, mistrust and suspicions should be considered as determining factors shaping civilian-military relation in Morocco. Neither does the king intend to negotiate the sharing of his power with the military and other security agencies, nor is he keen on seeing those actors play any political role. The implications of the Moroccan military in United Nations peace missions, in the NATO Mediterranean dialogue, and in the political reforms initiated in 2011, are among some of the factors favoring the subordination of the military to political authorities. However, the outcome of the Western Sahara conflict remains a key factor, which could determine the evolution of this question.

Libya: Revolutionary Committees versus the Armed Forces

The Libyan case is different from that of Algeria, Morocco, or Tunisia. The regime of Colonel Muammar Qaddafi structured its security apparatus around the Kata'ib, a sort of armed brigade recruited mainly from the different tribes around the country. The role of these Kata'ib in defending the regime of Colonel Qaddafi became evident during the rebellion in Libya, which broke out in the beginning of 2011. Instead of relying on the regular armed forces to contain the rebellion, Qaddafi trusted the Katai'b, which were headed by some of his own sons, namely, Khamis, Saadi, and Mouatassim.

The structure of the brigades is typical of the state model that the Qaddafi endeavored to establish: tribal affiliation and loyalty to the regime as a criterion for recruitment. Considering the sociological structure of the country, Qaddafi insisted on establishing a political and tribal network able to ensure the loyalty of the tribes,[22] even the ones originating from the eastern city of Benghazi, where the loyalty to the monarchy never completely subsided. By redistributing oil revenues and sometimes resorting to violence, as was the case in the early 1970s when the Libyan leader ordered the air force to neutralize the rebellious tribes that had remained loyal to King Idriss Sanussi, Qaddafi succeeded in imposing one of the most authoritarian political orders in the entire Maghreb region. Within this political configuration, the loyalty of a regular army could not be taken for granted. The Libyan leader was very much aware that he was under the threat of a military coup as the process that brought him to power rested on violence: a military coup against King Sanussi. He thus entrusted the Kata'ib and the revolutionary committees with the mission to protect his regime.[23] The February 2011 rebellion in Libya shed light on the role that these paramilitary troops played; they were at the forefront of the battle against the forces of the National Transitional Council, which was formed to lead the rebellion. However, the capacity of the Kata'ib to contain the NATO-backed rebellion proved to be limited despite the enrollment of mercenaries recruited from some African countries. NATO's weakening of the militias by targeting their bases and dropping munitions to the rebels undermined the security system that the regime had put into place, especially after the defection of many high-ranking officers, like Abdelfath Younes. Having noticed the weakness of the Kata'ib to stop the advancement of the rebellion, some tribes decided to distance themselves from the Qaddafi clan, thus precipitating the fall of the regime. A new political elite has emerged that will inevitably transform the nature of the relations that will exist between the military and politics. Despite the fact that the new political authorities displayed a willingness to change radically political practices by establishing a republic based on the rule of law, the future of Libya remains uncertain as the different factions still fight about what path to take in the coming future.[24] The radical factions represented by jihadist and former combatants who returned from Afghanistan seem less inclined to allow the secular wing to impose its vision regarding the management of the affairs of the future state.

Tunisia: The End of the Mukhabarat (Intelligence Services/Police) State?

Compared to the other Maghreb states, the number of academic works and studies devoted to the military's role in Tunisian political life is limited. Barring the works that examined the nature of the authoritarianism of the Tunisian regime,[25] works devoted to Tunisian security defense and different Tunisian security structures are rare. The difficulty in analyzing civilian-military relations in Tunisia lies in the nature of the Tunisian political regime where the police, rather than the armed forces, have been the key security institution whose role extended into the state-building process. Contrary to Algeria, the postindependence Tunisian state was not the product of a long process in which violence played a determining role. The Tunisian people did not wage a war of liberation in which the military could have taken precedence over politicians. As a lawyer and politician, President Habib Bourguiba had no difficulty in imposing his domination over the political and security apparatus. As Sorenson correctly pointed out, Bourguiba's elite came from the nationalist Neo-Destour Party, student and labor organizations, rather than a revolutionary military that would transform itself into the national army.[26] This is a quite different case from Algeria and Egypt where the military rested at the core of the political elite. The nonrevolutionary stance Bourguiba's Neo-Destour adopted may be considered as the main explanation of the nonmilitarization of Tunisian political life. Although in Algeria the military exploited the war of liberation as a source of legitimacy, in Tunisia violence was excluded as a structuring element of political identity. Habib Bourguiba shied away from socialist/radical ideology and opted instead for a liberal economic order, which opened the door for liberalizing actors and reformers to play a prominent role in the management of public affairs.

The decline of Bourguiba's health in the 1980s paved the way for General Zine al Abidin Ben Ali to emerge as Tunisia's strong man. The military coup orchestrated in November 1987 against an ailing Bourguiba inaugurated a new era in which the security services would impose themselves as the sole political actor while accentuating the marginalization of the armed forces. Following the coup, many in Tunisia anticipated that Ben Ali would democratize the regime; however, against expectation, the latter tightened control over political life. Using the Islamist threat as a pretext, the Ben Ali regime reinforced the role of the security services whose influence over the military grew considerably. As John Entelis contended, Tunisia's security apparatus has ballooned under Ben Ali,[27] a situation that was paradoxical since Ben Ali himself came from the military.

The securitization of Tunisian society did not, however, shield the Ben Ali regime from social unrest and political contestation. In 2008, riots took place in Gasfa; the mine workers of this poor region protested against the deterioration of their social conditions. The spark of the revolution in Tunisia was the immolation of Mohamed Bouazizi in December 2010. This event and the uprising that followed marked the end of an era and opened the way for a new one. Having failed to address the social unrest and ease the anger of the population, Ben Ali fled the country on January 14, 2011, after 23 years of ruthless authoritarianism. However, it is still too early to say whether the fall of the Ben Ali regime will put a definitive end to the security state in Tunisia.

A number of factors have, however, led us to believe that the fall of the Ben Ali regime has heralded the end of the Mukhabarat (security intelligence) state. First, although the military was deployed to maintain law and order following the social unrest throughout the country, the army did not use force. The chief of staff of the armed forces, General Rachid Ammar, disobeyed Ben Ali's order to shoot the protesters. The audacity in defying the president signaled the breakdown within the security apparatus; the military had decided to participate in the dismantling of the Mukhabat state. In many ways, the military's neutrality during the crisis could be interpreted as the revenge of the military over the police state.

Second, the legislative elections in October 2011 confirmed the rise of the Islamist movement, represented by the Ennahda, which was banished under Ben Ali, while the presidential election resulted in the election of Moncef Marzouki, a persecuted left-wing activist under the old regime. Against all odds, a new alliance has been forged between Marzouki and Rachid Ghannouchi's Ennahda Party. Both share a common objective: the dismantling of the Mukhabarat state. In addition to this, international pressure for further democratization of the regime entails the dismantlement of the security structures, which the old regime had set up to tighten control over the whole society. It is too early to conclude whether Tunisia is becoming the model of democratization in the Maghreb region and perhaps in the entire Arab world. However, we can assume that the security state is about to be dismantled, and the military, which maintains its neutrality, will not intervene in political affairs so long as the Islamist movement remains committed to respect the secular identity of the Tunisian state and the Salafists do not disrupt the transition.

FROM OLD TO NEW THREATS AND VULNERABILITIES: SECURITY DOCTRINES IN THE MAGHREB AT THE CROSSROADS

In the previous section we outlined, albeit briefly, the historical background underlying the emergence of the state in the Maghreb region. The state-centric model remains the dominant model with violence as a structural element explaining the propensity of the Maghreb ruling elites to amalgamate the security of the regime with the security of the state. The civilian-military relations model represents a materialization of this vision because the military in some of these countries is the manager of violence. Thus, the conceptualization of the national security model is centered on traditional threats such as foreign invasion, border disputes, and the protection of territorial integrity.

The emergence of terrorism in the 1990s has had a great impact on Maghrebi defense doctrines. Algeria, for instance, was compelled to rethink its security policy focusing on terrorism as the main threat to national security.[28] Morocco, Tunisia, and Libya also considered terrorism as the main threat to their national security following the September 2001 terrorist attacks against the United States. The new international context was among the key factors that induced Maghreb governments to refocus security and defense doctrines around terrorism, especially, because of the appearance of an Al Qaeda branch in the Sahara-Sahel region.

Sharing borders with four Sahel countries (Niger, Mauritania, Mali, and Libya), Algeria considers the presence of Al Qaeda in the Islamic Maghreb (AQIM) as a serious threat to the security of the region, not only because of terrorist activities, but also because of its arms and drugs smuggling activities and moreover the general association of the terrorist groups with traffickers of all kinds. However, these are not the only threats that challenge the security of the region. The Maghreb countries are also faced with new threats, particularly, illegal immigration. In this following section, we will examine the impact those new threats could have on the security of the region and if the Maghreb countries are prepared to face them.

Al Qaeda in the Islamic Maghreb

Terrorism is perhaps the greatest threat to the Maghreb countries. The 1990s witnessed the eruption of terrorist violence, which forced countries like Algeria to refocus their security doctrine to contain this threat. The Salafist Group for Preaching and Combat (GSPC), a splinter faction from of the Islamic Armed Group (GIA), created in 1998, faced many difficulties in legitimizing its `actions against the Algerian regime, especially after the government initiated the National Concord in 1999 and` the charter for peace and national reconciliation in 2005. These initiatives had prompted many terrorists to surrender: a decision that allowed them to be reintegrated into society. The Global Jihad Front headed by Osama bin Laden thus represented a golden opportunity for the GSPC to reinforce its political legitimacy. In 1998, Hassan Hattab, leader of the GSPC, made a public announcement in which he declared the group's allegiance to Al Qaeda and decided to restructure his organization in accordance with the requirements of global jihad. The most significant change in the GSPC's strategy was the new definition of the enemy that it adopted. The new strategy consisted of targeting only security forces while sparing civilians.[29] Since Hassan Hattab's group was a branch of a global organization he had to comply with Al Qaeda's ideology regarding attacks on security forces. However, the shift in the GSPC's strategy could not be interpreted as the beginning of close relations with Al Qaeda. Algerian terrorist groups had entertained relations with Al Qaeda since the beginning of the 1990s. But the ideological link was not so strong; Al Qaeda's support of the actions of those groups was limited to logistical and financial assistance. The terrorist attacks were confined to the Algerian territory, and targeting foreign interests was not yet part of the agenda of their alleged jihad. The 9/11 attacks led the GSPC/AQIM to rethink its modus operandi by enlarging the scope of targets to foreign interests. Abdelmalek Droukdel, who now headed the GSPC after the resignation of Hassan Hatab, said that, "it became our right and our duty to push away with all our strength this crusade campaign and declare clearly that American interests are legitimate targets to us. We will strive to strike them whenever we can. And we are sure that America is going to lose its war against us, like it lost it in Afghanistan and Iraq."[30]

Putting the near and the far enemy[31] in the same balance became henceforth the new strategic orientation of this group. Henceforth, so too did the Libyan and Moroccan Islamist fighting groups, albeit to a much lesser degree of success. The GSPC's strikes proved to be more efficient compared to the actions carried out by Islamist guerrillas in Libya and Morocco that faced many setbacks due to the tight control exerted by the local authorities.[32]

The scope of AQIM's actions in the region widened with the targeting of some military garrisons in Lamghiti, Mauritania in 2005, and in northern Mali in 2008, 2010, and 2012. However, one of the new developments in AQIM's strategy has been the kidnapping of foreigners, mainly Westerners. The strategy was inaugurated in 2003 when 32 German tourists were kidnapped by a terrorist group headed by Abderazak Al Para, whose real name is Amara Saifi. His action ignited a new market for ransoms that have yielded more than 50 million euros, according to the head of the Algiers-based African Center for Research and the Study on Terrorism. In any kidnapping operation, AQIM imposes the payment of ransoms for the release of the hostages. In some cases, refusal to pay the ransom results in the execution of the hostage, as was the case for Edwin Dyer, a British tourist who was kidnapped in 2007, and that of Michel Germaneau, a humanitarian worker who was executed in August 2010 during a failed rescue operation by French special forces in northern Mali. The amount of money collected from ransoms emboldened AQIM, especially, because some European countries continued to pay these ransoms despite calls for their nonpayment from Algeria and other countries. The reluctance of some European countries to support the call of the core countries or the countries of the field (Algeria, Mali, Mauritania, and Niger) to ban the payment of ransoms incited the terrorist groups to exert more pressure by enlarging the scope of their actions through the making of new alliances with similar groups located in Western Africa. Boko Haram, a Nigerian Islamist group, known for its rigorist interpretation of Islam, displayed great interest in establishing a connection with AQIM and paved the way for a new era of terrorism in North Africa. A connection between AQIM and Boko Haram will render the task of the Sahel countries ever more difficult. In addition to this, pressure from Western powers on the field countries to manage the security in the region efficiently has become stronger. Not only do the Sahara-Sahel states lack the military and technological equipment needed for such missions, but Western reluctance until 2013 to provide them with financial and technical assistance represented yet another challenge facing the field countries.

The GSPC shifting strategy toward internationalization has undoubtedly represented a real challenge for the Algerian antiterrorist strategy, with all the constraints that this implies. However, Algeria is not the only country facing such a threat; the other Maghreb states are confronted with the same menace. The Maghreb countries have adjusted their security strategies to contain this terrorist threat. Even with the experience gained in the 1990s in fighting terrorist groups, Algerian security forces remain incapable of eradicating this threat coming from the country's long southern borders. As shall be seen in Chapter Six, the geological nature of the Sahel region, its vast area, the social structures of the concerned countries, and tribalism, posing as the main factor determining political participation, are in fact all contributing factors in rendering the tasks of security forces of the Maghreb countries more and more arduous. The kidnapping of Western tourists has shed light upon the difficulty the security forces of the region are facing.

Illegal Immigration

Hundreds of sub-Saharan Africans have crossed hundreds of miles of desert and other perils trying to reach Europeans shores. The phenomenon is not new, but the 1990s were the period when illegal migration grew at an unprecedented rate. The new geography of immigration has been reshaped with North African countries becoming the crossroad for a massive influx of immigrants originating from different African countries.

The fall of the Iron Curtain in Europe resulted in an unprecedented movement of migration from Central and Eastern Europe to Western Europe as the European Community was perceived as the Promised Land for jobs and a better life. The deterioration of the political situation in some North African countries and the eruption of civil wars in many sub-Saharan African countries were considered as the main factors that triggered the migration influx toward Europe. Interestingly, the more European countries tighten controls on the access of immigrants to their territories, the more the numbers of candidates grow. This situation forces the Maghrebi states to rethink their policies regarding the management of human floods coming from sub-Saharan Africa. The task seems very hard to tackle because it is difficult for the countries of the region to fully control all their borders, especially along the southern rims. Migrants coming from sub-Saharan Africa use Libyan, Algerian, and Moroccan territories as transitory settlements. Before seeking to reach Europe, the migrants settle in the southern cities of Algeria, Libya, and Morocco, looking for jobs that would allow them to earn the money needed for paying the smugglers. However, more often than not the transitory sojourn becomes a permanent stay as the majority of African migrants face many difficulties to get the money they need to make their journey to Europe. In southern Algeria, especially in Tamanrasset, nationals from 52 countries reside. Each year, Algerian security services escort back 8,000 illegal African immigrants to the frontiers.[33] Despite the measures taken in recent years, the flood of immigrants coming from African countries remains constant. However, the real problem for the Maghrebi countries remains the control of the coastal borders where hundreds of illegal immigrants risk their lives to cross the Mediterranean on makeshift boats. According to some reports, the coast guards in Algeria and Morocco regularly intercept hundreds of potential immigrants. In 2008, the Algerian coast guards stopped 418 immigrants who were heading for European shores on small boats; 48 were found dead. Between 2001 and 2006, 32,000 illegal immigrants have been escorted back to the borders.[34] The number of immigrants escorted back to the borders is much more in Morocco; between 2005 and 2010, 83,000 persons originating from the Maghreb countries, South Asia, and Sub-Sahara Africa have been sent back.[35]

The figures in the previous paragraph reveal the pressure the Maghrebi countries have faced. Besides the foreign illegal migrants, Maghrebi governments have to deal with their native, young populations the majority of whom lack jobs and wish to migrate to Europe. The European Union has also put pressure on the Maghreb governments soliciting them to contain this illegal immigration. As European borders are about to be displaced to the south of the Mediterranean rim, EU members are seriously considering a burden-sharing option because tightening the control of the borders has proved to be insufficient. European countries have urged Maghrebi countries to take stringent measures to roll back the floods of immigrants. After the closing of some centers, where illegal immigrants have been gathered, particularly those of Sangat and Callé in northern France, the focus of EU members has turned to Maghrebi countries with the serious possibility that similar centers would be created there. In fact, what the northern Mediterranean countries have proposed to their neighbors of the south is merely an outsourcing of the protection of the northern borders, a proposition, which carried a heavy political price for the countries of the southern Mediterranean.

However, if some Maghrebi countries, especially Libya and Morocco, seemed very keen to fulfill this function, Algeria and Tunisia rejected such a scheme; they made it clear that they did not wish to play a proxy role for European security. If anything, this refusal shows how deep the divergences among the four North African countries regarding the management of this issue are. Expressing, as usual, his particularity from others leaders of the region, Qaddafi, went further by proposing to the members of the European Union to host those centers and asked for five billion euros to execute this mission. Despite the fact that none of those centers have been set up in any country of the region, especially after the revolts that overthrew two of them and the political changes that ensued, the Maghrebi countries did nonetheless partly respond to the expectations of the European countries by adopting legislations criminalizing illegal immigration. On July 26, 2003, the Moroccan parliament voted on a law criminalizing illegal immigration (both smugglers and victims) and gave greater power to police services and other authorities assigned to the mission of controlling the borders. In the same vein, the Algerian government issued on August 31, 2008, a law criminalizing any attempt to leave Algerian territory without official documents. This law has been enacted to express the Algerian will to comply with European demands regarding the fight against illegal immigration, as embodied in articles 82, 84, and 91 of the association agreement signed between Algeria and the European Union in 2002 and entered into effect on September 1, 2005. The Libyan government went even further in expressing its availability to respond favorably to European demands on this issue. On December 12, 2000, the Libyan government concluded with the Italian government a friendship agreement in which both parties agreed to cooperate in controlling the maritime and land borders while giving the management of this operation to a private Italian company. The agreement, signed on August, 30, 2008, endorsed this cooperation, thus giving to Libya the status of one of the main outsourcers for the EU in the Maghreb region. This demonstrates if need be that Libya, and to a lesser extent, Algeria and Morocco, are dependent on Europe.

CONCLUSION

In this chapter, our objective was to provide a general overview of the security equation in the Maghreb region. The problem facing the Maghrebi countries cannot be explained solely by the constraints that the external environment imposes upon them. The security order in the region has been to a great extent shaped by historical reasons, that is, the decolonization process where violence has been a determining factor, as was the case for Algeria in achieving independence. The prevalence of military institutions as primus inter pares and the control it has imposed upon the political process is the logical result of a process in which violence played a structural role. Despite the fact that the Maghrebi states chose different paths to gain their respective independences, the security state was a common feature of those countries. However, the propensity of Maghrebi regimes to rely on security forces and the military to maintain their domination over their societies has been weakened due to the uprisings that overthrew the dictatorships in Tunisia and Libya. Will the reforms undertaken in Algeria and Morocco loosen the authoritarian grips in these two countries?

The answer to this question is uncertain because the results of the last legislative elections in both countries, especially in the case of Algeria, have confirmed the prevalence of conservative ideology: in the sense that the Islamists in Morocco aspire to an Islamization of society with a less modernizing objective, while in Algeria, the 208 seats won by the FLN in May 2012 confirm, if need be, the status of that party as custodian of the authoritarian order.

NOTES

1. Stephen J. King, *The New Authoritarianism in the Middle East and North Africa* (Bloomington & Indianapolis, IN: Indiana University Press, 2009).

2. John Entelis, "The Democratic Imperative *vs.* the Authoritarian Impulse: The Maghrib State between Transition and Terrorism," *Middle East Journal,* Vol. 59, no. 4 (2005): 53–558.

3. With the terrorist violence exacerbating during the middle of the 1990s, some analysts predicted the fall of the Algerian regime and the erection of a fundamentalist state. See, for instance, Graham Fuller, *Algeria: The Next Fundamentalist State?* (Santa Monica, CA: The Rand Corporation, 1996).

4. Many interesting works have been published on the relationship between the monarchy and Islam in Morocco. For a deep and thoughtful analysis, see Mohamed Tozy, *Monarchie et Islam Politique au Maroc* (Paris: Presses de Sciences Po, 1999); Malika Zeghal, *Les Islamistes Marocains, le Défi de la Monarchie* (Paris, La Découverte, collCahiers libres, 2005).

5. Yahia H. Zoubir, "Les révolutions du Monde Arabe: la Fin du Mythe de L'exception," *Maghreb-Machrek,* no. 210 (2011–2012): 41–52.

6. Alistair Horne, *A Savage War of Peace: Algeria, 1954–1962* (London: NYRB, 2006).

7. Some analysts speak about a militarization of politics when analyzing the case of Algeria. See, for example, Elisabeth Picard, "Armée et Sécurité au Coeur de L'autoritarisme," in *Autoritarismes Démocratiques et Démocraties Autoritaires au XXIème Siècle,* ed. Olivier Dabène, Vincent Geisser, and Gilles Massardier (Paris: Editions La Découverte, 2008).

8. Lahouari Addi, *Algérie: Chroniques d'une Expérience Post-Coloniale de Modernisation* (Algiers: Brazakh Editions, 2012).

9. Moncef Djaziri, "Tribus et État dans le Système Politique Libyen," *Outre-terre*, 3, 23 (2009): 131.

10. Mustapha Mohamed, "State, Security and Reform: The Case of Algeria," *Arab Reform Initiative*, June 2012, http://www.arab-reform.net/state-security-and-reform-case-algeria.

11. Mohammed Hachemaoui, "Permanence du Jeu Politique en Algérie," *Politique Étrangère*, 2 (2009): 309–21.

12. Hugh Roberts, "Demilitarizing Algeria," *Carnegie Paper*, no. 86 (May 2007), http://www.carnegieendowment.org/files/cp_86_final1.pdf.

13. Mohammed Harbi, "L'armée est-elle une Institution de l'Etat ou une Caste?" *El Watan*, June 4, 2012, http://www.djazairess.com/fr/elwatan/373395.

14. Mohammed Harbi, "L'armée est-elle une Institution de l'Etat ou une Caste?" *El Watan*, June 4, 2012, http://www.djazairess.com/fr/elwatan/373395.

15. William B. Quandt, *Between Ballots and Bullets: Algeria's Transition from Authoritarianism* (Washington, DC: The Brookings Institution, 1998).

16. There are no accurate figures as to the number of casualties; estimates vary between 120,000 and 200,000.

17. The former powerful chief of staff of the Algerian Armed Forces, Mohamed Lamari, died of a heart attack in February 2012 at the age of 73.

18. Liess Boukraa, "Approche Sociologique de L'histoire de L'armée Algérienne: des Origines à Nos Jours," in *Les Premières Journées D'études Parlementaires sur la Défense Nationale* (Algiers: Editions ANEP, 2001).

19. Chafik Mesbah is a retired colonel from the Algerian intelligence services. He is a regular commentator on relations between the presidency and the military, especially the intelligence services. See, in particular, his interview, "Autant que Possible, Il Faut Tenir L'armée Loin des Démons de la Politique," *Le Soir d'Algérie* (May 16, 2011), http://www.lesoirdalgerie.com/articles/2011/05/16/article.php?sid=117184&cid=2.

20. Brahim Saidy, "Relations Civilo-Militaires au Maroc: le Facteur International Revisité," *Politique Etrangère*, 3 (2007): 589–603.

21. Quoted in Saidy, "Relations Civilo-Militaires au Maroc: le Facteur International Revisité," *Politique Etrangère*, 3 (2007): 599.

22. Luis Martinez, "La Sécurité en Algérie et en Lybie Après le 11 Septembre 2001," *Euromesco Papers* (May 22, 2003).

23. Luis Martinez, "Al Qaeda au Maghreb Islamique," *ISS Analysis*, European Union Institute for Security Studies, November 2007, http://www.iss.europa.eu/publications/detail/article/al-qaida-au-maghreb-islamique/.

24. Yahia H. Zoubir and Erzsébet Rózsa, "The End of the Libyan Dictatorship: The Uncertain Transition," *Third World Quarterly*, 33, 7 (June 2012): 1269–85.

25. For more details concerning the authoritarianism of the Tunisian regime during the Bourguiba and Ben Ali eras, see Michel Camau and Vincent Geisser, *Le Syndrome Autoritaire: Politique en Tunisie de Bourguiba à Ben Ali* (Paris: Presses de Sciences Po, 2003); Béatrice Hibou, *La Force de L'obéissance. Economie Politique de la Répression en Tunisie* (Paris: La Découverte, 2006).

26. Theodor Sorenson, "Civil-Military Relations in North Africa," *Middle East Policy*, 14, 4 (2007).

27. John Entelis, "Civil-Military Relations in North Africa," *Middle East Policy*, 14, 4 (2007).

28. Cherif Dris, "Rethinking Maghrebi Security: The Challenge of Multilateralism," in *North Africa: Politics, Region, and the Limits of Transformation*, ed. Yahia H. Zoubir and Haizam Amirah Fernández (London and New York: Routledge, 2008).

29. Yahia H. Zoubir, "Algeria," in *World Almanac of Islamism 2011* (New York: American Foreign Policy Council, 2011), 304–17.

30. Droukdel's interview in the *New York Times,* July 1, 2008, http://www.nytimes.com/2008/07/01/world/africa/01transcript-droukdal.html?pagewanted = all.

31. Guido Steinberg and Isabelle Werenfels, "Between the 'Near' and the 'Far' Enemy: Al-Qaeda in the Islamic Maghreb," *Mediterranean Politics,* 12, 3 (November 2007): 407–13.

32. Luis Martinez, "Between the 'Near' and the 'Far' Enemy: Al Qaeda au Maghreb Islamique," *Mediterranean Politics,* 12, 3 (November 2007): 407–13.

33. Saci Kheiredine, "Immigration Clandestine en Algérie: La Détresse des Naufragés du Désert," *El Watan* (July, 26, 2011), http://elwatan.com/reportage/immigration-clandestine-en-algerie-la-detresse-des-naufrages-du-desert-26–07–2011–133982_117.php. (no longer accessible online)

34. Hocine Labdelaoui, "La Gestion des Frontières en l'Algérie," *CARIM Rapports de Recherche,* no. 2, 2008/02.

35. Morocco extradited 83,000 illegal migrants between 2005 and 2010, http://www.kemisearch.com/maroc/forum/actualites-marocaines/2253/83–000-clandestins-extrades-du-maroc-entre-2005-et-2010.html. (no longer accessible online)

CHAPTER 2

Perceptions and Management
of the Violence

NEW FORMS OF VIOLENCE IN THE MAGHREB: THE POLITICAL
AND SOCIAL CHALLENGES

The social contract between citizens and the state provides the state with a monopoly on violence. Only a few select legal and institutional structures are permitted to use force under specific circumstances along constitutional prerogatives. This social contract, however, is no longer binding in the Maghreb. The state no longer holds a monopoly on violence; instead, violence has spilled over into the public sphere. One of the most notable phenomena has been urban riots, most prominently of all in Algeria.

Scholars have often considered riots to be short, disorganized, and spontaneous submovements, occurring in response to injustice. They have been characterized as violent reactions to social inequalities, not as the models of political expression. They have generally been regarded as the expressions of popular discontent, carried out not by organized groups such as associations or trade unions that would turn this discontent into political protest, but by unorganized submovements.[1] The dismissal of any political dimension to the riots comes from the pre-French revolution historians who refused to consider workers as political actors. The question that arises here is whether or not this is a valid consideration when analyzing the changes that have taken place since the outbreak of the Tunisian revolt in January 2011.

RIOTS: FROM SOCIOECONOMIC DEMANDS TO CALLS
FOR POLITICAL CHANGE

In Algeria, riots tend to bring districts (Bab El Oued in Algiers), communities (Illizi and Berriane), and/or tribes (Djelfa, Laghouat, Béjaïa, and so on) in opposition to one another. They can be provoked by trivial events, such as reactions to dissatisfaction with the result of a football match or the work of rival criminal gangs. They may also be the result of grim social conditions, such as unemployment, insecurity, corruption, and nepotism of the administration. The rioters often express themselves through the burning of tires, blocking roads, looting, and attacking municipal buildings. Occasionally, isolated incidents also occur between the rioters, who are more often than not of a young age, and the security forces. The gendarmerie has officially stated that 10,000 riots occurred in Algeria during 2010.[2] At the same time that the Tunisian uprising was in full swing, that is, in early January 2011, short-lived riots also began to break out across Algeria. This led the media to focus more attention on Algeria, which, many believed to be the next possible victim of the revolutionary wave. The pundits of the Middle East and North Africa (MENA) region did not envisage that Egypt or Syria could follow suit and were instead firmly convinced that Algeria would soon witness an upheaval of even greater magnitude than that of Tunisia. These recurrent riots were clearly the expression of a deficient system. In an efficient system, inputs reach decision makers through a number of institutionalized channels, such as trade unions, associations, political parties, elected representatives at the local and national level, and through mass media. All of these channels exist in Algeria; unfortunately, they do not operate as they should. Three reasons serve to explain this inefficiency. The first is linked to the nature of the system itself and the rules that manage those relations between the rulers and the people.[3] These rules include traditional constraints and repressive measures such as restrictions on the creation of political parties, associations, trade unions, newspapers, think tanks, the prohibition of demonstrations in the capital, and also the vetoing of the creation of private audiovisual media bodies. However, the Algerian ruling class has also modernized their way of controlling the public sphere without resorting to repressive measures. Hence, co-optation and clientelism have neutralized the trade unions and associations; the use of fraud has prevented the emergence of credible parties while public mass media continue to depict the conditions prevailing in the country in a positive manner. The state-owned media, particularly national television, minimize the socioeconomic tensions and strive to discredit the regime's political opponents. In other words, the government refuses to pacify social conflicts through their institutionalization, preferring to manage them without the involvement of autonomous mediators whose role could undermine the regime's control over society. Furthermore, the citizen's rebuke of the regime's legitimacy has forced the rulers to seek new allies causing the number of the regime's devotees and, consequently, the favors that need to be paid to increase considerably. The second reason why the channels of transmission of the inputs are ineffective is that there is a paternalistic relationship that exists between the government and the population. The independence gained in 1962 and the circumstances that surrounded it, that is, violent power struggles,[4] resulted in a strong, possessive, and dominating regime. However, revenues from hydrocarbons enabled the establishment of a welfare state that gave the population access to many privileges such as free education and health care, low costs of energy, and subsidized prices of essential food products.[5] Even if the quasi welfare state has become increasingly more costly to maintain, the regime nevertheless continues to pursue these same policies, especially, since the outbreak of the Arab revolts. Due to an increase in the population, consumer habits, and needs, these policies have resulted in more and more costly subsidies. In April 2011, the Algerian government revealed that food subsidies stood at a cost of 300 billion dinars and acknowledged that this figure was not sustainable over the long term. Between January and March, sugar and oil subsidies alone cost the state a total of three billion dinars.[6] The third reason relates to the weakness of the country's organized political opposition. For instance, on January 21, 2011, an attempt to channel the protest movement and mobilize the population was undertaken soon after the riots broke out, through the establishment of the National Coordination for Change and Democracy (CNCD), which incorporated a number of opposition groups, such as the Rassemblement pour la Culture et la Démocratie (RCD), the Ligue Algérienne pour la Défense des Droits de l'Homme, and some independent trade unions. The effective police crackdown, coupled with splits within the CNCD itself, resulted in the slow death of the movement that had attracted insignificant support within the population. In short, one could say that riots are the expression of an unorganized opposition to the current regime and that they are the by-product of a certain type of governance. As long as these riots entail the destruction of public and private properties, the regime will not consider them as a threat.[7] The fear of the regime comes from the idea of a Tunisian or Egyptian scenario breaking out, that is, where a politicization of the riots causes a swift downfall of the regime.

On the eve of the constitutional reforms that King Mohammed VI of Morocco announced in March 2011, reforms that were almost certainly prompted by the events taking place in Tunisia, Egypt, and Libya, the situation in the country was no different from the rest of the Maghreb; that is to say unemployment, especially among the youth, was rife. The government had been unable to fulfill the promise it made in 2007 to create 250,000 jobs per annum. By 2012 in fact, it had not even been able to achieve half that number. Unemployment officially hovers at around nine percent and affects 173,200 graduates (16.7 percent of total graduates).[8] Numerous, recurrent strikes occur across both the private and public sectors. The outskirts of major cities see sporadic outbursts of turmoil.

This is being generated by the sentiment that the people living in more remote areas do not enjoy the fruits of development. A prominent professor of economics, Driss Benali asserted that over the last ten years, the system has killed political parties. Morocco is much less authoritarian than Tunisia but we don't have the educated [people] of Tunisia, neither do we have the active business elite of Egypt.[9] Resentment against the political elite, even against those close to the king himself, has become apparent.

Morocco has a long tradition of bread riots;[10] groups, such as university graduates—of whom nearly 30 percent are unemployed—also stage demonstrations that sometimes turn violent. Like in Tunisia, Morocco has also experienced riots that have taken on a political dimension. For instance, the Movement of 20 February (2011) denounced King Mohammed VI's monopoly over power and called for a constitutional monarchy with more restricted prerogatives. The members of the movement have also criticized corruption practices in which people close to the king have been implicated. Several political parties, associations, and organizations, such as the Amazigh Congress, the Confederation of Labor, the Moroccan Association for Human Rights, and other Islamist opposition parties, have joined the movement.

However, despite these grievances, the once anticipated Tunisian style scenario did not come about, nor in fact did the Algerian scenario happen, that is, innumerable and replicating riots. The reason for this anomaly was due to the existence in Morocco of independent social forces that played mediating roles between the government and the population, thus reducing socioeconomic tensions. In 2011, worried about the possible snowballing effects of events in the rest of the Arab world, the monarchy instructed the government to take preventive measures. For instance, the government ordered, as in Algeria,[11] the riot police not to use lethal means against the demonstrators. The authorities also announced additional subsidies for basic products, such as sugar, cooking oil, wheat, gas, and oil, after having already spent, despite strains on the budget, more than two billion dollars on subsidies in 2010. The government nearly doubled the amount of the subsidy fund (Caisse de Compensation).[12] While the previous budget for 2011 called for a 17 billion dirham subsidy pool, the government announced on February 15, 2011 that another 15 billion dirhams would be injected into the fund. No additional reasons were provided by the finance ministry, letting analysts speculate that the government tried to prevent and contain the people's fury.[13]

Tunisia has shown that a shift from street demonstrations to political revolt, that is, a politicization of riots, is indeed possible. From spontaneous and ephemeral socioeconomic demands, the riots, which had lasted for several weeks, were transformed from mere socioeconomic grievances to calls for regime change. Local elites, associations, the leftist opposition, trade unions, and self-exiled intellectuals/opponents joined the demonstrations repressed by security forces. After a month and a half, abandoned by his own military, which had refused to shoot at protesters, and his Western allies, President Ben Ali fled Tunisia on January 14, 2011. The downfall of Ben Ali brought upon by persistent riots raised the question of possible domino effects across the other countries in the Maghreb, which undoubtedly showed many economic, social, and political similarities with Tunisia. All have been governed by authoritarian regimes, the most despotic being those of Tunisia and Libya. In all of them, economic governance did not lead to development but resulted instead in increased frustrations of youth-dominated populations, well integrated into the workings of globalization.

Unlike Algeria, Morocco, and Tunisia, where riots take place frequently, Libya, under Qaddafi's rule, witnessed only a few uprisings, the most notable being the armed uprising led by jihadists in the mid-1990s.[14] The absence of upheavals in Libya can be explained by the benefits of the welfare state that the population at large enjoyed under Qaddafi's rule. However, soon after Mubarak's resignation in Egypt and not long after Ben Ali's downfall in Tunisia, turmoil began in neighboring Libya. Tens of thousands of Libyans demonstrated in the streets of the eastern city of Benghazi[15] expressing their discontent with four decades of authoritarian rule by Muammar Qaddafi. The riots then spread to other cities in the country. The protests had begun in January when demonstrators, unhappy with construction delays, broke into and occupied a government housing project. The government responded with a $24 billion fund for housing and development. However, this decision did not appease the anger of the population. Indeed, a month later, more demonstrations took place when the police detained relatives of those killed in an alleged massacre, which, according to Human Rights Watch, had taken place in 1996 at the Abu Salim prison. This was not the only grievance that sparked the riots; high unemployment had also fueled the protests, which provided the opportunity for the anti-Qaddafi groups to encourage a mass-scale upheaval. These riots took on a political dimension with the emergence of a leadership, made up of secular and Islamist opponents, members of the government who broke ranks with the regime immediately following the riots, and jihadist fighters who were members of the Al Qaeda and/or of the Libyan Islamic Fighting Group. This heterogeneous group constituted itself into the National Transition Committee (NTC), which eventually coordinated the uprising and proclaimed on October 22, 2011 the liberation of Libya.

TERRORISM: FROM A NATIONAL TO TRANSNATIONAL THREAT

Terrorism is both a national and transnational phenomenon. At the national level, Algeria is one of the countries that have witnessed some of the most violent forms of domestic terrorism.

Algeria

Various Islamist opposition groups emerged under quite complex conditions from the 1970s to the present day.[16] The first Islamist association was named El-Qiyam al Islamyya (Islamic values) and was founded in 1963, enjoying a practically legal existence until 1970. The association demanded the full implementation of the Shari'a (Islamic Law), the prohibition of the sale of alcohol, the exclusion of non-Muslims from public jobs, and the introduction of religious teaching in schools. However, the real radicalization of Islamism started in the 1980s. The most violent radical Islamist group was rallied around Mustapha Bouyali, who founded the Armed Islamic Movement (MIA) in 1982 and served as its emir (commander) until his violent death in 1987. His strategy consisted of creating a small but disciplined organization, able to carry out pinpointed operations like political assassinations and acts of sabotage. In the 1990s, some members of this organization joined the post-1991 Islamist armed groups.[17] Algeria is a country where terrorism still constitutes national threat and causes immense worries to the authorities. Since the early 1990s, armed groups claiming to be fighting the infidels have threatened both state and society. They fought under the pretext that the regime had robbed them of their electoral victory when the Islamic Salvation Front (FIS) won the majority of the seats in the National Popular Assembly (APN). Since then, several armed Islamist groups have launched attacks against political and military targets, as well as civilians.

In 1996, there were 14 autonomous armed Islamist groups known to be active in Algeria, all using different tactics. Six of these groups obtained support from radical militants based in Europe.[18] A bloody battle pitted security forces, made up of regular and auxiliary troops, against extremist groups. The successful conduct of the antiterrorist campaign compelled one of the major groups, the Islamic Army of Salvation (AIS) of Madani Mezrag to stop fighting in September 1997. The deal resulted in an agreement whereby the AIS forces would assist the military in the fight against the other armed groups, such as the GIA, which refused to surrender. In addition to military means, Algeria initiated political processes, such as the Rahma (Forgiveness) Law (1994), the Civil Concord (1999), and the Charter for National Reconciliation (2005) in order to restore security in the country and weaken the remaining fighting groups.

Morocco

Radical Islamism and terrorism have been less of a concern to Morocco than they have been for Algeria. The continuous dialogue between the monarchy and Islamists provides a partial explanation as to the relative absence of these two phenomena in Morocco. In fact, this dialogue has been maintained and consolidated through the special attention placed upon it by the king for centuries. As the alleged descendant of the Prophet Mohammed, the king claims the title of Commander of the Faithful, and thus represents spiritual as well as secular authority. Some other institutions play a key role in this religious-political system. One of these institutions, the Ulema Council (council of religious scholars), serves as a tool in legitimizing the religious status of the king and spreading the government-approved version of Islam throughout the 32,000 mosques in the country.[19] In order to counter and contain the radical Islamist trends, new bureaus have been set up within the Ministry of Religious Affairs to oversee the administration of the kingdom's mosques and provide rational religious education. The king has also encouraged the emergence of Islamist political parties, such as the moderate Party for Justice and Democracy (PJD) and the Alternative Civilisationnelle, an Islamic party.

Undoubtedly, Morocco has drawn upon lessons from the Algerian experience of the early 1990s, that is, before the Algerian government co-opted moderate Islamists into the political process. Hence, the Moroccan monarchy seized an opportunity early on to consolidate moderate Islamists. For their part, the moderate Islamist parties avoided any action that would represent a threat to the status quo.[20]

Beyond these specific issues, Moroccan radical Islamism has, like its Algerian counterpart, grown in strength due to harsh socioeconomic conditions and the lack of reforms. This explains why although Morocco has been much less concerned with terrorism than Algeria, it is not totally immune to its threat. In fact, some small violent groups have sought to destabilize the monarchy, most notably the 16 August Movement, constituted by officers who plotted against King Hassan II in the 1970s and the Frontistes, El Djihad, and the Islamic Youth (made up of the fighters who returned from Afghanistan in the early 1990s). In 1993, the Islamic Youth changed its name to the Islamic Group of Moroccan Combatants (GICM). The GICM recruited in Morocco as well as within the Moroccan community in Europe. The salafia jihadia groups have emerged in Morocco and constituted a real threat to national security. The most spectacular attack led by the salafists and the GICM occurred in 2003 in Casablanca. In 2007, several other suicide bombings took place in the same city.[21]

However, noteworthy is the fact that, unlike the attitude toward Algeria, the international community condemned more strongly terrorism in Morocco, linking the activity to international networks and thus propelling the notion that the international community and Morocco were engaged in the same fight. Indeed, an antiterrorism judge testified that there are more than 100 Al Qaeda cells in Morocco that pose a great threat to Europe. The suspects who were arrested after the attacks allegedly confirmed that they acted under Al Qaeda's guidelines and that they had connections with the perpetrators of the train bombings on March 11, 2004 in Madrid[22] and the July 2005 attacks in London.

Tunisia

Compared to Algeria and Morocco, Tunisia has been less preoccupied about radical Islamism. However, this is not to say that the country has been altogether free of Islamist tendencies. As was the case in Algeria and Morocco, Islamists, under Habib Bourguiba's rule (1956–1987), were involved in the educational and cultural sectors, encouraged in working there by the government in order to counter the leftist opposition. However, the 1984 riots in Gafsa gave Islamists a new and growing visibility. In this unstable context, Islamism spread from social organizations into the state security institutions (army, police, and administration, and so on). Even the trade union federation, a traditional government ally, witnessed an increased Islamist influence. The perceived Islamist threat prompted the government to react swiftly and firmly. General Zine al Abidine Ben Ali, the then minister of the interior, decided on November 7, 1987, to remove from office President Bourguiba under the pretext that he was senile. The decision was dubbed a medical coup. The new president used a carrot-and-stick approach to deal with the Islamist movement. Henceforth, he launched a reconciliation policy through amnesty and co-optation, allowing Islamists to adhere to the High Islamic Council and allowing the tolerated, but not officially recognized, Ennahda party to participate in the legislative election of April 1989. The party founded the General Union of Tunisian Students and the al-Fajr (the dawn) newspaper. The government created in 1989 the Center for Islamic Studies and restored the autonomy of the prestigious al-Zaytouna University.[23] For some observers today, Ben Ali's initial moves are considered a prelude to the Arab Spring. However, the honeymoon between the government and Islamists was momentary, primarily because Ben Ali decided soon after to base his legitimacy on his capacity to play the role of bulwark against Islamism, which had begun to rise spectacularly in Algeria. In a sudden change of course, the Tunisian authorities imprisoned and tortured thousands of Ennahda sympathizers and forced the Ennahda party leader, Rached Ghannouchi, into exile. The regime used its fight against the Islamists to ban any form of opposition, secular or Islamist. In contrast to what happened in Algeria, the United States and France supported the Tunisian government's policy of the eradication of the Islamists.[24]

Despite or perhaps due to this eradication policy, Tunisia then witnessed the surfacing of several violent Islamist groups throughout the 1990s. The 1980s were a particularly difficult period for Tunisians. Economically, the country had experienced a drop in revenues because of the decline of the tourist industry as well as a high rate of unemployment. Politically, the country was suffering from Bourguiba's inability to run the country efficiently due to his age and deteriorating mental health. Regional tensions prompted by the 1985 Israeli attack against the Palestinian representation in Tunis, coupled with the social turmoil that plagued the neighborhood, constituted additional strains on the country. What is more, members of Hizb el Tahrir el Islami (Islamic Liberation Party, created in Jerusalem in 1948)[25] had set up a branch in Tunisia that attracted military officers to its membership.[26] The members of this organization were tried for forming an illegal organization and defaming the president. Some other groups emerged in that period and thereafter: The Islamic Trend Movement (MTI in its French acronym), the Popular Revolutionary Movement (MPR), and the Tunisian Armed Resistance (RAT) based in Algeria and Libya. In 1989, a crucial year, the MTI was charged with attempting to overthrow the government and for plotting with Iran.

The Tunisian Combatant Group (GCT), founded in 2000, was the most active terrorist organization in Tunisia. The GCT is similar to the GICM and the Algerian Salafi Group for Preaching and Combat (GSPC), which succeeded to the barbaric GIA in 1998. All of these groups share the same objectives and the same modus operandi even if the GCT and the GCM are much less active than the GCSP.[27] On December 23, 2006 and on January 3, 2007, salafist groups in the town of Slimen, located just 20 miles south of Tunis, broke out in violent clashes with the security forces, made up primarily of the police, the National Guard, the gendarmerie, and the army.[28] Other violent groups, such as the Zarzis, operate in Tunisia. Several members of this group, who originated from the Zarzis region located along the Libyan border, were arrested, tried, and imprisoned for 26 years in 2004.[29] Some of them were pardoned in 2006 under a government amnesty program. The Prophet Brigades group is also active in the Zarzis region and boasts, like other salafist groups, a large network in Europe.[30]

Libya

Qaddafi's 42-year authoritarian rule did not go unopposed. Many opponents from different ideological standpoints had contested his regime. In the 1980s, the Libyan regime accused its opponents of being members of the Muslim Brotherhood.[31] The accusation coincided with the emergence in that period of the Muslim Brothers of Libya, Mohammed Ben Ghali's al-jamaa al islamiya (Islamic Group),[32] and, most importantly, the Party of Islamic Liberation and the Party of God. These opponents exploited the international pressures and the internal socioeconomic difficulties inflicted upon the regime to seek its overthrowing. In 1989, armed clashes between security forces and Islamist groups occurred in Benghazi, Misrata, and Ajdabiya. The radical groups, whose members included foreigners, assaulted mosques, killing and wounding scores of worshippers. Drawing from the jihadist ideology, the groups committed crimes against Muslims they considered as heretics. The regime responded to these actions in an equally cruel fashion, arresting and torturing Islamists. This repression had no dissuasive effect.

During the 1990s, the Islamist opposition became more apparent, owing to internal socioeconomic difficulties due to international sanctions[33] and regional factors, such as the Algerian internal conflict. In addition to the Islamist groups already enumerated, other violent organizations emerged in the country—the Jama'a al-islamiya al-muqatila (Libyan Islamic Combatant Group) and the Harakat al-Shuhada a-libiya (Libyan Martyrs' Movement). Similar to what had occurred in Algeria[34] and Egypt, the most violent jihadist groups were made up of veterans of the war in Afghanistan, the Arab Afghans. For instance, the Jama'a al-islamiya al-muqatila and the Harakat al-Shuhada a-libiya were composed of Afghan war veterans; while the Jama'a al-islamiya a-libiya radicalized people under the influence of the Afghans. Both launched various attacks against security forces and other targets in 1996. The Harakat al-Shuhada launched attacks in spring 1996. The Libyan Islamic Fighting Group, created in 1995, was apparently inspired by the Algerian GSPC and supported by the Egyptian Jama'a Islamiya. Like the other Maghreb salafi groups, the LIFG joined the Al Qaeda networks. The most significant of the attacks targeted Qaddafi himself in Benghazi in 2003.

In the late 1990s and early 2000s, the Libyan regime performed a shift in its foreign policy; indeed, Libya renounced the use of terrorism and decided to join the regional and global war against it[35] and cooperate with the United States in combating Al Qaeda even before the 9/11 attacks.[36] This decision was motivated all the more because Qaddafi himself was the target of assassination attempts by Al Qaeda. Libya became the first country to release proof and a request for an Interpol arrest warrant for the Al Qaeda leader, five months before the 1998 attacks on the U.S. embassies in Kenya and Tanzania.[37] In counterpart, the United States added one of Libya's most radical factions, the LIFG, onto the list of terrorist organizations in December 2001.[38]

THE MAGHREBIZATION OF TERRORISM

Due to their experience, Algerian salafists have become the central figures of Maghrebi armed groups. Even if the terrorist attacks in other Maghreb countries may not be as spectacular as those seen in Algeria, they reveal a horizontal expansion. From the very beginning of the turmoil in Algeria, regional networks were established. Hence, investigations into the Guemmar attack on the Algerian-Tunisian border in November 1991 revealed that the perpetrators of the attack had accomplices among Tunisian Islamists.[39] In 2001, specialists estimated that 200 Islamists linked to Ennahda were trained by the GSPC. Some of them may have been the group that had attacked a border post in Oum Ali (Kasserine region) and a group of Tunisian soldiers in October 2001. This region saw all kinds of trafficking: weapons, red mercury, and banknotes to name but a few.[40] Algerian authorities arrested in 2001, 2005, and 2007 many Tunisians whom they suspected of having joined the GSPC.[41] According to security forces in Morocco, members of the GICM had been trained and supported by the LIFG.[42] In recent years, numerous Maghrebi terrorist networks have emerged.[43]

Since 9/11, terrorism in the North Africa region has increased astronomically. The main characteristic of this terrorism is its transnational dimension. Terrorist groups, most notably, Al Qaeda in the Land of the Islamic Maghreb, known as AQIM, started in early 2007, have established themselves not only in northern Algeria but also in the Sahara-Sahel region. Owing to the difficulties of operating in northern Algeria, AQIM has established a stronger presence in the Sahara-Sahel, which it uses as a base for its operations and for fund-raising through trafficking and kidnappings.

With respect to the number of terrorist attacks, Algeria has suffered the greatest number annually; since 2004, terrorist attacks have increased by 240 percent. Algeria concentrates 80 percent of the total attacks (938) in the North Africa-Sahel region. Comparatively, Libya was targeted once, Morocco seven times, and Tunisia three times.[44] Despite these deadly attacks, the Algerian regime has not seemed to be threatened by radical Islamism, at least in the short term.[45]

The sudden increase in terrorist actions can be linked to the 2003 GSPC decision to associate itself with Al Qaeda in the hope of obtaining an ideological blessing and international financial support, which would break the isolation imposed by the security forces inside the country.

Table 2.1 Table of Terrorist Attacks in the Maghreb between 2001 and 2011

	Algeria	Libya	Morocco	Tunisia
2001	20			1
2002	54			1
2003	28		2	
2004	39			
2005	93			
2006	120	1		
2007	110		5	
2008	121			1
2009	185			
2010	168			
2011	164		2	1
Total	1102	1	9	4

Source: Yonah Alexander, "Special Update Report Terrorism in North, West, & Central Africa: From 9/11 to the Arab Spring," The International Center for Terrorism Studies (ICTS), January 2012, 27.

VIOLENCE: A REAL THREAT TO SECURITY IN THE MAGHREB?

The answer is undoubtedly difficult to come by, especially if the following two considerations are taken into account:

1. The definition of security must be detailed and analyzed in depth so that one is clear about what is meant by state security, internal security, national security, and regime security.

2. The nature of the threats needs to be clarified in order to determine whether or not the threats are virtual or real, hard or soft, classical or asymmetric.

The remarkable evolution of the threats, on the one hand, and the extraordinary alteration in the state's functions and powers on the other, has created a novel situation where exceptions to the rule have become more common than the rule itself. For instance, the idea that the Islamist threat was merely an excuse to justify the status quo is confirmed in the Tunisian case under Ben Ali, but does not apply to Qaddafi's Libya. In the first case, the authoritarianism of the regime did not prevent the emergence of institutions and administrative structures that preserve the survival of the state, for "both the regime and the Islamists serve each other. The regime holds the Islamists up as justification for restrictions on democracy, and the Islamists use the regime's repression as a claim to legitimacy."[46] Contrarily, the whole confusion between Qaddafi's power and the nation-state resulted in the collapse of the state as soon as Qaddafi's power was undermined by the rebellion. The frontal attack on the regime also brought down the state. The survival of the Jamahiriya state was linked to Qaddafi's fate; thus, the risk of a tribal war following the collapse of the regime was real. The revolt against the regime could not have been peaceful simply because the conditions of the political fight—elections, trade union activities, and political parties—were never permitted and, what is more, the building of the nation-state was never completed. The historical regional tensions between Tripolitania and Cyrenaica never disappeared and neither have the associated tribal loyalties.[47]

The confusion between state security and regime security has implications at yet another level. The security vacuum left in Libya after the collapse of the regime results in a security threat for the region as a whole.[48] For the European countries in general and above all for Tunisia, the refugees fleeing Libya represented the main concern in the short term. For northern and western African countries, terrorism represented, and still represents, the main danger to their national security.[49] Their economic security is of concern because refugees constitute an additional economic and social burden. The fate of the small Tunisian island Djerba illustrates the social impact of the war.[50] Furthermore, trade between Tunisia and Libya has declined considerably. Tunisia's exports to Libya fell by 32 percent in the first quarter of 2011, compared with the same period in 2010. This fall is due to the interruption of imports of crude oil from Libya, which represents the major part of Tunisian imports.[51] It should however be pointed out that Tunisian exports to Libya increased during the same period due to the consumption requirements of the Libyan population.[52] The flow of refugees from Libya also impacted Algeria because 200,000 people found refuge in the country between February and August 2011, in addition to the 500 Tuareg families who fled the country due to the threat from the rebels.[53]

The fight in Libya caused collateral damages owing to the military escalation along the bordering countries and led the British government to invoke the possibility of sending British troops to the Libyan border with Tunisia to help protect refugees from attacks by Qaddafi's forces. Actually, all of Libya's neighbors had to send reinforcements to their security forces at the borders to ward off arms trafficking and control the refugee situation. Hence, 40,000 troops and gendarmes were sent to strengthen the borders in July 2011.[54] Algeria, which shares a 1,000-kilometer border with Libya, took political and military measures to reinforce security in the area with close cooperation with the desert tribes. What is more, in order to ensure control of this lawless region, the government decided to create two new military subregions in the south (Ouargla and Tamanrasset) in order to facilitate the integration of local populations in their security agenda.

Undoubtedly, the Libyan, Yemenite, and Syrian experience have worked as a deterrent against the potential opponents in many Arab countries and offered some comfort to the rulers. Governments convey the message that uncontrolled opposition can easily lead to military escalation, heavy human and material losses, and destruction of a country's unity. In the 1990s, for example, the Moroccan government regularly used the civil unrest in Algeria to justify the choice of restricted reforms. Since the beginning of the Arab turmoil, the official Algerian political discourse has focused on the view that Algeria has already experienced political changes and paid a heavy price for it. Moreover, Algerian rulers have sought to strengthen their legitimacy through the security principle. This security legitimacy linked to the war on terror came at an opportune time to revive the revolutionary legitimacy inherited from the war of independence (1954–1962).

In summary, the political instability in Tunisia and the civil war in Libya represent a challenge for Algeria's national security, but at the same time, a political opportunity for the Algerian regime.

As we shall see in Chapter Five, the same comparison could be made with the role that the Western Sahara conflict plays in the Moroccan national security conception and the monarchial security vision. Supporting a long-term war, even of low intensity, is an economic burden;[55] this conflict has cost one percent of the country's GDP. Morocco has mobilized between 130,000 and 160,000 troops in occupied Western Sahara, which represents between 52 and 64 percent of the total number of its armed forces. Morocco has also invested $2.4 billion since its occupation of the disputed territory to build basic infrastructures. In addition, before the year 2005 several hundred Moroccan POWs were being held in POLISARIO jails while others had died in captivity since the conflict erupted in 1975. The political cost has also been consequential as no country recognizes Morocco's sovereignty over the territory. Furthermore, the conflict has poisoned relations with Algeria, thus undermining the potential development of greater economic and commercial cooperation. More importantly, the monarchy has linked its fate to that of the future of Western Sahara by making the issue as one of the core constituents of the country's national identity. Thus, in order to convince outsiders to support the Autonomy Plan of 2007 as an alternative to a referendum on self-determination for the Sahrawi people, the monarchy has had to initiate a wide decentralization project for the kingdom.

Although the Western Sahara issue incurs heavy costs on the kingdom, the conflict offers a good opportunity for the king to strengthen his powers. Since gaining independence, the royal family and the armed forces have had tense relations. King Hassan II escaped two military coups in 1971 and 1972. The conflict in Western Sahara provided him with the opportunity to move the military away from the centers of power in Rabat and keep the forces held up far away, thus reducing considerably any influence they may have. To a large extent, this strategy, continued under his son Mohammed VI, who succeeded him in July 1999; the policy has been rather successful.

NOTES

1. RatibaHadj-Moussa, "Riots: Protest from the Margins or the Margins of Protest? Reconsidering Riots in the Mediterranean and Beyond," Twelfth Mediterranean Research Meeting, 2011.

2. Sofiane Ait-Iflis, "Les Émeutes de la Fin? " *Le Soird'Algérie,* January 7–8, 2011, http://www.lesoirdalgerie.com/pdf/2011/01/08012011.pdf.

3. Louisa Dris-Aït Hamadouche, "Algérie Face au Printemps Arabe: L'équilibre par la Neutralisation des Contestations," *Confluences Méditerranée,* N° 81 (Spring 2012): 55–67.

4. On the events in the aftermath of independence, see Ali Haroun, *Algérie 1962: la Grande Dérive* (Paris: L'Harmattan, 2005).

5. Charif Mustapha et Benmansour Abdallah, "Le Rôle de l'Etat dans L'économie Sociale en Algérie," *Revue Internationale de L'Economie Sociale,* no. 321, July 2011, http://recma.org/node/1360.

6. Kamel Hamzi, "La Subvention des Produits Alimentaires Coûte 300 Milliards de Dinars," *Maghreb Emergent,* April 12, 2011.

7. Louisa Dris-Aït Hamadouche, "L'Algérie Face au Printemps Arabe: Pressions Diffuses et Résilience Entretenue," *L'Annuaire IEMed de la Méditerranée* (Med., 2012).

8. Christian Lowe and Souhail Karam, "Will Other N. African States Go Way of Egypt and Tunisia?" http://af.reuters.com/article/energyOilNews/idAFLDE7130EC20110216?page Number = 5&virtualBrandChannel = 0.

9. Ibid.

10. See, in particular, Florence Beaugé, "Troubles Sociaux Meurtriers au Maroc et en Tunisie," *Le Monde,* June 10, 2008 and "Maroc: Événements de Sidi Ifni ou L'échec de l'État de Droit," *Le Nouvel Observateur,* June 15, 2008.

11. Yahia H. Zoubir, "The Arab Spring: Is Algeria the Exception?" *Euromesco-IEMed Brief,* no. 17 (October 20, 2011).

12. Kouichi Shirayanagi, "North Africa under Stress: Latest Developments," *The North Africa Journal* (February 10, 2011), http://www.north-africa.com/social_polics/security_politics/1northafricaunderstress46.html.

13. Kouichi Shirayanagi, "North Africa under Stress: Latest Developments," *The North Africa Journal* (February 10, 2011), http://www.north-africa.com/social_polics/security_politics/1northafricaunderstress46.html.

14. Yahia H. Zoubir, "Contestation Islamiste et Lutte Antiterroriste en Libye, 1990–2007," *L'Année du Maghreb 2008* (Paris: CNRS Editions, 2008), 267–77.

15. Benghazi, an industrial and commercial center, is the principal city of eastern Libya and is one of the country's major economic centers. The city has an important port which is vital to the economy; most of the food and manufactured products are imported into Libya through that port. Finance is also important to the city's economy with the Libyan Bank of Commerce and Development maintaining branches in there. The city has historically boasted the main opposition to Qaddafi's rule.

16. Yahia H. Zoubir, "Resilient Authoritarianism, Uncertain Democratization, and *Jihadism* in Algeria," in *Democratic Development and Political Terrorism: The Global Perspective,* ed. Bill Crotty (Boston, MA: Northeastern University Press, 2004).

17. Louisa Aït-Hamadouche and Yahia H. Zoubir, "The Fate of Political Islam in Algeria," in *The Contemporary Maghrib,* ed. Bruce Maddy-Weitzman and D. Zisenwine (Gainesville, FL: University Press of Florida, 2007), 103–31.

18. Carlos Echeverria, "Radical Islam in Maghreb," *Orbis* 48, no. 2 (Spring 2004): 3.

19. Malika Zeghal, "Religion et Politique au Maroc Aujourd'hui," *Policy Paper* no. 11 (Institut Français des Relations Internationales, IFRI, March 2005), 32–50; Mohamed Tozy, *Monarchie et Islam Politique au Maroc* (Paris: Presses de Sciences Po, 1999).

20. Michael J. Willis, "Morocco's Islamists and the Legislative Elections of 2002: The Strange Case of the Party That Did Not Want to Win," *Mediterranean Politics,* Vol. 9, no.1 (Spring 2004): 53–81.

21. Alexander Yonah, "Maghreb & Sahel Terrorism: Addressing the Rising Threat from al-Qaeda and Other Terrorists in North and West/Central Africa," *International Center for Terrorism Studies at the Potomac Institute for Policy Studies,* January 2010, 18.

22. Ilhem Rachidi, "Morocco Tempers Islamists," *Christian Science Monitor,* July 19, 2004.

23. Aziz Enhaili and Oumelkheir Adda, "State and Islamism in the Maghreb," *Middle East Quarterly,* 7, 1, (March 2003), http://www.social-sciences-and-humanities.com/PDF/etat-et-islamism-au-maghreb.pdf.

24. John P. Entelis, "Political Islam in the Maghreb: The Non-Violent Dimension," in *Islam, Democracy and the State in North Africa,* ed. John P. Entelis (Bloomington, IN: Indiana University Press, 1997), 49.

25. He claimed responsibility for the attack against the synagogue of Djerba, in 2002.

26. Annelli Botha, "Terrorism in the Maghreb, the Transnationalisation of Domestic Terrorism," Pretoria/Tshwane: Institute for Security Studies, 2008, ISSS Monograph Series, no. 144, (June 2008), 113.

27. "Morocco Tempers Islamists," *Islam Daily,* July 20, 2004, http://www.islamdaily.org/en/wahabism/1562.morocco-tempers-islamists.htm.

28. Aamza Belloumi, "La Tunisie Face au Terrorisme," *Islamiqua,* January 18, 2007, http://islamiqua.canalblog.com/archives/2007/01/18/3728127.html.

29. "La Torture et la loi Antiterroriste du 10 Décembre 2003," Association de Lutte Contre la Torture en Tunisie, 2008, http://www.fidh.org/IMG/pdf/crldht-altt-torture-en-tunisie-rapport.pdf.

30. Anneli Botha, "Terrorism in the Maghreb, the Transnationalisation of Domestic Terrorism," *ISS Monograph Series,* no. 144 (June 2008), 118–19.

31. François Burgat and William Dowell, *The Islamic Movement in North Africa* (Austin, TX: University of Texas Press, 1993), 158.

32. Bruno de Callies de Salies, *Le Maghreb en Mutation-Entre Tradition et Modernité* (Paris: Maisonneuve et Larose, 1999), 147.

33. Tim Niblock, *Pariah States' and Sanctions in the Middle East—Iraq, Libya, Sudan* (Boulder, CO: Lynne Rienner, 2001).

34. Yahia H. Zoubir, "Resilient Authoritarianism, Uncertain Democratization, and *Jihadism* in Algeria," in *Democratic Development and Political Terrorism,* ed. William J. Crotty (Boston, MA: Northeastern University Press, 2005), 280–300.

35. Ronald E. Neumann, "Libya: A US Policy Perspective," *Middle East Policy,* Vol. 7, no. 2 (February 2000): 142–45.

36. Ronald Bruce St John, " 'Libya Is Not Iraq': Preemptive Strikes, WMD and Diplomacy," *Middle East Journal,* 58, 3 (Summer 2004): 391–92.

37. Yahia H. Zoubir and Louisa DrisAït-Hamadouche, "The United States and the Maghreb: Islamism, Democratization, and Strategic Interests," *Maghreb Review,* Vol. 31 (2006): 2–4.

38. Foreign Terrorist Organizations, http://www.state.gov/j/ct/rls/crt/2008/122449.htm.

39. Carlos Echeverria, "Radical Islam in Maghreb," Orbis: *A Journal of World Affairs,* Vol. 48, no. 2 (Spring 2004): 354.

40. Anneli Botha, "Terrorism in the Maghreb, the Transnationalisation of Domestic Terrorism," *ISS Monograph Series,* no. 144 (June 2008), 119.

41. Anneli Botha, "Terrorism in the Maghreb, the Transnationalisation of Domestic Terrorism," *ISS Monograph Series,* no. 144 (June 2008), 120–23.

42. "L'UMA du Terrorisme," *Le Quotidien D'Oran,* June 15, 2005.

43. Louisa Dris-Aït Hamadouche, "Les Relations Euro-maghrébines sous le Prisme de L'islamisme," in *Europe et Maghreb. Voisinage Immédiat, Distanciation Stratégique,* ed. Abdennour Benantar (Alger: Centre de Recherche en Economie Appliquée pour le Développement, 2010), 199–228.

44. Yonah, "Maghreb & Sahel Terrorism: Addressing the Rising Threat from al-Qaeda and Other Terrorists in North and West/Central Africa," *International Center for Terrorism Studies at the Potomac Institute for Policy Studies,* January 2010, 14.

45. David Gray and Erik Stockham, "Al Qaeda in the Islamic Maghreb: the Evolution from an Algerian Islamism to Transnational Terror," *African Journal of Political Science and International Relations,* Vol. 2, no. 4 (December 2008): 91–97.

46. Neila Charchour Hachicha, "Tunisia's Election was Undemocratic at all Levels," *Middle East Quarterly,* 12, 3 (Summer 2005): 77–81. http://www.meforum.org/article/732.

47. Moncef Djaziri, "Tribus et Etat dans le Système Politique Libyen," *Outre-terre,* Vol. 3, no. 23 (2009): 127–34.

48. Arslan Chikhaoui, "La Menace Jihadiste en Libye: un Intérêt Stratégique pour al Qaïda," *Liberté* (August 18, 2011). Swami Praveen and Duncan Gardham, "Libyan Rebel Commander Admits his Fighters Have Al-Qaeda Links," *The Telegraph,* March 25, 2011; James Dorsey, "Libyan Islamists Stand to Gain with or without Gadhafi," Deutsche Welle, March 24, 2011; Noman Benotman and James Brandon, *The Jihadist Threat in Libya,* Briefing paper, Quilliam Foundation (2011), http://www.rivagessyrtes.com/ext/http://www.quilliamfoundation.org/images/stories/pdfs/libya24march11.pdf 24/03/2011.

49. Andrew Stroehlein and Kimberly Abbott, "Libya: Achieving a Ceasefire, Moving toward Legitimate Government," International Crisis Group, May 13, 2011, http://www.crisisgroup.org/en/publication-type/media-releases/2011/libya-achieving-a-ceasefire-moving-toward-legitimate-government.aspx; "Popular Protest in North Africa and the Middle East (V): Making Sense of Libya," *Middle East/North Africa Report* N°107 International Crisis Group, http://www.crisisgroup.org/en/regions/middle-east-north-africa/north-africa/libya/107-popular-protest-in-north-africa-and-the-middle-east-v-making-sense-of-libya.aspx (June 6, 2011).

50. From February to August 2011, almost 50,000 Libyans escaped to Tunisia, 5,000 of them settling in Djerba. In this famous tourist destination, Qaddafi's supporters and rebels lived side-by-side, *La Stampa,* June 7, 2011.

51. http://rawlinsview.wordpress.com/2011/05/24/tunisias-exports-to-libya-down-32-tap-reports-economic-impact-of-libyan-civil-war-on-tunisia/.

52. "Tunisie Libye Reprise des Exportations," Tunisieprojet.tn, http://www.tunisieprojet.tn/actualites-et-news/tunisie-libye-reprise-des-exportations/.

53. "Pourchassés par des Libyens, 500 Touaregs se réfugient en Algérie," *Agence France Presse* (AFP), August 31, 2011, http://www.dna-algerie.com/fil-rouge/pourchasses-par-des-libyens-500-touaregs-se-refugient-en-algerie-2.

54. Nabil Belbey, "L'Algérie Renforce sa Sécurité à ses Frontières," *L'Expression,* July 6, 2011.

55. Abdelmoumni, Fouad, "The Cost of the Conflict," *Middle East/North Africa Report,* No 65, *International Crisis Group* (June 11, 2007), 9.

CHAPTER 3

Human Security within the Maghreb: Contrasted Conditions

ECONOMIC DEVELOPMENT: MAGHREB PARADOXES AND DISPARITIES

One could distinguish among the Maghreb economies according to the degree of their openness, their per capita income, or according to the existence of their rentier[1] status, and the accountability of the rulers. These factors, along with other variables, are able to provide us with a comparative grasp on the economies of the Maghreb. In order to portray these paradoxes and imbalances, this chapter will focus on the poor social benefits of economic growth due to diverse monopolies.

The Disparities

Disparities in Individual Countries

All of the Maghreb countries suffer from internal disparities between the coastal areas and the interior (Tunisia and Algeria), between the north and the south (Algeria, Morocco, and Libya), and between the cities and the rural areas (all of them). Several geographical areas are propitious to economic activities because of the presence of adequate infrastructure and the availability of labor, which contribute to the development of these regions whereas other areas do not attract investors at all because investors tend to look for a suitable environment (good facilities, less bureaucracy, skilled labor, and so on), thus putting the residents of these areas at a significant disadvantage especially in terms of unemployment and social exclusion.

In Morocco, for instance, data for 2010, provided by the High Commission for Planning, indicates that five regions generated more than 60 percent of the entire country's income: Greater Casablanca, Rabat, Marrakech, Tangier-Tetouan, and Sousse-Massa-Draa. The populations in these regions enjoy the highest purchasing power.[2] The figures that the Financial Forecasting and Research Division published in 2010 confirm the existence of interregional disparities in GDP per capita income. In Greater Casablanca, for example, it is on average 3.6 times greater than in Taza-Al Houceima-Taounate.

In Tunisia, as in Algeria, social as well as regional disparities are evident. Hence, unemployment, particularly among new graduates, has continued to increase since 2006 (to 18.2% in 2007 and 21.9% in 2009) whereas job creation has slowed down (from 80,000 jobs created in 2007 to only 57,000 in 2009). Some regions in Tunisia have been excluded from access to capital and investments altogether. It is for this reason that riots broke out in Sidi Bouzid in the central region.[3] The number of graduates looking for jobs against the total number of unemployed has grown from 20 to 55 percent in less than 10 years. The proportion of unemployed young people under the age of 30 has reached 69 percent in Morocco, 72 percent in Tunisia, and 75 percent in Algeria.[4] In Morocco, 31.8 percent of the youth under the age of 24 are unemployed. The Tunisian youth, aged between 20 and 24 face an unemployment rate of 31 percent whereas 25 percent of those between the ages of 25 and 29 are jobless. Young Algerians under 24 face a jobless rate of 23 percent. Throughout the Maghreb, urban areas report a 27.5 percent rate of youth unemployment.[5] The period of unemployment among the Maghreb youth lasts longer, extending from two to three years in Morocco, Algeria, and Tunisia. The informal sector offers the most job opportunities, a form of safety valve; however, the workers enjoy practically no benefits, no social protection, no retirement plans, and so on.

Undoubtedly, youth joblessness produces insecurity and instability. In Tunisia, the unemployed made up the bulk of the protesters in December 2010 and January 2011. In Algeria, the situation is more serious because Islamist armed groups recruit unemployed young men; the desire to adhere to these groups is no longer ideological or political but mostly economic because these armed groups provide financial security to their members. This is in fact the most attractive aspect of Al Qaeda for the new militants who join the organization.[6] Young men are often contacted through electronic messages and guided toward Islamist Internet sites. In order to motivate them to join the movements, Islamists offer to help the families of the potential recruits.[7]

Disparities among Maghreb Countries

The United Nations Human Development Report ranks Libya 53rd, Tunisia 81st, and Algeria 84th: rankings considered to be somewhat high. Morocco, on the other hand, is ranked 114th, placing it within the medium band of human development rankings. This classification reveals a stark difference between the best ranked Maghreb country (Libya) and the worst one (Morocco). However, the relatively good Libyan ranking did not prevent the eruption of social protests, nor did it prevent the civil war. Morocco on the other hand, has remained comparatively stable. An analysis of the different variables will provide an explanation as to some of the causes of these disparities.

The 2010 World Bank's report *Doing Business* placed Tunisia among the 10 best ranked countries in the Arab World owing to the country's significant reforms of the tax system, the welfare system, and trading across borders. Tunisia introduced electronic payment processes (including filing and settlement), which have reduced the frequency of payments, tax-payment compliance times, tax evasion, and transaction costs.

Table 3.1 Tunisian Macroeconomic Indicators

	2008	2009	2010	2011
Real GDP Growth	4.6	3.1	4.0	4.5
CPI Inflation	5.1	3.5	3.1	3.4
Budget Balance % GDP	–0.8	–3.9	–3.5	–2.8
Current Account % GDP	–4.2	–2.7	–1.1	–1.3

Source: African Economic Outlook, Tunisia Profile, http://www.africaneconomicoutlook.org/en/countries/north-africa/tunisia/.

Unlike Tunisia, Morocco has had greater difficulty in overcoming the consequences of the economic crisis. There are persistent worries about the health of the balance of trade, and the competitiveness of its exports, as well as the strong concentration of exports on the European markets. In addition, the crisis has had a negative impact on the revenues from tourism and the remittances from Moroccan residents abroad. The dwindling of these two principal sources of foreign currency has aggravated the economic conditions of the country.

Table 3.2 Moroccan Macroeconomic Indicators

	2008	2009	2010	2011
Real GDP Growth	5.6	5.0	4.3	4.9
CPI Inflation	3.9	1.0	2.9	2.5
Budget Balance % GDP	0.4	–2.9	–4.0	–3.4
Current Account % GDP	–4.9	–6.3	–4.0	–3.7

Source: African Economic Outlook, Morocco Profile, http://www.africaneconomicoutlook.org/en/countries/north-africa/morocco/.

The World Bank's reports *Doing Business* published in 2009 and 2010 indicated that Morocco continues to face great challenges in improving its business environment. Among these challenges is modernizing the judicial system, facilitating small to medium-sized enterprises (SMEs) access to credit, and increasing labor market flexibility.

While both Morocco and Tunisia share a traditional commitment to liberal economics, Algeria and Libya, both rentier economies, share common features and have initiated a number of reforms. Algeria has increased its tax revenue thanks to an improved system of collection in ordinary taxation and oil taxes. In 2008, the tax revenue rose by 57 percent; the rate of oil taxes increased by 76 percent while nontax revenue has increased annually since 2000.[8] Nevertheless, this has not lessened the country's dependency on hydrocarbons; this dependency will certainly not decrease in the foreseeable future especially because investments in that sector are gaining more and more momentum. Gas exports will increase thanks to the 250-kilometer Medgaz gas pipeline, which has been operational since October 2011; the pipeline links Algeria to Almeria in Spain. The pipeline will have an annual transit capacity of eight billion cubic meters. On completion in 2015, the gas pipeline between France and Spain will have an interconnection capacity of seven billion cubic meters to transport gas to France. This link will enable Algeria to increase its exports to Europe, which has become increasingly dependent on Algerian gas. In addition, $45 billion has been planned for the development of projects for the processing of raw hydrocarbons, most notably refining, gas liquefaction, and petrochemicals.

According to the World Bank's 2010 report *Doing Business*, Algeria has dropped two places to 136th. Despite this mediocre position, the country is doing better in terms of competitiveness, having risen from 99th in 2008–09 to 83rd in 2009–10, in the World Economic Forum's global competitiveness ranking.

Table 3.3 Algerian Macroeconomic Indicators

	2008	2009	2010	2011
Real GDP Growth	2.4	2.2	3.9	4.3
CPI Inflation	3.9	5.7	3.4	4.5
Budget Balance % GDP	6.0	−8.3	−6.3	−4.6
Current Account % GDP	17.6	−3.1	4.9	5.2

Even if Algeria and Libya are both rentier economies, the latter, with a population of barely six million, is in a far better financial situation than the former.

Libya boasts the continent's largest proven oil reserves and is the third biggest producer behind Angola and Nigeria. Libya was only moderately affected by the global economic and financial crisis. Despite significant efforts over the past two decades to diversify its economy, Libya remains highly dependent on hydrocarbons, which account for close to 70 percent of GDP and generate more than 90 percent of government revenues and 95 percent of export earnings. Libya has since 2003 struggled with an unemployment rate estimated to be between 20 and 30 percent. At the same time, however, Libya enjoyed, according to the UN Development Program, the highest Human Development Index (HDI) on the African continent, rising steadily between 2000 and 2008 by 0.44 percent annually from 0.821 to 0.847. What is more, its Human Poverty Index (HPI-1) only slightly decreased from 13.6 percent in 2008 to 13.4 percent in 2009 despite the impact of the global economic crisis. Seventy-eight percent of the population live in urban areas, with an average life expectancy of more than 77 years and an average literacy rate of 82.6 percent, which puts Libya on the right path to achieving the UN Millennium Development Goals (MDGs).[9]

Regarding the taxation policy, the 2009 Africa Competitiveness Report assigned a score of 4/7 on the perceptions of business executives on the level of taxes, placing Libya in 37th position out of 134 countries. The main source of nontax revenue is the returns from investments made by the Libya Investment Authority (Libya's major sovereign wealth fund) and other investments located abroad. Like Algeria, Libya suffers from juridical instability, which increases uncertainty and investors' distrust. For instance, in January 2009, Qaddafi threatened to nationalize the hydrocarbon industry.[10] Although he did not carry out this threat, the announcement did cause a stir among oil and gas operators in Libya. The following month, Qaddafi suggested that all the ministries should be dismantled; the General People's Congress, the equivalent of parliament, ultimately rejected the proposal.

Table 3.4 Libyan Macroeconomic Indicators

	2008	2009	2010	2011
Real GDP Growth	3.8	2.1	5.2	6.1
CPI Inflation	10.4	2.5	5.3	5.6
Budget Balance % GDP	29.6	10.6	14.8	21.6
Current Account % GDP	40.7	16.8	32.6	37.3

Source: C. Helman, "Is Libya Going To Boot U.S. Oil Companies? Muammar Gaddafi Looks Ready to Launch a New Round of Energy-Sector Nationalism," *Forbes*, January 22, 2009, http://www.forbes.com/2009/01/22/libya-gaddafi-oil-biz-energy-cx_ch_0122libya.html.

Monopolies and Corruption

Economic liberalization without a concomitant political liberalization inevitably leads to the creation of monopolies and allows the exploitation of wealth through political means in various ways. For instance, in Morocco, the king must approve large economic contracts. The royal family is the largest entrepreneur and the biggest owner of agricultural operations in the kingdom. The monarchy secures these operations through the industrial and financial holding, Omnium Nord Africain (ONA), which generates a significant percentage of Morocco's GDP.[11] Under the pretext of forming powerful conglomerates to protect the Moroccan economy, the king's business has grown exponentially. Siger, King Mohammed VI's holding company, controls the largest bank, the biggest insurance company, and one of the three main telecom operators.[12] In a published Wikileaks cable, it has been reported that the "major investment decisions are made by three individuals: Fouad al-Himma, former deputy interior minister who now heads the Party of Authenticity and Modernity, Mohammad Mounir al-Majidi, head of the king's private secretariat, and the king himself."[13]

Privatization of state-owned enterprises is expected to continue, but most of the funds from the sale of state firms will be used to cover government expenditure and debt repayments, leaving little for productive investments. The king established 16 regional investment centers, headed by an appointed governor, to circumvent bureaucratic opposition and stimulate new investments. Furthermore,[14] the government put together a joint (public-private) committee in 2009 with the aim of identifying measures that could improve the business environment. Tunisia has witnessed a series of privatizations since 1986, which have been highly instrumental in instituting a market economy, developing private investment, enabling the state's withdrawal from a number of competitive sectors, and relieving public finances of the burden of a number of enterprises in constant deficit. Between 1987 and 2009, 219 enterprises were privatized, amounting to 5.976 billion Tunisian dinars. Nearly 90 percent of the investment came in the form of foreign direct investments (FDI). In 2009, a further five public enterprises were privatized, adding nearly 100 million Tunisian dinars to the state budget. In 2010, the privatization program targeted 12 new enterprises, including three as concessions.[15] Before the revolution, little progress was made in the banking or telecommunications sectors because these sectors were viewed as strategic industries by Tunisian decision makers. It is for this reason that Tunisia's two largest banks remain state-owned. The government however, was seeking a strategic investor in 2006 to take a 35 percent share of the state-owned Tunis Telecommunications Company. The company owns all fixed telephone lines in the country, as well as 60 percent of the mobile or cellular network.[16]

In comparison, in Libya, the state remained in control during Qaddafi's reign, posing as the country's primary employer and primary investor. Indeed, the Economy Watch estimated in 2010 that industry and services (mainly under the government control) represented 82 percent of the national economy.[17] In August 2009, the Privatization and Investment Board established its new one-stop streamlined business license application procedure to improve the overall business climate and enhance investor confidence in the non-oil sectors of the economy. The opening up of Libya's economy has triggered the interest of foreign investors attracted by opportunities in energy and construction and to a lesser extent by the potentially promising new tourism sector. According to the UN Conference on Trade and Development 2009 World Investment Report, FDI in Libya quadrupled between 2005 and 2008.[18] Prior to this, in 2002, Seif-al-Islam Qaddafi indicated that the objective was to transform the Libyan economy into a market economy through liberalization and privatization. One year later, the government called for the privatization of all sectors, including the oil sector. Three hundred public enterprises then went on to be sidelined in preference for privatization.

As for the impact of the revolution, increasing wages in the public sector resulted in a 60 percent increase of the state wage bill in 2011. The cost of subsidies has also gone up significantly.[19] The IMF has already informed the Libyan government that the issue of unemployment should not be resolved by providing employment through the public sector. This message clearly indicates that the private sector is being encouraged to take a more active role in society. From this perspective, since January 2012, the IMF and the World Bank have started working with the authorities to strengthen public financial management and, what is more, reform the central bank.

With respect to Algeria, the business climate is still hindered by a complex bureaucracy and sudden changes in public policies. Some indicators have improved such as the following: the terms and conditions for granting building permits; the adoption of a new civil code for procedures, which reduces the time needed to process lawsuits; the reduction of the cost of land and property transactions; and the nontaxation of capital gains on the stock market.[20] In the 2010 World Bank's *Doing Business* report, Algeria dropped two places year on year to 136th. The country is doing better in terms of competitiveness, however, having risen from 99th in 2008–09 to 83rd in 2009–10 in the World Economic Forum's global competitiveness ranking. Currently, Algeria's financial sector is still dominated by public banks; therefore, clearly there is a need to further modernize and deepen the financial sector to facilitate access to credit. Furthermore, the 2009 Complementary Law of Finance (CLF) has had a negative impact on business because businesses must now submit a letter of credit to pay for imports; the law exempts companies importing raw materials and equipment from this requirement. The 2009 CLF also compels foreign importers to transfer 30 percent of their capital to Algerian partners. "While the point of these regulations was to encourage new partnerships with domestic investors, what we've actually seen is a significant decline of already scarce foreign investment flows to Algeria."[21]

Corruption

Corruption is another way of creating monopolies and preventing the redistribution of wealth.

Due to the volume of Algerian imports, international trade is frequently subject to corruption, tax fraud, and capital flight, often related to false declarations of the quantities of imports and price transfers. The illegal transfers have increased considerably from four billion dollars in 2009 to $16 billion in 2010.[22] The authorities therefore decided to impose systematically the use of a letter of credit as the only mode of payment for imports as of 2010. However, corruption has affected many other strategic sectors, such as the national oil company Sonatrach, the National Highway Agency's huge corruption case, and the big financial scandal of the private Khalifa Bank. The collapse of the Khalifa Bank resulted in losses of billions of dollars for the state. With regard to the huge east–west highway project, each kilometer has cost three times more than that of the average cost of similar projects in other countries. The revelations in February 2013 concerning the bribes received by Algerian senior executives from Italian and Canadian companies to secure access to the lucrative oil sector illustrate the high degree of corruption in the granting of contracts.

Neighboring Libya suffered under Qaddafi's rule from a business environment that was totally unpredictable, with weak coordination, a complex decision-making process, and opaque legal and institutional frameworks. Like in Algeria, nepotism and clientelism undermined the pace and efficiency of economic development.

Corruption in the Maghreb countries has been so pervasive that it is no longer an economic phenomenon but has simply become common cultural practice. Has civil society been concerned with this phenomenon and if so how has it tried to fight it? Before the overthrow of Qaddafi, Transparency-Libya, administered by Libya around the Human and Political Development Forum, was "dedicated to exposing all kinds of corruption in the country." It published the 2004 *Libya Human Development* report, which included a chapter on "Corruption and Lack of Transparency in Governing." In Tunisia, due to the restrictions the Ben Ali regime imposed on associations and on Internet usage, civil society initiatives against corruption took the form of blogs and news commentaries posted on the Internet from sites based outside the country. Active civil societies have on the other hand been present in Algeria and, more forcefully, in Morocco. The most active groups in Algeria are Transparency International and the Algerian Association against Corruption. Officers of the Cour des Comptes (National Audit Court) protested publicly against being marginalized in their efforts to audit the government's finances. The independent press has played a leading role in revealing corruption affairs—among them those that involve senior officials. Morocco is the country where most of the anticorruption actions have taken place. Transparency-Morocco established a "National Observatory of Corruption" in June 2007; during its first year of activity, it publicized 1,500 instances of corruption. The members of this organization maintain a highly visible profile, organizing public marches, and launching campaigns on television. Forty-six nongovernmental organizations (NGOs) make up the Network against Corruption (NAC), which works actively to reduce corruption in the bureaucracy. The General Confederation of Moroccan Enterprises (CGEM) has taken the lead in devising a code of ethics, which it adopted in 2008.

Revealing corruption scandals is only useful if concrete measures are taken to eradicate corruption practices. In this respect, Qaddafi never launched any initiative or established any structure to fight corruption. In Tunisia, the Interior Ministry had an economic crimes brigade in addition to trade and financial regulatory authorities, but both were greatly ineffective. Both Algeria and Morocco have multiplied anticorruption governmental institutions and initiatives. After the 1999 and 2004 Algerian presidential elections, a committee was established to study corruption; the government enacted the anticorruption law in June 2005, and in November 2006 it decreed the creation of a government agency to fight corruption. However, it was not until the end of 2011 that this agency became operational, probably, because the independent media denounced its existence in name only. In 2008, presidential ordinance extended the authority of the Inspection Générale des Finances (the government auditing office). Despite these seemingly concrete initiatives, one can question their effectiveness and success in fighting corruption. In early 2005 dozens of customs officials and at least 33 judges were sacked. The clean hands campaign also put powerful prefects in jail and prohibited chief executive officers from leaving the country. In February 2006, 100 agents were fired, and 530 were prosecuted. However, one of the most symbolic anticorruption operations was the Khalifa Bank affair. Before the revelations regarding the corruption within Sonatrach, the Khalifa affair was dubbed the scandal of the century. At least five former ministers and 40 CEOs of state enterprises were heard by judges, but none of them were prosecuted. Likewise, except for a few scapegoats, who received jail sentences, senior officials, such as the minister of energy and mines, left office unscathed.

As was the case in Algeria, anticorruption initiatives have proliferated in Morocco with basically the same low level of efficiency. In 2001 the government promised the creation of an independent authority to monitor corruption, and in May 2007 it formally established the Central Agency for the Prevention of Corruption (ACPC). Attached to the prime minister's office, the ACPC has never been independent and only has limited powers and resources, lacking investigative, auditing, and monitoring prerogatives. In April 2005, the government announced a six-point plan to fight corruption, which included, inter alia, the obligation for all high-ranking officials to disclose their assets before and after holding public office. The Special Court of Justice (CSJ) was replaced in 2004 by five courts of appeal. Officially, this change was aimed at giving greater independence in the pursuit of justice against officials and any other citizens accused of corruption, but, again, its effectiveness has been questionable.

However, with many of the initiatives put forward by the government, the result on the ground has been weak or deficient. Table 3.5 related to corruption perception confirms this observation.

Table 3.5 Corruption Perception Index

Corruption Perception Index 2011			
Algeria	**Morocco**	**Tunisia**	**Libya**
Algeria Scored 2.9, Rank 112	Morocco Scored 3.4, Rank 80	Tunisia Scored 3.8, Rank 73	Libya Scored 2, Rank Rank 168

HUMAN RIGHTS AND DEMOCRACY: A MIXED RECORD

Human rights cannot be guaranteed without the existence of the rule of law which constitutes a fundamental condition for the erection of a democratic order; the rule of law ensures the application of the same rights and duties for all. Since the end of the Cold War and the emergence of Human Rights and Democracy as key universal values, one could divide the Maghreb countries into two categories: Morocco and Algeria on the one hand, and Tunisia and Libya on the other. The countries constituting the first group have made some political reforms whereas the countries in the second group were reluctant to initiate such reforms. Of course, Tunisia no longer belongs to this second group; since the Jasmine Revolution of 2011, it has made considerable progress. The current president Moncef Marzouki is himself a former human rights activist and a staunch opponent of former president Ben Ali. Hence Tunisia has not only caught up with the first group, but has taken the lead in the Maghreb in implementing reforms. Before the Arab Spring, the types of reforms in the Maghreb in the late 1980s and 1990s had different characteristics; these reforms at various points can be lumped into three categories: Liberal reforms (Algeria); limited reforms from above (Morocco, Algeria, and Tunisia); and undecided reforms (Libya).

Liberal Reforms

In 1989, Algeria initiated the first genuine political reforms in the Maghreb and in the Arab world as a whole. Freedom of speech, association, and demonstration was instituted shortly after the 1988 riots. Pluralism was established, allowing the emergence of political parties, independent labor organizations, and freedom of the press whereas economic reforms allowed the private sector to expand its economic activities. The first free and pluralistic municipal elections took place in June 1990 and led to the overwhelming victory of the Islamic Salvation Front (FIS) and the transformation of the old single ruling party, the National Front of Liberation (FLN), into an ordinary party. The legislative elections in December 1991 confirmed the Islamist popularity; the cancelation of the election by the military-civilian establishment resulted in a political crisis and eventually to quasi civil war.[23]

The post-1988 political reforms were historical, but devoid of any political maturity and institutional regulation. The popular anger against the FLN gave the FIS an absolute victory; the absence of institutional democratic counter-powers would have allowed the FIS to institute a totalitarian/despotic regime. This paradox was managed by reverting to authoritarian tools and then military intervention on January 11, 1992. This military intervention gave Islamists the justification to move from a radical discourse to an extremist behavior. The decade-long bloody civil war caused nearly 200,000 deaths, stagnated economic development, isolated the country, and created the Algerian syndrome.[24]

Morocco, under Hassan II's rule, was the first regime to use the Algerian syndrome in order to maintain the internal political status quo, while speaking of Algeria as an interesting laboratory,[25] that is, an experiment in a neighboring country to see what type of outcome it would produce if Islamists were allowed to govern. In fact, the tragic evolution of the Algerian experience was an unexpected gift for all Arab rulers, which they would eventually use for another decade following the 9/11 attacks on the United States. Certainly, the use of the Algerian experience as a scarecrow against democratic reforms lost its pertinence after the Tunisian revolt.

Limited Reforms

The Tunisian revolt, which led to the overthrow of Ben Ali has inaugurated a rational negotiated transition[26] period during which numerous important changes occurred in a short period of time. Hence the High Commission for the Realization of the Revolutionary Goals, Political Reforms, and Democratic Transition, headed by the brilliant scholar Iyad ben Achour, was established to examine laws related to political organization, propose specific reforms, lead the interim government, and prepare the first post–Ben Ali election of a constituent assembly. In addition, several committees were set up to brainstorm on issues, such as dialogue on political reforms, electoral laws, and corruption among Tunisian officials. The Tunisian League for Human Rights (LTDH) and the Association of Tunisian Magistrates (AMT) were among the first groups allowed to engage in free activities, and the government freed in March 2011 all of the remaining 800 political prisoners, dissolved the much-feared political police, abolished the general directorate of public security, and disbanded the former ruling party—the RCD. Additionally, 50 political parties were created just two months after Ben Ali's removal; the number of political parties reached 112 by September 2011.[27] The majority of these parties participated in the election of the constituent assembly in October 2011.

In Morocco, the limited reforms that King Mohammed VI has initiated since 1999 were accelerated by the turmoil started in Tunisia. Between 1999 and 2010 he instituted greater media freedoms, allowed the media to report on sensitive issues, such as corruption, released political prisoners, and amended the penal code to ban torture. Some taboos, like human rights, political Islam, and corruption, have been broken. Furthermore, Mohammed VI conducted a reconciliation policy under which he recognized the previous government's responsibility for thousands of disappearances and human rights abuses and compensated victims and their relatives. He ordered the Royal Consultative Council on Human Rights (CCDH) to resolve cases of forcible disappearances and compensate victims of human rights violations.[28] In order to prevent the domino effect from the Arab Spring and contain the street protests that had erupted in the country, Mohammed VI announced on June 17, 2011 major constitutional reforms, which were approved overwhelmingly through a referendum held on July 1, 2011. Although the political and religious supremacy of the monarch remains intact, the constitutional reforms have reinforced the power of the prime minister who is no longer appointed at the discretion of the king but is chosen by the king from the victorious party at the polls. Thus, following the elections of November 25, 2011, Mohammed VI appointed Abdelilah Benkirane, secretary general of the moderate Islamist Party of Justice and Development (PJD), as prime minister. The PJD won 27.08 percent of the popular votes, conferring 107 out of 395 seats in the parliament. The question remains as to whether these reforms are tactical or are the prelude of a genuine democratization process. In other words, will the monarchy move toward a genuine constitutional monarchy or will it continue to exert its ascendency over the political system without fundamental changes to the structures of power?

Algeria was not immune to the events that took place in Tunisia. Even though political street demonstrations were not as important as in Morocco, the multiplication of riots and strikes have raised serious concerns for the regime, forcing it to make concessions in light of socioeconomic requests from teachers, doctors, students, and legitimate defense groups. The government provided the following: new housing to dozens of families who lived in precarious homes; subsidized and set (by law) prices of basic food products; and disbursed between four billion and five billion dollars to finance facilities to the jobless youth.[29] These decisions have been concurrent with the huge economic projects that had been launched across various sectors. The revamping of infrastructure coupled with industrial projects has cost the state $16 billion,[30] arguing that economic growth was linked to the modernization of its industrial infrastructure.[31, 32] Furthermore, the government extended the tax exemption period from three to five years on company profits for promoters having generated 100 permanent jobs when launching their projects. The government established a national investment fund of more than $14 billion and planned an investment fund of one billion dollars for each of the country's 48 wilaya (administrative regions) to contribute to the capital stock of new small to medium-sized enterprises (SMEs). The banks financial guarantees for young investors became a state guarantee and increased fivefold from 50 million Algerian dinars to 250 million Algerian dinars.[33] All of these reforms had a double effect; first, they prevented the general unrest that had taken place in Tunisia and Egypt; second, they encouraged the multiplication of social demands and labor strikes.[34] The consequences of the socioeconomic concessions that the government made under pressure resulted in increasing less legitimate demands, thus undermining the real economy. For instance, when confronted with protests, the government trebled the employees' salaries without due regard for the logic of such decisions, which were politically motivated.

At the political level, the most important decision that the authorities made during the Arab Spring was the lifting of the state of emergency, which had been in place since February 1992. On April 15, 2011 President Bouteflika announced comprehensive political reforms in an unexpected speech he delivered despite his poor health. He read a written speech, in which he announced different reforms concerning political parties, associations, media, and a revision of the electoral law. The president set up a three-member commission to engage in a wide dialogue with civil society's representatives, former political policy makers, retired officials, intellectuals, and so on. However, the initiative lacked credibility, especially since the three-member commission was made up of members of the regime.

Undecided Reforms

After Qaddafi seized power in a bloodless coup on September 1, 1969, Libya experienced a long period of internal stability with no political openness. The State of the Masses that Qaddafi put into place aimed at making al jamahir (the masses) the real rulers through a large number of people's committees and congresses. Actually, the Jamahiriya (state of the masses) was not only an authoritarian state but also a state devoid of any formal institutions. Previous institutions were replaced by popular committees, which mediated among the various tribes; compromises constituted one of the foundations of the system in which Qaddafi and his tribe (the smallest in the country) played a mediating role. The Code of Honor of March 1997 instituted a system of collective punishment for wrongdoing whereby families, towns, and municipalities were held responsible for the actions of individuals in their midst. Violators of the code were subject to punishment in the form of dissolution of the local people's congress or denial of government services, including utilities, water, or infrastructural projects.[35] Despite a 1972 law that permitted the constitution of associations, Libya had absolutely no independent organizations. In Qaddafi's eyes, such independence was contrary to the revolution and so was any practice of politics outside of the revolutionary committees or the country's borders. Thus, political activity was defined in articles 2 and 3 of Law 71 of 1972 as "any activity based on a political ideology contrary to the principles of the Al-Fateh Revolution of September 1, 1969." Libyans were free, but within the framework of the Third Universal Theory, the Green Book, which Qaddafi completed in 1977. This theory rejected both the class exploitation of capitalism and the class warfare of communism, which allow for a small elite domination. According to the Third Universal Theory, classes are an artificial colonial import; this is why Qaddafi's theory was aimed at eliminating class separation. The theory embodied shura (the Islamic principle of consultation), by which community or even national affairs would be conducted through mutual consultation in which the views of all citizens were exchanged.[36]

The Jamahiriya system had reached its limitations in the late 1980s, compelling Qaddafi to introduce economic reforms. The government introduced limited privatization through the self-management of enterprises. In 1988, 140 SMEs were created while state monopoly on imports and exports was abandoned. From 1990 to 1993, new laws opened the internal market to foreign companies and investments, making the national currency convertible and encouraging foreign tourism, thus sending a significant signal of openness in a country known for its conservatism and tribalism. These reforms proved ineffective and quite restricted. This was due to three primary reasons: most of the laws were never implemented; the banking system was archaic; and, finally, the government failed to include political reforms in infitah (the pseudo liberalization). The second wave of reforms from 2003 onward also focused on economic liberalization. One of the most important measures was the inclusion of private and foreign companies in the strategic oil sector[37] and the acceptance of the obligations under the article VIII of the IMF. Despite hopes that Libya would initiate the necessary political and economic reforms following the country's rehabilitation, this did not happen.[38] On the contrary, Qaddafi had been as adamant as ever to allow reforms of the authoritarian regime. A contradictory discourse could be perceived; despite talks about reforms, the regime also referred to some old socialist policies of the 1970s. In opposition to his father's discourse, Saif-el-Islam, the agent of Libyan would-be reformers, used all the buzzwords that appealed to Western governments: civil society, good governance, rule of law, and so on. Although Libya set out to resolve some human rights cases (mostly to respond to some domestic and international pressure), Qaddafi never allowed meaningful political reforms to be implemented. The attempt to produce a constitution was shelved in early 2010.[39] Attempts to create independent media fell through; not only were the independent newspapers and the private TV eventually banned, but journalists critical of the regime were also arrested. Similar to the other dictators in the MENA region, once confronted with the uprising in February 2011, Qaddafi promised that he would initiate reforms and respond to the demands put forth by the demonstrators.

The revolutionary logic of the Qaddafi regime from the 1970s onward resulted in violations of human rights against those who did not share the regime's vision. The violations compiled by human rights organizations included arbitrary arrests, detentions without trial, torture, disappearances, unfair trials, and the death penalty. However, in 2009, the regime did introduce some modifications to its foreign affairs, the economy, finance, health, communications, and education. By then, Libya had been rehabilitated and become an important partner in the fight against terrorism and also illegal immigration.[40] Like the other Maghreb countries, Libya is a signatory to the 1998 *Arab Agreement against Terrorism,*[41] which defines terrorism, on paragraphs 2 and 3 of article one of the agreement, as "any act of violence or threat to use it, regardless of its causes and motives taking place in implementation of an individual or collective criminal project, and aiming at terrifying people, harming them, or exposing their lives, freedom or security to danger." This definition depoliticizes terrorism and reduces it to an ordinary criminal act.

ENVIRONMENTAL CHALLENGES: FROM NEGLECT TO PRIORITY?

The Challenges

The Maghreb countries face several environmental challenges linked to the following: climate, health, sustainable development, desertification, urbanization, and water resources.

Like other regions in the world, the Maghreb climate has known various changes in the last 20 years. One of these changes has produced a paradoxical phenomenon: the reduction of annual precipitation resulting in water shortages and devastating floods, particularly in Morocco, Algeria, and Tunisia. These cataclysms cause casualties, destruction of infrastructure, and disruption of social structure. Some studies on climate change predict that the Maghreb will, at the end of the 21st century, be one of the world's worst hit regions in terms of the reduction of water resources. Water deficiency will increase by 10 to 20 percent, while the extreme temperature of the hot season will increase in the order of more than six degrees celsius.[42] Indeed, the temperature increase in the Maghreb will be twice that of the rest of the world.[43] This important difference is due to the massive exploitation and waste of water resources, agricultural activities, demography, and droughts.

Undoubtedly, these climate changes will have considerable consequences for agriculture but also for the food security of the Maghreb countries. It is estimated that the agricultural production in Morocco will drop as of 2020 by 10 percent and as high as 50 percent during the years of drought. The same calamity will affect Algeria and Tunisia whose production will decrease by 15 and 20 percent, respectively. If that was not enough, Algeria and Morocco will annually lose 25,000 hectares of arable lands.[44]

Urban Challenges

The Maghreb cities are highly vulnerable to all kinds of natural and technological risks, especially because of demographic density and its concentration in major political and economic centers.

Table 3.6 Percentage of Urban Populations

	2005	2006	2007	2008	2009	2010
Morocco	55	55	56	56	56	57
Algeria	63	64	65	65	66	67
Tunisia	65	66	66	67	67	67
Libya	77	77	77	78	78	78

Source: http://data.worldbank.org/indicator/SP.URB.TOTL.IN.ZS.

In addition, the vulnerability of the cities derives also from anarchic urbanization, owing to the lack of planning and control, as well as urban mismanagement (see Appendix E, demographic profile). Casablanca, Algiers, and Tunis face a demographic growth of five percent. The absence of efficient management explains why 40 percent of housing construction in these three cities has been undertaken illegally. This deficiency in urban planning intensifies and aggravates the consequences of natural disasters.

Table 3.7 Classification of Urban Major Risks

Classification	Material Causalities	Human Causalities €M
Accident	+1 Injured	0.3–3
Serious Accident	1–9 Deaths	3–30
Very Serious Accident	10–99 Deaths	30–300
Catastrophe	100–900 Deaths	300–3,000
Serious Catastrophe	+1000 Deaths	+ 3000

Source: Riadh Hadh Taib, "Les Responsabilités des Maires et Responsabilités Locales," Seminar on urban major risks, Algiers, June 13–16, 2005.

Regarding the climate impact on urban life, Libyan and Tunisian cities are more at risk than those in Algeria and Morocco because of the rising sea levels. Hence, between one and five percent of the inhabitants are threatened in Algeria and Morocco, whereas the rate is between five and 10 percent in Tunisia and Libya.[45] Flooding has become a recurrent phenomenon, resulting in heavy casualties, particularly those in Algiers (2001, 2008), Tunis (2003, 2007), and Casablanca (2008, 2010).

Water

Access to water resources refers to the percentage of the population with reasonable access to an adequate amount of water from an improved source, such as a household connection, public standpipe, borehole, protected well or spring, and rainwater collection. Unimproved sources include vendors, tanker trucks, and unprotected wells and springs. Reasonable access is defined as the availability of at least 20 liters a person a day.[46] In Morocco, the available water resources reach 21 billion cubic meters a year, but this availability is becoming scarcer since agriculture consumes 80 percent of water resources. In addition, bad water management results in the loss of 35 percent of delivered waters.[47]

Table 3.8 Access to Water

	2000	2008
Morocco	96%	98%
Algeria	88%	82%
Tunisia	87%	91%
Libya	55%	NA

Source: World Health Organization/UNICEF, Joint Monitoring Program (JMP) for Water Supply and Sanitation, op. cit.

Desertification

Since the independence of South Sudan in July 2011, Algeria has become the largest country in Africa. However, the Saharan desert makes up 80 percent of Algeria's total land area. Consequently, the population distribution is somewhat uneven; 63 percent of the population is concentrated in four percent of the immense territory—five times the size of France. In Morocco, deforestation now causes the country total losses of 31,000 hectares of forest every year.[48] This constitutes a serious problem because forests constitute 12 percent of the Moroccan territory and provide critical economic support to its development.

National Approaches to Environmental Questions

The Maghreb countries have drawn up national plans and bolstered up police forces in order to protect the country against environmental disasters.

The Algerian government has grappled for a long time with serious environmental challenges, notably, increased desertification. However, the measures that the authorities have taken to resolve the problem have been inadequate; most often, these measures have been ad hoc, without long-term remedies and have lacked structured management. Consequently, sand from the desert reaches the coastal cities, such as the northwestern Mediterranean city of Oran. Recently, the government dedicated 60 billion Algerian dinars to fight desertification; Algeria and Brazil rank first in terms of financing efforts of antidesertification.[49] The National Planning Scheme (PNS) is a global project, which aims at rural renewal, based on the integration of the different actors and ministries (ministry of hydraulics, interior, agriculture, finance, education, and youth). The Rural Renewal Program (RRP) includes 1,440 communes (municipalities) across 43 million hectares. The PNS has full responsibility over 28 million hectares in 2011; 300,000 hectares (6%–7%) were recovered at a cost of $50,000 per hectare. In addition, 600,000 hectares of forests (50%) were reforested, and the Green Dam was reinforced with 100,000 new hectares.

The objectives of the PNS and the RRP are not limited to saving the forests and the agricultural land in the south, but also aim at keeping the populations settled in these regions. This is a strategic plan that requires providing transportation, health care services, schools, administration, security, and infrastructure for the residents in those areas.

In Morocco, sustainable development and environmental issues have become core concerns. A national strategy has been elaborated to face these challenges through a global action plan whose central objective is to protect the environment and preserve the national resources. The strategy also includes a Clean Development Mechanism, which gives priority to clean technology transfers and environmental conservation.[50] Thus far, the efforts that the authorities have deployed against deforestation have salvaged only 30 percent of the 31,000 hectares lost every year.

The government has adopted several laws whose objectives are to ensure good quality environmental governance; concurrent to these laws, the authorities set up a special fund within the framework of the National Action Plan (PAN). The PAN rests on a number of priorities: protecting water resources (18 actions); reducing wastes and improving their management; ameliorating air quality; reducing atmospheric pollution; and protecting the ground and the coast (12 actions). In cooperation with the UNDP, Morocco has improved its development mechanism, which focuses on the following:[51]

- expanding renewable energies (solar and windmill) because Morocco imports 96 percent of the energy it consumes, which, obviously, constitutes a security vulnerability;
- improving energy efficiency, which requires focus on new technologies;
- improving transport efficiency and reorganization of the transport sector to reduce the consumption of energy and the production of pollution;
- enhancing waste management because the current management of waste has been unable to ecologically handle the six million tons of municipal waste or the 975,000 tons of industrial debris;
- accelerating reforestation because only 30 percent of the lost forests are currently replaced.

Regional Approaches to Environmental Questions

The World Bank has given priority to increasing the public's awareness on issues such as the following: environment, prevention, education, and energy saving. In the MENA region, the World Bank supervises 17 investment projects, amounting to about U.S.$2.1 billion. Two Maghreb countries are involved through several projects: Morocco's ONE Support project and the Integrated Solar Project; and Tunisia's Energy Efficiency project. Other projects are under preparation through the new Climate Investment Fund and the Clean Technology Fund, which has allocated U.S.$1.2 billion to MENA: $750 million to design and implement a MENA Concentrated Solar Power (CSP) and $200 million to develop wind power and energy efficiency in Morocco.

The World Bank has carried out analytical and advisory energy work in most countries of the region, including a strategic dialogue on the environment with several countries. In the Maghreb, Tunisia and Morocco are involved the most in this strategic dialogue. The first is interested in developing energy efficiency and renewable energy and reviewing energy management policy whereas the latter wishes to develop a framework for wind power, energy supply strategy, and an investment plan. The World Bank has undertaken regional studies on the Maghreb Energy Market as well as on the Maghreb Energy Integration and Trade.

Finally, the Middle East and North Africa Energy Group is involved in a technical cooperation program with the Gulf Cooperation Council (GCC) countries on a refundable basis, notably in Saudi Arabia, Kuwait, Oman, Israel, Malta, and Libya.[52] Tunisia secured a $55 million loan from the World Bank that is intended to stimulate investment in the country's energy conservation pursuits.[53] The Energy Efficiency Project for Tunisia is worked out through the National Energy Control Agency (NECA) and the World Bank. Tunisia's solar plan aims at reducing carbon dioxide emissions by 1.3 million tons and raising the share of renewable energies in the country's total energy consumption from 0.8 percent in 2009 to 4.3 percent by 2014.

Energy

Energy consumption is disparate among Maghreb countries and quite different from that of the northern Mediterranean countries.

Table 3.9 Maghreb Energy Consumption

	Consumption Million Tons	Population Million	Consumption Per Capita
1. Libya	18	6	3
2. Algeria	34	33	1
3. Tunisia	8.9	10	0.9
4. Morocco	12	30	0.4

Source: Mustapha Kaïd, "The Importance of Energy Issues in Intra-Maghreb Relations and in the Relationships between the Maghreb and Europe," 47–61, 50, http://www.isn.ethz.ch/isn/Digital-Library/Articles/Detail//?ots591=4888caa0-b3db-1461-98b9-e20e7b9c13d4&size544=10&lng=en&id=123106.

Libya is the biggest per capita consumer of energy, followed by Algeria, Tunisia, and Morocco. This consumption will unavoidably increase in the future. Algeria and Libya represent 50 percent of the proven African oil reserves, and they represent—with Egypt—56 percent of the proven natural gas reserves in Africa. Morocco for its part is the largest phosphate exporter.[54]

However, what is rather surprising with respect to energy needs is the fact that in spite of the proximity and the existing energy resources intra-Maghreb energy trade is poor. For instance, in 2005, Tunisia imported no oil from Algeria, 12 tons from Morocco, and 779 tons from Libya; Morocco imported 975 tons from Algeria and 37 tons from Libya. Algeria and Libya do not import any energy resources from any Maghreb country.[55] Electricity connections remain insufficient; Algeria sells less than one percent of its gas exportations and less than two percent of electricity production to its neighbors.[56]

The most abundant energy source is solar power; a mere 0.3 percent of the North African desert could provide the electricity and desalinated water needs for the entire MENA-EU region.[57]

Table 3.10 Renewal Energy Consumption in Maghreb Countries

	1999	2008
1. Tunisia	16.1	
2. Morocco	3.9	4.8
3. Libya	0.9	1
4. Algeria	0.2	0.3

Source: David Ramin Jalilvand, "Renewable Energy For The Middle East and North Africa," Friedrich Ebert Stiftung, February 2012, p4, http://library.fes.de/pdf-files/iez/08959.pdf

This table shows that the less fossil energy the country holds the more that country tends to develop renewable energy. In fact Tunisia was the first country involved in developing renewable energies in the Maghreb.

Any one of the many energy resources found there could constitute a strategic way of improving cooperation among the countries of the Maghreb and thus advance the prospects for regional integration. Morocco could import between 35 and 40 percent of the needed oil from Algeria by 2020 whereas Algeria could increase its imports of lubricants from Morocco. Oil transactions could be multiplied threefold within a 10-year period. The same applies for gas; Algeria could provide by 2020 up to 70 percent of Morocco's estimated needs.[58] The energy trade between Algeria and Tunisia is as undervalued as trade between Algeria and Morocco and could be better exploited in the interests of both Algeria and Tunisia. To achieve these goals, multiproduct pipelines need to be built, linking production and distribution units, in eastern and western Algeria. In addition, the increase of gas use, the development of cross-border electricity lines, and cooperation in the phosphate and nitrogen fertilizer industries would strengthen an integrated energy market.[59]In order to execute such projects, the Maghreb countries can simply create joint ventures among Maghreb companies in many semifinished sectors, such as packaging, plastic bottles, and polyester, and promote subcontracting expertise and capacities instead of importing them. As an analyst put it, "Is it logical for Morocco and Tunisia to purchase ammonia from distant markets, while Algeria and Libya are producing and exporting it?"[60] Electricity provides a potentially favorable instrument of integration among Maghreb countries. In June 2010, the energy ministers of Morocco, Algeria, and Tunisia officially announced the acceleration of an integrated electricity market, strongly encouraged by the European Union, which funds a number of interconnecting Mediterranean energy projects:[61]

- MED-REG II—energy regulators: Supports the development of a modern and efficient energy regulatory framework in the Mediterranean partner countries and strengthens their cooperation with EU energy regulators;[62]
- MED-EMIP—energy cooperation: A platform for energy policy dialogue and exchange of experiences, leading to enhanced Euro-Med cooperation, integration of the energy markets, improved security, and sustainability;[63]
- MED-ENEC II—energy efficiency in construction: Encourages energy efficiency and the use of solar energy in the construction sector through capacity building, fiscal and economic instruments, and pilot projects;[64]
- Electricity market integration: Supports the development of an integrated electricity market among Algeria, Morocco, and Tunisia and between these three Maghreb countries and the EU, through the harmonization of their legislation.

Cooperation in renewable energy resources is as important as it is with fossil fuels. Producing electricity from solar power (photovoltaic and solar concentrator) requires that the Maghreb countries make greater efforts to secure financial support and technical knowhow. Exploiting Europe's great interest in solar and clean energy could provide a lucrative market for the Maghreb countries.[65] The Desertec Industrial Initiative (DII) launched in 2009 is supported by German companies; this project needs between 400 and 570 billion euros for the construction of North African solar power plants. Some 20 underwater, high-voltage, direct current cables costing up to one billion dollars each would then transmit the electricity under the Mediterranean Sea to Europe. This project has a double advantage; it has attracted the EU's interest because it would provide Europe with 15 percent of its total energy needs by 2050; at the same time, it would allow the North African countries to desalinate seawater and produce electricity in a region that has growing energy, industrial, and agricultural needs.[66] If we consider that up to 80 percent of the electricity generated from the solar installations would be used in the North African region itself, these countries will also reduce their dependence on oil and gas. Morocco has expressed enthusiasm whereas Algeria appears hesitant, despite the engagement of Cevital, a privately owned company, which has subscribed to the Desertec project.

The Mediterranean Solar Plan (MSP) is yet another project, which has been put forth as one of the flagships of the Union for the Mediterranean (UfM) initiated by France's former president Nicolas Sarkoy in 2007. The MSP plans to develop 20 gigawatt of renewable electricity capacity on the southern shore of the Mediterranean, as well as the necessary infrastructures for electricity interconnection with Europe. The plan also envisages saving and energy efficiency, as well as the transfer of technology. A key element for the development of this plan is the establishment of a new, suitable regulatory framework to promote the establishment of renewable energies and facilitate the exchange of electricity.

NOTES

1. A rentier state applies to states which derive all or a substantial portion of their national revenues from the rent of local resources to external clients.

2. Sarah Touahri, "The Natural Wealth Gap between Cities and Rural Areas is Widening in Morocco," *Magharebia,* November 21, 2010, http://magharebia.com/cocoon/awi/xhtml1/en_GB/features/awi/features/2010/11/21/feature-01.

3. Silvia Colombo, "The Tunisian Riots and the Risk of a Domino Effect," January 31, 2011, http://www.heptagonpost.com/node/32.

4. Siham Ali, "Maghreb Jobless Rate Highest for Women, Youth," *Magharebia,* February 4, 2010, http://magharebia.com/cocoon/awi/xhtml1/en_GB/features/awi/features/2010/02/04/feature-01.

5. Siham Ali, "Maghreb Jobless Rate Highest for Women, Youth," *Magharebia,* February 4, 2010.

6. Lamine Chikhi, "Al Qaeda Recruiters Target Algeria's Young Jobless," *Reuters,* June 24, 2010, http://www.reuters.com/article/2010/06/24/us-security-qaeda-algeria-idUSTRE65N27520100624.

7. Lamine Chikhi, "Al Qaeda Recruiters Target Algeria's Young Jobless," *Reuters,* June 24, 2010.

8. African Economic Outlook, Algeria Profile, http://epri.org.za/wp-content/uploads/2011/03/1-Algeria.pdf.

Economic Outlook, Algeria Profile, http://www.africaneconomicoutlook.org/en/countries/north-africa/algeria/.

9. African Economic Outlook, Libya Profile, http://www.africaneconomicoutlook.org/en/countries/north-africa/libya/.

10. C. Helman, "Is Libya Going to Boot U.S. Oil Companies? Muammar Gaddafi Looks Ready to Launch a New Round of Energy-Sector Nationalism," *Forbes,* January 22, 2009, http://www.forbes.com/2009/01/22/libya-gaddafi-oil-biz-energy-cx_ch_0122libya.html.

11. Ignace Dalle, "Maroc: La Monarchie," http://www.bibliomonde.com/donnee/maroc-monarchie-40.html.

12. Aboubakr Jamai, "Morocco after Benalization, The Tunisation?" http://www.bitter-lemons-international.org/previous.php?opt = 1&id = 326#1333.

13. "Palace Coercion Plagues Morocco's Real Estate," *Wikileaks,* ID 239525, December 11, 2009, Released December 6, 2010, http://wikileaksarab.com/Casablanca/Cable%20Viewer3.pdf.

14. African Economic Outlook, Morocco Profile, http://epri.org.za/resources/country-profiles/.

15. African Economic Outlook, Tunisia Profile, http://epri.org.za/resources/country-profiles.

16. UNDP, Program on Governance in the Arab Region. http://www.pogar.org/

17. Ronald Bruce St John, "The Changing Libyan Economy, Causes and Consequences," *Middle East Journal,* Vol. 62, no. 1 (Winter 2008): 75–91, 80, http://www.relooney.info/SI_Routledge-Oil/Authors_48.pdf.

18. African Economic Outlook, Libya Profile, http://epri.org.za/resources/country-profiles.

19. "Libya on Recovery Path but Faces Long Rebuilding Effort," *IMF Survey online,* April 16, 2012, http://www.imf.org/external/pubs/ft/survey/so/2012/CAR041612A.

htm. For more details, see Ahmed Al-Darwish, Serhan Cevik, Joshua Charap, Susan George, Borja Gracia, Simon Gray, and Sailendra Pattanayak, *Libya beyond the Revolution: Challenges and Opportunities,* Directed by Ralph Chami http://www.imf.org/external/pubs/ft/dp/2012/1201mcd.pdf.

20. Algeria Profile, http://www.africaneconomicoutlook.org.

21. "Algeria Should Reduce Reliance on Oil, Create More Jobs," IMF Survey online, January 26, 2011, http://www.imf.org/external/pubs/ft/survey/so/2011/INT012611A.htm.

22. Interview of Mohammed Abdou Bouderballa, Managing Director of the Algerian Customs, *Alger Chaine 3,* April 10, 2011.

23. Yahia H. Zoubir, "Stalled Democratization of an Authoritarian Regime: The Case of Algeria," *Democratization,* Vol. 2, no. 2 (1994–1995): 109–39.

24. Kamel Beniaiche, "La Tunisie Post-Révolution: La Crainte du Syndrome Algérien," *El Watan,* March 28, 2011.

25. Cherif Ouazani, "Chronique d'un Dégel Annoncé," *Jeune Afrique,* February 18, 2003.

26. This type of transition is the result of a pact between the forces that cause and want political changes and members of the previous ruling elite through a compromise aimed at initiating a gradual and peaceful democratization. This is the reason why some former officials who served under Ben Ali remain present and active in the political system.

27. Hassen Ayadi, "Les Indépendants Face au Règne des Partis," *La Tunisie Vote,* October 4, 2011, http://www.latunisievote.org/fr/politique/item/322-les-independants-face-au-regne-des-partis.

28. Initially established in 1990 by King Hassan II, the CCDH compiled a list of only 112 cases of forcible disappearances in 1998. Once it achieved its autonomy, the Council compiled a total of 4,750 claimants against the state and had received a total of $100 million in compensation for past violations.

29. Younès Djama, "Mécanismes d'aides à l'emploi des Jeunes en Algérie," *La Tribune,* January 18, 2012.

30. Aïda Amari, "Algérie, l'Etat a consacré 16 milliards de dollars à la relance du secteur industriel public,"*Maghreb Emergeant,* March 29, 2011.

31. Youcef Benabdallah, "Le Développement des Infrastructures en Algérie: Quels Effets sur la Croissance et l'Environnement de l'Investissement ?"http://www.gate.cnrs.fr/unecaomc08/Communications%20PDF/Texte%20Benabdallah.pdf..

32. Benabdallah, "Le Développement des Infrastructures en Algérie: Quels Effets sur la Croissance et l'Environnement de l'Investissement ?," http://www.gate.cnrs.fr/unecaomc08/Communications%20PDF/Texte%20Benabdallah.pdf.

33. Algeria Profile, http://www.africaneconomicoutlook.org/en/countries/north-africa/algeria/.

34. In March 2011, no less than 70 social protest actions occurred (2.3 movements a day), *El Watan,* March 31, 2011.

35. UNDP, Program on Governance in the Arab Region.

36. Ronald Bruce St-John, *Libya: Continuity and Change* (London: Routledge, 2011).

37. Eleven of the 15 oil exploration licenses went to U.S. companies, including Occidental, Amerada Hess, and Chevron Texaco. Some European companies won some licenses, among them the French Total.

38. For details on the reforms, see Diederik Vandewalle, "Libya: Post-War Challenges," *African Development Bank Economic Brief* (September 2011), http://www.afdb.org/fileadmin/uploads/afdb/Documents/Publications/Brocure%20Anglais%20Lybie_North%20Africa%20Quaterly%20Analytical.pdf.

39. Ronald Bruce St John, "The Slow Pace of Reform Clouds the Libyan Succession," *Real Instituto Elcano,* ARI45/2010, March 11, 2010, http://www.realinstitutoelcano.org/wps/portal/rielcano_eng/Content?WCM_GLOBAL_CONTEXT = /elcano/elcano_in/zonas_in/ari45–2010.

40. Yahia H. Zoubir, "The United States and Libya: The Limits of Coercive Diplomacy," *Journal of North African Studies,* Vol. 16, no. 2 (June 2011): 275–97; Y. Zoubir, "Libya and Europe: Economic Realism at the Rescue of the Qaddafi Authoritarian Regime," *Journal of Contemporary European Studies,* Vol. 17, no. 3 (2009): 401–15.

41. The agreement was signed by Arab ministers of the Interior and Justice on April 22, 1998, at the headquarters of the General Secretariat of the Arab League, during the extraordinary session of Arab Ministers of the Interior and Justice. See the excellent commentary of the Arab Center for the Independence of the Judiciary and the Legal Profession (ACIJLP) on the Arab Agreement against Terrorism, http://www.derechos.org/human-rights/mena/acijlp/terr.html.

42. https://docs.google.com/fileview?id=0B2QVTLK6dgpKMWU2Njk3MjUtMzkzNy00NDUzLTliM2MtODFmM2ViMTkwYjU5&hl=en.

43. Frédéric Lejeal, "Sale Temps pour le Maghreb," *Jeune Afrique,* November 13, 2008, http://www.jeuneafrique.com/Article/ARTJAJA_2493-94_p064-065.xml0/.

44. Frédéric Lejeal, "Sale Temps pour le Maghreb," *Jeune Afrique,* November 13, 2008, http://www.jeuneafrique.com/Article/ARTJAJA_2493-94_p064-065.xml0/.

45. Mohammed Amin Hammas, "Ville et Changement Climatique, La Vulnérabilité des Villes du Maghreb aux Risques de Changements Climatiques. Applications aux Villes de Tunis, d'Alger et de Casablanca," Fifth International Symposium on Energies, Climate Change, and Sustainable Development, Hammamet (Tunisia), June 15, 16, and 17, 2009. "Adaptation aux Changements Climatiques et aux Désastres Naturels des Villes Côtières d'Afrique du Nord," Rapport d'Etablissement, World Bank, September 2009, www.bceom.fr/Documents_en_ligne/Inception_Report_Fr.pdf.

46. World Health Organization and United Nations Children's Fund, JMP, http://www.wssinfo.org/.

47. Mohammed Boussetta, "Protection de L'Environnement et Stratégie du Développement Propre: Leçons et Perspectives de L'expérience Marocaine,"http://www.francophonie-durable.org/documents/colloque-ouaga-a3-boussetta.pdf 47–52.

48. Mohammed Boussetta, "Protection de l'Environnement et Stratégie du Développement Propre: Leçons et Perspectives de L'expérience Marocaine," 48.

49. Abdelkader Khalifa, Chargé de la Désertifcation au Ministère de L'agriculture. Alger Chaine 3 (April 7, 2011).

50. Boussetta, "Protection de l'environnement . . . ," 47.

51. Boussetta, "Protection de l'environnement et Stratégie du Développement," 50–51.

52. Energy in MENA, http://go.worldbank.org/88TPPX6OF0.

53. Amber Skinner, "World Bank Lends $55 Million for Energy Projects in Tunisia," *Politics Africa*, January 2, 2010, http://www.politicsafrica.com/2010/02/01/world-bank-lends-55-million-for-energy-projects-in-tunisia/.

54. Till Stenzel, "Solar Energy and the Maghreb region," *CIDOB,* 63–74, http://www.isn.ethz.ch/isn/Digital-Library/Publications/Detail/?ots591=cab359a3-9328-19cc-a1d2-8023e646b22c&lng=en&id=123105.

55. Mustapha Kaïd, "The Importance of Energy Issues in Intra-Maghreb Relations and in the Relationships between the Maghreb and Europe," 47–61, 50, http://www.google.com/url?sa=t&rct=j&q=&esrc=s&source=web&cd=1&ved=0CDQQFjAA&

url=http%3A%2F%2Fwww.cidob.org%2Fen%2Fcontent%2Fdownload%2F24706%2F 304891%2Ffile%2F5_MUSTAPHA%2BKAID.pdf&ei=WvobT4v2A5TT4QSm2OTC DQ&usg=AFQjCNHJ8HC65NVWGzSBxJ9DZDKHAriWmw&sig2=3d17aAMtZuepr l42dGTGLQ, 52. (No longer accessible on Internet)

56. Mustapha Kaïd, "The Importance of Energy Issues in Intra-Maghreb Relations and in the Relationships between the Maghreb and Europe," 47–61, 50, http://www. google.com/url?sa=t&rct=j&q=&esrc=s&source=web&cd=1&ved=0CDQQFjAA&url= http%3A%2F%2Fwww.cidob.org%2Fen%2Fcontent%2Fdownload%2F24706%2F304 891%2Ffile%2F5_MUSTAPHA%2BKAID.pdf&ei=WvobT4v2A5TT4QSm2OTCDQ &usg=AFQjCNHJ8HC65NVWGzSBxJ9DZDKHAriWmw&sig2=3d17aAMtZueprl42 dGTGLQ, 53. (No longer accessible on Internet)

57. Till Stenzel, Institute of Technological Thermodynamics, German Aerospace Center, 65.

58. Till Stenzel, Institute of Technological Thermodynamics, German Aerospace Center, 119.

59. Mustapha Kaïd, "The Importance of Energy Issues in Intra-Maghreb Relations and in the Relationships between the Maghreb and Europe," 47–61, 50, http://www. google.com/url?sa=t&rct=j&q=&esrc=s&source=web&cd=1&ved=0CDQQFjAA&ur l=http%3A%2F%2Fwww.cidob.org%2Fen%2Fcontent%2Fdownload%2F24706%2F 304891%2Ffile%2F5_MUSTAPHA%2BKAID.pdf&ei=WvobT4v2A5TT4QSm2OT CDQ&usg=AFQjCNHJ8HC65NVWGzSBxJ9DZDKHAriWmw&sig2=3d17aAMtZ ueprl42dGTGLQ, 56.

60. Mustapha Kaïd, "The Importance of Energy Issues in Intra-Maghreb Relations and in the Relationships between the Maghreb and Europe," 47–61, 50, http://www.google.com/ url?sa=t&rct=j&q=&esrc=s&source=web&cd=1&ved=0CDQQFjAA&url=http%3A%2F% 2Fwww.cidob.org%2Fen%2Fcontent%2Fdownload%2F24706%2F304891%2Ffile%2F5_ MUSTAPHA%2BKAID.pdf&ei=WvobT4v2A5TT4QSm2OTCDQ&usg=AFQjCNHJ8H C65NVWGzSBxJ9DZDKHAriWmw&sig2=3d17aAMtZueprl42dGTGLQ, 57. (No longer accessible on Internet)

61. http://desertec-mediterranee.over-blog.com/article-maghreb-energy-ministers-commit-to-electricity-market-integration-in-meeting-with-eu-52738951.html.

62. European Neighborhood Partnership Information, http://www.enpi-info.eu/ mainmed.php?id = 304&id_type = 10. (no longer available online)

63. Euro-Mediterranean Energy Market Integration Project, http://www.medemip.eu/.

64. Energy Efficiency in the Construction Sector in the Mediterranean, http://www.med-enec.com/.

65. The Japanese nuclear catastrophe of Fukushima has reinforced the antinuclear clan in Europe and especially in the Mediterranean countries.

66. Pamela Ann Smith, "$570 billion: Maghreb Solar Energy Project to Light Up Europe," *Middle East,* December 2009.

PART II

Maghreb Common Security: Regional Dilemmas

The second level of security in the Maghreb is linked to interstate relations. The question is to what extent do the regional tensions impact upon the idea of a coherent common Maghreb security.

The Arab Maghreb Union (UMA) between Algeria, Libya, Mauritania, Morocco, and Tunisia that was launched in February 1989 aimed at improving economic and security cohesion. The signatories of the UMA agreed that any aggression against any one member would be considered as aggression against the other member states. The member states promised not to permit any activity or organization on their territory that could endanger the security or territorial integrity of another.

CHAPTER 4

Interstate Relations: Rivalries, Alliances, and Counter-Alliances

ROOT CAUSES OF THE RIVALRIES

Each Country Defends Its Self-Perception

Morocco's perception of its relations with other Maghreb countries is dominated by the Western Sahara conflict, which represents a key issue that determines its relations with its peers in the region. Historically, the Maghreb countries entered into alliances with one another, which were later severed according to whose side they took in the conflict—that is, the side of the Polisario Front or Morocco. This primary strategic objective can partially explain why Morocco has always maintained such strong relations with Europe—France, in particular, and with the United States. The northern Mediterranean countries have provided continuous support to Morocco's position on the Western Sahara conflict.

The leading principle of the Algerian policy in the Maghreb is the "good neighborliness policy." One of the key arguments set forth by Algerian policy makers is the recognition of the borders inherited from the colonial period; any dispute should thus be negotiated bilaterally through peaceful means. Algeria shares thousands of miles of borders with its neighboring Maghreb states—borders that are inevitably difficult to control. They also advocate nonintervention in the internal affairs of other countries, nonparticipation in any alliance against neighbors, and the strict application of international law. These quasi obsessive principles derive from Algeria's history: the military-civilian leaders hold the view that if Algerians had maintained good relations with their neighbors, France would not have occupied the territory as easily as it did in 1830 and that the Emir Abdelkader, considered the founder of the Algerian state, would have obtained support from the neighbors to carry out war against the occupation.[1] The question remains however as to whether Algeria has succeeded in enforcing these principles.

Libya's relations in the Maghreb have been determined by the extravagant ambitions of Qaddafi, who has always sought to enlarge the country's power through unification plans with the neighbors. Initially, Qaddafi looked to the Machreq, thus paying scant attention to the Maghreb. Indeed, in 1970 Libya withdrew from the Permanent Maghreb Consultative Committee, an organization founded in 1964 by the Maghreb economic ministers to foster the eventual development of an economic community.

Qaddafi had a unique, very personal view of what an African social and political organization ought to be. Similar to his conception of Libya's ideal polity, he sought to establish a distinct type of direct democracy in which citizens govern themselves through grassroots activism. Accordingly, in this organization, there was to be no place for state institutions or other organizational hierarchies. All governmental and social structures were to be dismantled. It is precisely this model that Qaddafi planned for the region as a whole through his merger projects.

THE MANIFESTATIONS OF RIVALRIES

Despite talks of unity, Morocco, Algeria, and Libya all sought to ascertain their hegemony in the region. This chapter will focus on the relations that these countries entertained with one another and on how their competition affected the other countries.

Algeria versus Libya: Dealing with Instability

Like most other countries, Algeria has had very unsteady relations with Muammar Qaddafi. On the positive side, Libya appreciated Algeria's support for Qaddafi's revolution in 1969, which overthrew the Senoussi monarchy. This support was derived from ideological convergence. Algeria, which belonged to the Steadfastness group on the Arab-Israeli conflict, sided with Libya during its 1977 short border war with Egypt, which had moved to the Western camp under Anwar Sadat. In return, Tripoli supported Algiers when the government decided in February 1971 to nationalize the hydrocarbons sector, and the two countries tried to coordinate their respective positions and defend their common interests inside of OPEC. The Western Sahara issue, which erupted in 1975, was also a point of convergence when both countries supported the nationalist movement, the Polisario Front. In the early 1990s, Libya was one of the few countries which extended financial backing to the Algerian government, which was facing a very severe economic crisis. The two countries developed an important economic cooperation, especially in the hydrocarbons sector. Algeria's Sonatrach and Libya's Lipetco—renamed the National Oil Company (NOC) in 1972—engaged in an extensive partnership whereby the two companies exchanged technical information, technicians, and experts; they even envisaged the setup of joint ventures in exploration, production, and transportation in order to face competition from foreign companies.[2] The Arab Libyan-Algerian Exploration and Production Company (ALEPCO) was established in the 1980s and was followed by the Libyan-Algerian Geophysics Company (LAGC). NOC pursued policies inspired by Sonatrachs' dealing with domestic and international challenges; it built a model based on state control of national resources.[3] Undoubtedly, Algerian-Libyan relations were relatively stable in the 1970s.

However, bilateral relations were impacted by geopolitical and security issues. Qaddafi manipulated, supported, and financed rogue Tuareg groups, a policy that generated risks of secessionism in Algeria's southern border regions. Libya maneuvered around the borders' issue in the hope of compelling Algeria to accept a union with Libya.[4] Worse still, in the early 1990s, during the Islamist uprising, the Algerian government charged Libya with supporting the armed groups and providing them with weapons to fight the Algerian security forces.[5] Such security differences were not new. In the 1980s, the two countries had already been at loggerheads when Libya entered in 1984 into an alliance with Morocco, Algeria's main rival. The 1984 Treaty of Oujda, an unholy unity pact between revolutionary Libya and conservative Morocco, was in fact a response to the Treaty of Concord and Fraternity that Algeria, Tunisia, and Mauritania had signed the previous year. Libya's military intervention in Chad and the unilateral annexation of a disputed territory, the Aouzou Strip, were yet another source of tension. Libya had annexed the uranium-rich Aouzou Strip in 1976, and a war between Libya and Chad lasted until the late 1980s; tensions between the two countries lasted until 1994 when the International Court of Justice ended Libya's claim. Algerian security analysts were of the conviction that Libya supported the Islamist insurgents in Algeria as retaliation against the latter's opposition to Libya's policy in Chad. Furthermore, security issues were not the only problems that the two countries faced. Libya and Algeria were also engaged in open competition in the energy trade sector. Both are oil and gas exporters with Europe being their main client. Until 2011, Algeria was the main Maghreb supplier of natural gas to Europe, but it is likely that the foreign military intervention in Libya will change that, tipping the balance in favor of the new Libyan regime, especially since Libya boasts significant reserves.[6] Foreign investments will certainly focus on modernizing the energy infrastructure, which still needs revamping; this will transform Libya into a major competitor to Algeria. According to the International Energy Agency, before the civil war, the 520-kilometer pipeline exported 26 million cubic meters a day of natural gas from Libya to Italy.

As of today, the three main northern Mediterranean countries through which gas is distributed to Europe import more gas from Algeria than from Libya. Algeria is Spain's most important supplier of gas whereas Libya ranks just eighth. Algeria is Italy's first provider of gas whereas Libya is its third. Algeria is France's third provider of gas whereas the supply coming from Libya is insignificant.[7]

Table 4.1 Gas Imports of Some European Countries from the Maghreb

French Gas Imports				
By Country of Origin (in Mcm)	**2006**	**2007**	**2008**	**2009**
1. Norway	12,286	13,683	14,653	14,142
2. Netherlands	9,420	8,837	9,073	8,262
3. Russia	7,311	5,955	6,772	6,400
4. Algeria	**6,827**	**7,254**	**7,044**	**7,038**
5. Nigeria	3,966	2,929	2,245	1,159
6. Egypt	2,109	1,067	938	1,416
7. Qatar	-	-	-	445
Other	3,582	4,091	5,721	8,248
Total	45,501	43,816	46,446	47,120

Source: Natural gas information 2010 and OECD/IEA, 2010.

Spanish Gas Imports				
By Country of Origin (in Mcm)	**2006**	**2007**	**2008**	**2009**
1. Algeria	11,107	12,858	13,156	12,046
2. Nigeria	7,116	8,162	7,846	4,153
3. Qatar	5,012	4,196	4,858	4,285
4. Egypt	4,512	3,978	4,391	4,273
5. Trinidad & Tobago	3,369	2,071	4,728	4,220
6. Norway	2,013	2,092	2,596	3,314
7. Oman	775	306	162	1,347
8. Libya	661	742	517	719
Total	34,650	34,492	38,629	34,672

Source: Natural gas information 2010 and OECD/IEA, 2010.

Italian Gas Imports				
By Country of Origin (in Mcm)	**2006**	**2007**	**2008**	**2009**
1. Algeria	27,646	24,584	25,992	22,711
2. Russia	22,520	22,667	23,486	22,971
3. Libya	-	9,241	9,871	9,168
4. Netherlands	9,372	8,038	7,050	7,213
5. Norway	5,745	5,581	5,535	4,809
Other	12,116	3,839	4,933	2,403
Total	77,399	73,950	76,867	69,275

Source: Natural gas information 2010 and OECD/IEA, 2010.

Algeria-Morocco: Historical Tensions

Algerian-Moroccan tensions have deep historical roots. The September 1844 Tangiers agreement between France and the Moroccan Sultan Moulay Abderrahmane made the Emir Abdelkader an outlaw and prevented the Algerian resistance to France from using Moroccan territory to secure human and material support despite the tribal and religious cross-border links in the region.

Before Algeria's independence in July 1962—132 years after its colonization by France—Moroccans raised the border issue with Algeria. The issue was discussed in a meeting between Ferhat Abbas, president of the Provisional Government of the Algerian Republic (GPRA) and King Hassan II, which resulted in the signing of an agreement in July 1961. The agreement contains three important points: 1) the Kingdom of Morocco pledged to respect Algeria's territorial integrity; 2) the parties recognized that the borders that France had drawn were arbitrary and imposed by the colonizer; 3) any discussions regarding the border issue should be postponed until after Algeria's independence.[8] The two sides provided two opposite interpretations of the 1961 agreement. While Rabat felt that the GPRA promised to open negotiations immediately after independence to correct the consequences of colonization, Algiers adopted the position of the Organization of the African Union (OAU) on the inviolability of the borders inherited from the colonial period. Algerians also firmly believed that they had fought hard and paid a heavy price for the whole territory; it would thus be considered treason to give up any portion of that territory. The question was how to reconcile two opposite, yet legitimate claims. The idea of reconciling these opposite positions through a global project of codevelopment gained some attraction. Therefore, limited, timid attempts were made repetitively but with very inconsequential results. Algeria and Morocco signed in 1972 a bilateral political agreement, including the border issue, concurrently with two other agreements on Maghreb integration and the joint exploitation of the Ghar Jbilet iron mine. Not until 1989 did the Moroccan government ratify the treaty. Although an agreement could have been the starting point of a Maghreb community, such hope was dashed despite the launch of the Arab Maghreb Union in 1989 because the UMA came to a brutal standstill in 1994 due to the Western Sahara conflict and other bilateral issues.

Morocco-Libya

Libyan-Moroccan relations have also undergone many tensions. Soon after Qaddafi seized power, the two countries experienced a head-on collision. Rabat accused Tripoli of having conducted subversive acts against the monarchy; more precisely, Morocco accused Libya of having helped the plotters of the attempted military coup in 1971 against King Hassan II. The positions of Libya and Morocco differed on major international issues. Their respective political and ideological orientations set them apart especially in the context of the Cold War when Morocco belonged decidedly in the pro-Western camps whereas Libya supported anti-Western, anti-imperialist forces. For instance, during the Angolan civil war in the mid-1970s, Qaddafi supported Angola's MPLA government whereas Morocco supported pro-Western UNITA and FLNA rebels allied to Zaire. Libya and Morocco's positions on the Western Sahara conflict were in total opposition and resulted in permanent tensions. Although Libya's position on this conflict shifted at times, Qaddafi was one of POLISARIO's first political and financial supporters. At times, Libya, when confronted with regional or international isolation, would reconsider its position vis-à-vis the Sahrawis as it did in 1984 when it signed the Oujda Agreement. Its position shifted again after it broke the treaty in 1986. In exchange for abandoning the Sahrawis in 1984–1986, Libya received Moroccan backing in its conflict with Chad.

Relations between the two countries warmed up again after Qaddafi decided in December 2003 to renounce the MDW program. More importantly, Moroccans appreciated Libya's attempts to help resolve the conflict on the basis of Morocco's autonomy plan initiated in 2007.[9] However, Qaddafi shifted on the Western Sahara issue by reverting to his support for the right of self-determination of the Sahrawis, which then led to tension between the two countries; by 2010, Mohammed VI had refused any direct contact with Qaddafi.[10]

Tunisia: Dealing with More Powerful Neighbors

Tunisia-Algeria

Historically, there has not been any rivalry between Algeria and Tunisia; however, Tunisia was subject to the regional power politics game that Maghrebi states are known to play. Before analyzing this point, one should point out that Algeria and Tunisia had, in the past, had border disputes of their own: Carquey Fort and two wells at the end of the southern frontier near Algeria and Libya of Fort Saint (renamed Bordj-el-Khdra). The disputes ended with a bilateral agreement that allowed Algeria to pay one billion French francs in exchange for the acquisition of the disputed territory.[11] In March 1983, Algeria and Tunisia signed the Treaty of Fraternity and Concord agreement, which Mauritania signed in December of the same year. Morocco and Libya, for their part, joined the Arab-African Federation, known as the Oujda Treaty, as a counterweight to the Treaty of Fraternity and Concord.[12] Tunisia's attitude toward the Sahrawis during that period seemed more sympathetic.

Tunisia-Morocco

In the 1970s, Morocco secured Tunisian neutrality, which in many ways translated into implicit support for Morocco's claims. As to Morocco's relations with

Libya, they had been tumultuous from 1969 onward, except for the interlude in 1984–1986 or when Qaddafi sporadically changed his views on Western Sahara. The ideological tendency of the *Jamahirya* exacerbated the bilateral tensions, and Qaddafi was one of the first supporters of the Polisario Front.

Tunisia-Libya

Relations between the two countries have experienced various ups and downs. On an economic level, Libya had for some time been antagonized by oil trafficking across its borders with Tunisia. The problem between the two countries regarding maritime boundaries was settled by the International Court of Justice ruling in favor of Libya in 1982 and, again, in 1985. In August 1985, relations worsened when 40,000 Tunisian workers were expelled from Libya, not only due to the downturn of the Libyan economy (the price of oil having dropped), but also for political reasons because Qaddafi considered expelling guest workers as a political weapon he could use against uncooperative governments. In retaliation, Tunisia reacted to Libya's decision to expel its workers by ousting 300 Libyans, including 30 diplomats.

On a political level, Tunisia, like the other Maghreb neighbors, constantly complained about alleged Libyan subversion attempts. In 1976, for instance, Tunisia charged Libya with attempting to assassinate Prime Minister Hédi Nouira. In February 1980, the Tunisian government accused Libya of instigating the failed uprising led by Tunisian insurgents in the town of Gafsa in central Tunisia, a charge Libyans denied.[13]

THE CONSEQUENCES OF THE RIVALRIES

Rivalries among states can have a positive function in terms of boosting productive economy, reinforcing internal cohesion, and creating a productive competition dynamic. Destructive regional rivalries can be transformed into constructive regional competition. However, in order to achieve this, the contenders must conclude that the real costs of their rivalries are far greater than their potential results.

Undoubtedly, the extent of rivalries in the Maghreb demonstrates their irrationality in terms of costs versus benefits. Officially, the Maghreb countries seem aware of such truths. All political speeches and statements emphasize the necessity of moving forward through the unification of their efforts in the face of globalization and cooperating to defeat new threats. Governments declare in their agendas that Maghreb unity is a strategic priority. In 1994, however, although the Maghreb Free Trade Zone was stillborn due to renewed tensions between Algeria and Morocco over the Western Sahara issue, several free trade agreements were signed between Morocco and Tunisia in 1999, among

Morocco, Tunisia, Libya and Jordan in 2004, and between Tunisia and Algeria in 2008. In 2010, after 19 years of negotiations, the five Maghreb countries reached an agreement on the establishment of a Maghreb free trade zone for agricultural products, which was supposed to take effect in 2011.[14] This is yet to materialize.

Dependence on Europe

Beyond their official declarations and the agreements they enter into, the situation on the ground is still held hostage to hostile perceptions and narrow-minded calculations of the Maghreb governments. For instance, all the Maghreb countries prefer to import goods from Europe than from their neighbor who may be producing the same product and at a cheaper price. Thus, 80 percent of Tunisia's total exports and 70 percent of Morocco's end up in Europe.[15] This has two main consequences. First, the exchange ratio among the Arab Maghreb Union countries does not exceed three percent; second, the European economic situation impacts upon the Maghreb economies. Hence, the recent economic and financial crisis has resulted in the slowing down of nonagricultural activities in Morocco and Tunisia in 2009. Manufacturing, which represents 17 percent of GDP in both countries and employs 12 percent and 20 percent of the labor force in Morocco and Tunisia, respectively, has shrunk. Because of their high dependence on European markets Europe's severe recession has translated into lower demand for the manufactured goods from Morocco and Tunisia. Morocco's trade deficit worsened to such extent that its foreign reserves, which cover about seven months of imports, were affected by the deterioration of foreign direct investment inflows (–34.5 percent). In Tunisia, before the revolt, although the foreign exchange reserves covered only five months of imports, the country's external position remained relatively sound. Its import coverage (79 percent) dropped only by three percent in 2010 whereas tourism revenues increased almost five percent with FDI dropping 36 percent in the first half of 2009.[16] However, after Ben Ali's downfall, the economy has faced major challenges and it remains to be seen whether tourism can remain the life preserver of the country.

Libya and Tunisia tried to increase their exchanges; the commercial developments were such that Libya had become Tunisia's first Maghreb partner, ranking fifth after France, Italy, Germany, and Spain.[17] In comparison, Tunisia's trade with Mauritania did not exceed $28.7 million, a totally negligible figure.[18] In the last few years, Tunisia was the most dynamic economic actor in the Maghreb. For instance, during the 2010 Second Maghreb Businessmen's Forum, 630 Maghreb companies were present including 394 from Tunisia, 116 from Libya, 47 from Morocco, 45 from Algeria, and 30 from Mauritania.[19]

The Maghreb States and the War in Libya: No Coherent, Common Position

All the Maghreb countries were conscious that the Qaddafi regime was a source of instability in the region and that the war in Libya would have dire consequences for regional security. They were also cognizant of the fact that NATO's intervention in North Africa would constitute a problematic precedent. Although the member states in the Maghreb did in fact attempt to form a unified position on the issue, with the aim of managing what is after all a Maghreb crisis, they, in reality, each dealt with the issue in their own way, rendering the attempts on forming a common policy, obsolete. It was not until later on that the Maghreb started to focus its attention on the consequences that a regime change in Libya may bring about.[20]

During the Libyan civil war, Tunisia took a neutral position; it did not openly support the rebels, but did decide to open its borders with Libya to allow in the massive influx of civilian refugees fleeing the war. The Qaddafi regime, however, interpreted this as support for the Transitional National Council (TNC) that led the uprising against it. The Tunisian government waited patiently until the irreversible defeat of Qaddafi before sending the first official delegation to Benghazi. The prime minister's spokesman Moez Sinaoui described the visit as historic. Pleased, the TNC said that Tunisia would definitely be considered to take part in future reconstruction projects, which came as good news in light of the post–Ben Ali economic crisis.[21]

In addition to the influx of refugees, the battles taking place inside Libya itself at times spilled over into Tunisian territory as rebel and government forces chased each other across the border. For instance, in April 2011, 15 Libyan military vehicles, carrying troops armed with antiaircraft guns and rocket launchers reached the Tunisian town of Dehiba (Dhuheiba), where many Libyan rebels had found shelter. The Tunisian army drove back many of Qaddafi's brigades to the Libyan border. The interior Tunisian ministry also spoke about a number of pistols, rifles, AK47s, and thousands of live ammunitions that had been seized from Libyans crossing into Tunisia as well as from Tunisians who obtained arms in order to protect themselves during the chaos in Tunisia.[22] Given their geographic proximity to Tunisia, the Nafusa Mountains constitute one of the most important sources of illicit weapons. The biggest depots are located in the areas of Tiji and al-Badr, only 40 kilometers away from the Tunisian border. Besides, in late August, Libyan Brigadier General Abderazzak Rajhi confirmed to Tunisian authorities that he had managed to come into possession of large quantities of explosives and store them in the al-Nasr neighborhood in Tunis. Later on, arms and ammunitions were found in the possession of a Libyan citizen, who was about to board a plane en route to Tripoli.[23]

For its part, Algeria's policy toward the war in Libya has been the subject of much criticism because it was interpreted as support for the Libyan dictator. Algeria's official position rested on strict neutrality, which drew from two of the most sacrosanct principles of Algeria's foreign policy,[24] that is, the noninterference in the internal affairs of another sovereign state and the notion that Algeria recognizes states not governments. Overall, the refusal to support the rebellion was considered as support to Qaddafi. Libya's Transitional National Council (TNC), which declared itself on March 5, 2011, the legitimate representative of the Libyan people and the Libyan state, alleged that Algeria allowed weapons, fuel, and fighters to be shipped to Qaddafi's military forces. Despite repeated denials, the TNC allegations were widespread in the media, thus confirming the adage that, "in a war, if you are not with me, you are against me." The TNC, though, never provided any proof to corroborate the accusations it brought against Algerian authorities. In fact, the head of the U.S. Command for Africa, General Carter Ham, declared that there was no evidence that Algeria sent mercenaries to support Qaddafi's forces.[25]

In conflict management, scholars refer to what is known as positive and negative neutrality.[26] During the Libyan civil war, Algeria chose to remain neutral in order to propose, through the African Union, political mediation based on inclusive negotiations and peaceful solutions. This strategy failed simply because France, the United Kingdom, the Arab League, and some members of the Security Council chose the military option. For Algerian policy makers, neutrality meant that they would neither support Qaddafi nor the rebels because they believed that security problems would emanate from both parties. Hence, they refused to allow Muammar Qaddafi and his close associates to find refuge in Algeria, and they closed the border with Libya to prevent the entry of weapons and fighters into the country. By the time Algeria had recognized, quite reluctantly, the TNC, the position of Libya had not changed much because it tied official recognition to the TNC to the inclusion of all political forces in Libya.[27]

What about Morocco's position on the Libyan war? Could the establishment of a new regime in Tripoli now bring about more cooperative bilateral relations? At the official level, the declarations of the TNC were very optimistic. It has more than once expressed the country's willingness to build strong relations with the kingdom. Morocco's recognition of the TNC as the sole representative of the Libyan people and the official visit of the Moroccan delegation to the city of Benghazi was probably linked to the TNC's potential recognition of Western Sahara as a Moroccan territory.[28] It should be pointed out that as soon as the Libyan rebels announced their victory toward the end of August, Morocco was one of the first countries to send its foreign minister, Taeib Fassi Fihri, to Benghazi to express support for the new regime. In this respect, the TNC's official praised Morocco's honorable stance regarding the Libyan revolution, saying that the new Libya is committed to establishing solid relations with all of the brotherly Arab countries.

Finally, it seems that the core security challenges have not in fact brought about a coherent and cooperative Maghreb front. If we consider that the reason for this failure is due to the inabilities of the decision makers, then is it conceivable that certain political changes have succeeded where security has failed? This question is linked to the Tunisian policy of reviving the UMA. President Marzouki is undoubtedly the most enthusiastic leader in renewing support for the UMA. For example he proposed the opening up of the borders to Maghreb nationals (i.e., allowing the presentation of a simple form of ID for entering Tunisia) and what is more, to simplify the conditions of working inside the Tunisian territory for holders of Maghreb nationalities. The Maghreb official reactions were prudent because it is widely known that these propositions are dictated by the economic crisis in Tunisia. Nevertheless, it is worthwhile to point out that President Marzouki is the first Maghreb leader to ask for support from the Maghreb states in resolving a crisis, instead of asking for this kind of backing from Europe. Interdependence and integration must start from somewhere. Why not from here?

NOTES

1. Ismail Hamdani, "El jazair wa housn el jiwar," *Publications of the Senate,* Algiers, 2009, 14.

2. Luis Martinez, "Algeria, the Arab Maghreb Union and Integration," *Euromesco Paper 59* (October 2006), 11, http://www.euromesco.net/images/59_eng.pdf.

3. Luis Martinez, "Algeria, the Arab Maghreb Union and Integration," *Euromesco Paper 59* (October 2006), 11, http://www.euromesco.net/images/59_eng.pdf.

4. Luis Martinez, "Algeria, the Arab Maghreb Union and Integration," *Euromesco Paper 59* (October 2006), 11, http://www.euromesco.net/images/59_eng.pdf, 23.

5. Interview of Yahia Zoubir with National Security Advisor, Presidency of the Republic, Algiers, March 6, 1993.

6. According to the International Energy Agency, Libya has 54.7 billion cubic feet of proved reserves in natural gas. That makes Libya the fourth largest natural gas reserves holder in Africa after Nigeria, Algeria, and Egypt. PetroStrategies, Inc. " Libya," http://www.petrostrategies.org/Learning_Center/libya.htm.

7. Energy Delta Institute, Italy http://www.energydelta.org/mainmenu/energy-knowledge/interactive-world-gas-map.

8. Ismail Hamdani, "El jazair wa housn el jiwar," *Publications of the Senate,* Algiers, 2009, 29.

9. Mohammed El Bazzaz, "Les Relations Maroc-Tunisie et Maroc-Libye et les Perspectives de Règlement de la Question du Sahara," *Sahara du Maroc,* http://saharadumaroc.net/spage.asp?rub=2&Txt=101&parent=&parent1=1.

10. *Maghreb Intelligence,* "Kadhafi: le Roi du Maroc m'a Trahi," March 10. 2011.

11. Ismail Hamdani, "El jazair wa housn el jiwar," *Publications of the Senate,* Algiers, 2009, 27.

12. Mary-Jane Deeb, "Inter-Maghrebi Relations since 1969: A Study of the Modalities of Unions and Mergers," *Middle East Journal,* 43, no. 1 (Winter 1989): 20–33.

13. http://countrystudies.us/libya/84.htm.

14. Algeria expressed reservations regarding the project; it refused to extend the agreement to the free movement of people.

15. Lahcen Achy, "The Maghreb and the Global Economic Crisis: When Does the Tunnel End?," *International Economic Bulletin,* September 17, 2009, http://carnegieendowment. org/2009/09/17/maghreb-and-global-economic-crisis-when-does-tunnel-end/oox.

16. Lahcen Achy, "The Maghreb and the Global Economic Crisis: When Does the Tunnel End?," *International Economic Bulletin,* September 17, 2009, http://carnegieendowment. org/2009/09/17/maghreb-and-global-economic-crisis-when-does-tunnel-end/oox.

17. http://www.africanmanager.com/articles/118027.html.

18. Mona Yahia, "Calls Grow for Maghreb Economic Integration," *Magharebia,* February 24, 2010, http://www.magharebia.com/cocoon/awi/xhtml1/en_GB/features/awi/ features/2010/02/24/feature-02.

19. Monia Ghanmi, "Maghreb Business Leaders Call for Economic Integration," *Magharebia,* May 12, 2010, http://www.magharebia.com/cocoon/awi/xhtml1/en_GB/features/awi/ features/2010/05/12/feature-02.

20. Yahia H. Zoubir, "Tilting the Balance Towards Intra-Maghreb Unity in Light of the Arab Spring," *International Spectator: Italian Journal of International Affairs*, Vol. 47, no. 3 (September 2012): 64–80.

21. Emanuele Santi, Saoussen Ben Romdhane et Mohamed Safouane Ben Aïssa, "Nouvelle Libye, nouveau voisinage: Quelles opportunités pour la Tunisie ?," BAD, Note analytique trimestrielle pour l'Afrique du Nord, N 1, 2012, http://www.afdb.org/fileadmin/uploads/ afdb/Documents/Publications/Santi%20quarterly%20f%C3%A9vrier%202012%20(bis)_ Santi%20quaterly%20f%C3%A9vrier%202012%20(bis).pdf.

22. Monia Ghanmi, "Libyan Arms Pose New Dangers for Maghreb," *Magharebia,* http:// www.eurasiareview.com/03112011-libyan-arms-pose-new-dangers-for-maghreb/03/11/ 2011.

23. Monia Ghanmi, "Libyan Arms Pose New Dangers for Maghreb," *Magharebia,* http:// www.eurasiareview.com/03112011-libyan-arms-pose-new-dangers-for-maghreb/03/11/ 2011.

24. Yahia H. Zoubir, "The Dialectics of Algeria's Foreign Relations, 1992 to Present," in *Algeria in Transition: Reforms and Development Prospects,* ed. Ahmed Aghrout and Réda Bougherira (New York: Routledge, 2004).

25. "Le Général Carter Ham Dit N'avoir Aucune Information sur L'envoi par l'Algérie de Mercenaires en Libye," *AlgériePlus,* June 1, 2011, http://www.algerie1.com/actualite/ le-general-carter-ham-dit-navoir-aucune-information-sur-lenvoi-par-lalgerie-de-mercenaires-en-libye/.

26. Kamil Kazan, "Culture and Conflict Management: A Theoretical Framework," *International Journal of Conflict Management,* Vol. 8, issue 4 (1997): 338–60.

27. This condition was officially expressed during the Conference of Paris on September 2, 2011 and confirmed later on.

28. "The Future of the Sahara Can Only be Conceived under the Sovereignty of Morocco," TNC spokesman in London Guma al-Gamaty said on regional television in Laayoune, the capital of Moroccan-occupied Western Sahara.

CHAPTER 5

The Western Sahara Conflict and Its Impact on Regional Security

The conflict in the Western Sahara has been the most important factor in hindering Maghreb integration; the Arab Maghreb Union initiated in 1989 has been at a standstill since 1994 because of renewed tensions between Algeria and Morocco over the issue. In this chapter, we will focus on how this conflict has affected relations between the states and, more importantly, the arms race it has generated.

THE WESTERN SAHARA CONFLICT: A BRIEF OVERVIEW

Despite Moroccan claim that had it not been for Algeria's support for POLISA-RIO the question of Western Sahara would not exist,[1] this conflict remains a question of decolonization for which the United Nations has legal responsibility. Western Sahara is a former Spanish colony (1884–1976) whose native population is made up of Arab-Berber–speaking Sahrawis. The territory, a desert land, contains considerable mineral deposits, mainly phosphates; its Atlantic coast boasts of one of the richest fishing waters in the world.[2]

The right to self-determination of Western Sahara, a nonautonomous territory, already exists within the framework of international law and UN resolutions. The right to self-determination is inscribed in the Declaration of the Granting of Independence of Colonial Countries and Peoples contained in General Assembly Resolution 1514 (XV) of December 14, 1960. In 1963, the United Nations recognized the Sahrawis' right to independence, and it has restated that right in every resolution since. Based on the opinion from the International Court of Justice on October 16, 1975,[3] UNSC resolutions have reaffirmed "the inalienable right of the people of Spanish Sahara to self-determination, in accordance with General Assembly resolution 1514 (XV)." Regardless, Morocco and Mauritania invaded Western Sahara; Mauritania withdrew in 1979 and gave up any claim over the territory ever since. Morocco for its part annexed the area evacuated by Mauritania. On April 19, 1991, the UNSC finally passed resolution 690, which outlined a detailed plan for the holding of a free and fair referendum and the setting up of a UN mission (MINURSO) to conduct the referendum. The referendum was scheduled to take place in early 1992, but the UN postponed it repeatedly, primarily because of Morocco's hindrance. Morocco reneged on the conditions of the UN peace plan by adding thousands of individuals to the list of potential voters to be identified by MINURSO, thus delaying indefinitely the holding of the referendum. The stalemate over Western Sahara[4] has continued to this day despite attempts by successive UN special representatives to find a resolution; all these attempts have failed following nine rounds of preliminary negotiations held between the Polisario Front and Morocco, with Algeria and Mauritania as observers. The last round of fruitless negotiations in Manhasset, New York, in mid-March 2012 confirmed the diametrically opposed views of the two parties. Morocco is firm in its position that it can only grant autonomy to the Sahrawis whereas the latter insist on the holding of a referendum for self-determination, which includes the option of independence, as inscribed in UN resolutions.

The objective for providing a brief background to the conflict in this chapter is not to delve into the intricacies of the dispute but to simply set the stage for the discussion on the opposite positions between Algeria—the Sahrawis' main supporter—and Morocco, the occupying power.

WESTERN SAHARA IN THE ALGERIAN-MOROCCAN STRUGGLE FOR REGIONAL HEGEMONY

Algeria and Morocco's Competing Interests

Since the inception of the Western Sahara conflict in 1975, both Morocco and Algeria have been unwavering in their respective positions; the fundamental arguments of both governments have not changed. Algeria maintains that Western Sahara is a question of decolonization and that international legality should prevail; in addition to financial and political support, it continues to back the Polisario Front and defend the Sahrawi cause at multilateral organizations. The basic premise is that Sahrawis are entitled to partake in a referendum on self-determination as prescribed in UN resolutions. Moroccans have rejected the option of self-determination and oppose the possibility of Sahrawi statehood. They contend that Algerians have created an artificial conflict over Western Sahara to weaken the Kingdom of Morocco, its main rival in the region, and thwart the recovery of Morocco's southern provinces. The other accusation is that Algeria's determination for an independent Western Sahara rests on an ulterior strategic motive: free access to the Atlantic to export its iron ore from Gara Djebilet in the Tindouf area through Western Sahara. This accusation is tenuous because it overlooks the fact that Algeria and Morocco had signed a convention in 1972 whereby the two countries would exploit jointly the mine in Gara Djebilet, which Algeria had nationalized in 1966, provoking Morocco's anger. Undoubtedly, whether Western Sahara had remained under Spain or under Morocco, this would not have undermined the agreement between Algeria and Morocco on the transport of iron ore through Morocco—an argument that even some Moroccan nationalists agree with;[5] the best illustration of this point is the transportation of the Algerian gas to Europe via the Pedro Duran Farell Gasline that crosses northern Morocco. Surprisingly enough, in 2002, Moroccan officials reiterated accusations that Algeria sought the partition of Western Sahara in order to create "a microstate that will be under the protection of Algeria," which, as Mohammed Bennouna, Moroccan Ambassador to the UN put it, "covets an access to the Atlantic Ocean."[6]

There are historical, geopolitical, ideological, and psychological reasons that have strained Algerian-Moroccan relations since Algeria's independence in 1962.[7] Although there is a regional leadership struggle between the two countries and various contentious issues between the two states,[8] Moroccan irredentism is a weightier factor in the Western Sahara equation, which has exacerbated Algeria's apprehensions and suspicions toward Morocco. Moroccan irredentism emerged in the 1950s when Mohammed Allal al-Fassi, leader of the nationalist Istiqlal Party, developed the concept of Greater Morocco.[9] Al-Fassi endeavored to persuade the monarchy and the population to wage a struggle to liberate the region. In June 1956, three months after Morocco's independence, he declared: "If Morocco is independent, it is not completely unified. The Moroccans will continue the struggle until Tangier, the Sahara from Tindouf to Colomb-Béchar, Touat, Kenadza (the four in Algeria), and Mauritania (whose independence in 1961 Morocco did not recognize until 1969) are liberated and unified. Our independence will only be complete with the Sahara! The frontiers of Morocco end in the south at Saint-Louis-de-Sénégal."[10] Contributing greatly to rising Moroccan nationalism, the Istiqlal movement also instilled suspicions among the leaders of the Algerian nationalist movement.[11] Morocco was becoming a potentially hostile neighbor intent on amputating parts of the territory Algerians had fought fervently to liberate through a fierce war against French colonialism.

Despite the geographic proximity, a number of differences between the two countries during the colonial era were transformed into conflicting ideologies after independence. Inevitably, Moroccan irredentism, though gradually watered down, resulted in border conflicts with its eastern neighbor. In the 1970s, border issues were by and large resolved; however, since 1975, the conflict in Western Sahara has remained the main bone of contention in Algerian-Moroccan relations. It is important to note that although the boundaries separating these countries were agreed upon in 1972, unlike Algeria, which ratified the treaty in 1973, the Moroccan parliament did not ratify the decision until 1992, that is, 20 years after it had been signed. King Hassan, as the absolute sovereign had confirmed the treaty in 1989. This change of heart on the part of the Moroccans not only put pressure on Algeria to settle the Western Sahara dispute, but also indicated that Morocco was not willing to relinquish the territory and rather would eventually simply annex it to the kingdom. The Moroccan-Algerian border treaty did not mean the end of Moroccan irredentism, its ratification notwithstanding. Thus, in January 2009, for instance, Moroccan prime minister Abbas al-Fassi repeated the same arguments as the ones his father pronounced 53 years earlier, claiming that the western part of Algeria belonged to Morocco,[12] thus reinforcing Algeria's long-held apprehension about Morocco's irredentism.

Algerian leaders used Morocco's occupation of Western Sahara as an instrument in their own struggle against Moroccan irredentist aspirations. Above and beyond the Western Sahara conflict, additional factors have contributed to the rivalry between the two powerful neighbors, visible not only in the Maghreb itself, but throughout the rest of the African continent. Algeria's support for liberation movements was motivated primarily by its commitment, as a former colony, to achieving national self-determination.[13] Nevertheless, Algeria's approach to some African countries derives from its determination to thwart Morocco's ambitions and muster support for creating an independent Sahrawi state.

The Algerian military-civilian establishment was greatly affected by the Algerian-Moroccan border dispute of 1963, particularly because the better equipped Moroccan troops outperformed the Algerian war of national liberation veterans. Algeria drew a few lessons from the Sand War: Morocco was the most plausible security threat; there was an urgent need for Algeria to modernize its armed forces, which included the necessity to acquire enough weapons to counter Morocco in case of war, a vision that has persisted to this date. Such security assessment partly explains why Sahrawi self-determination in the 1970s was so important to Algerian policy makers, particularly the national security apparatus. Algeria saw the conflict in Western Sahara as a threat on its western border. This resulted in the modernization of the armed forces and the acquisition of more equipment to maintain the regional balance of power and deter Morocco from waging war against Algeria.[14]

As in other cases of countering expansionism, in Algeria, support for Sahrawis derived from fears that Western Sahara would be absorbed into the Moroccan kingdom and would thus upset the regional balance of power in Morocco's favor, which would threaten, according to officials, Algeria's national security. As Damis rightly pointed out long ago, "Algerians fear that the absorption of the (Western) Sahara by their neighbors would only encourage Moroccan expansionist tendencies and whet the Moroccans' appetite for pursuing their unfulfilled and frequently articulated irredentist claim to territory in western Algeria."[15] The absorption of Western Sahara through military means would also create a precedent that could undermine the whole logic of the inviolability of borders—a sensitive issue not only for Algeria, but also for most members of the African Union (formerly Organization of African Unity, OAU until 2002).

Moving beyond a historical analysis of the Western Sahara conflict, certain structural discrepancies in Algerian-Moroccan relations have contributed to the policies of the two countries.[16]

The Kingdom of Morocco

Morocco has felt empowered through its control of two-thirds of the territory, which it has preserved through the walls that it erected to thwart attacks from POLISARIO fighters. Morocco has also established its domination over the territory's resources.

Securing Occupation in Western Sahara through the Wall

The performance of the Algeria-backed POLISARIO fighters in the early years of the war startled Morocco and its foreign supporters. Despite their numerical superiority, which increased from 55,000 in 1975 to 130,000 in 1984, the Royal Armed Forces experienced heavy losses.[17] The successful guerrilla tactics of POLISARIO compelled Morocco to adopt a new strategy. Within occupied Western Sahara, Moroccans began setting up a multitude of cordons de sécurité (security rings) that cordoned off what they called the useful triangle, made up of the cities of Laayoune and Smara and containing the rich phosphate mines of Bu Craa. The fortifications consist of sand and stone walls or berms about three meters in height with bunkers, fences, and landmines throughout. The barricade mine strip that runs along the structure is considered the longest continuous minefield in the world.[18] The reason for the construction of the wall, which stretched over 1,700 miles (2,700 kilometers), was to prevent POLISARIO from repossessing it and also to exploit its resources, which are of strategic importance to Morocco. Inside the walls, Morocco installed military bases equipped with electronic warning systems and radars.

About four km behind each major post there is a rapid reaction post, which includes backing mobile forces (tanks, etc). A series of overlapping fixed and mobile radars are also positioned throughout the berm. The radars are estimated to have a range of between 60 and 80 km into the POLISARIO controlled territory, and are generally utilized to locate artillery fire onto detected POLISARIO forces. Information from the radar is

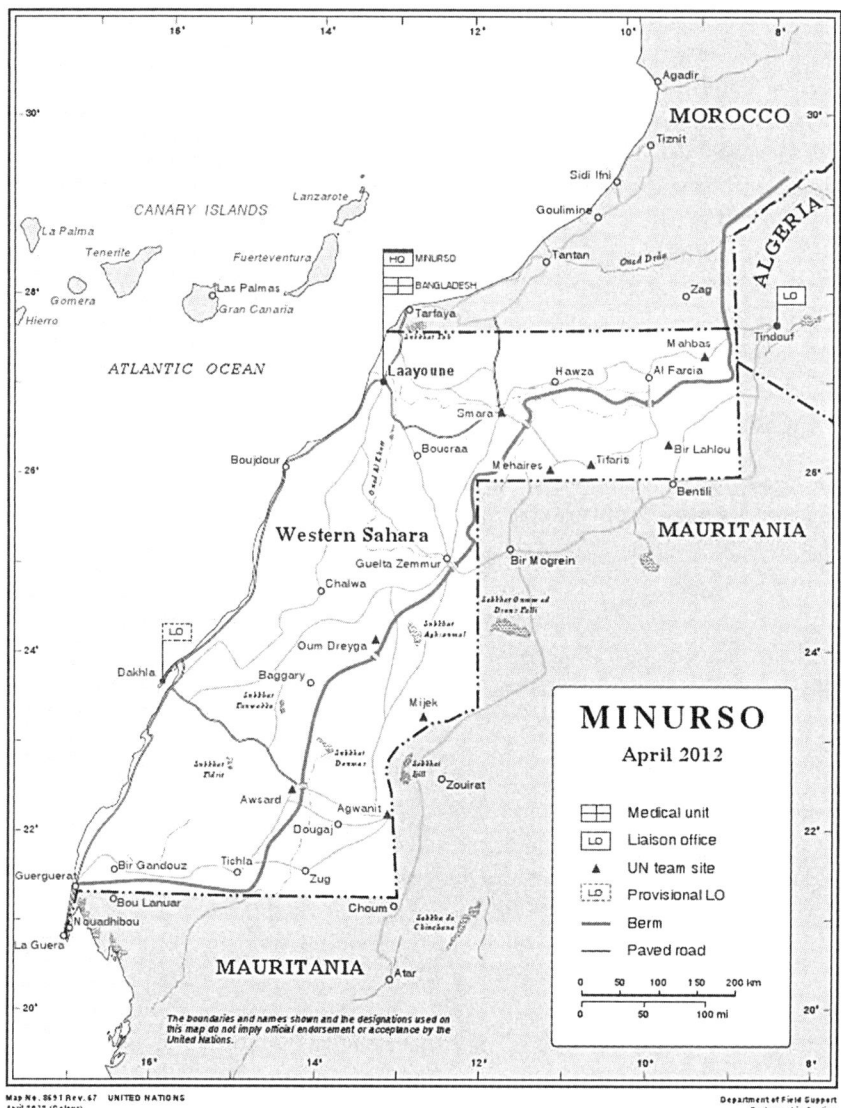

MINURSO, Map No. 3691 Rev. 67, April 2012 (Courtesy of the United Nations Cartographic Section)

processed by a forward-based commander, who contacts a rear-based artillery unit. The Skyeye recently acquired by Moroccan forces, and the anticipated Israeli Hunter craft, will play a similar role in the detection of targets for artillery fire. These same sources provided a degree of insight into the tactics utilized by the POLISARIO to counter the berm, which are generally reflected by the principles of surprise and speed.[19]

The construction of the walls took many years. The construction of the first wall, which surrounded the useful triangle, lasted from 1980 to 1982. The sixth and last wall, which encircled the cities of Awsard, Tichla, and Bir Ganduz, was completed in 1987 (See map). Despite the ceasefire of 1991, Morocco continued fortifying the walls, rendering any potential POLISARIO attack ineffective. Although Morocco has not succeeded in obtaining the recognition of sovereignty over the territory, it has nonetheless succeeded in establishing a fait accompli in Western Sahara. Furthermore, the monarchy has exploited the resources of the territory while keeping its mistrusted military forces busy in Western Sahara.

Strengthening Morocco through Exploitation of Western Sahara's Resources

Morocco's objective for colonizing Western Sahara rests on various objectives: irredentism, the unification of the country following two coup attempts and consolidation of the monarchy's legitimacy. Another factor concerns the economic benefits that Morocco can extract from the occupation of the territory and the exploitation of its resources when it secured a ceasefire.[20] Western Sahara is considerably rich in natural resources and the huge phosphate deposits inspired heavy Spanish investment. Regardless of the territory's disputed status, Western corporations have contributed to its exploitation either through shipments of phosphates on behalf of the Moroccan government[21] or through exploration for oil by major companies, such as Kerr-McGee and the French TotalFinaElf. In 2001, the Moroccan state oil company, Office National des Hydrocarbures et des Mines (ONHYM), signed agreements with these two companies for pre-exploration of oil off the coast of Western Sahara.[22] However, because of the negative publicity their involvement elicited and compulsions from NGOs, both companies ceased their activities there.[23] However, this did not deter several other companies, such as Kosmos Energy, San Leon Energy, Longreach Oil and Gas Ventures, and DMV International from operating in the exploration of oil in Western Sahara,[24] although insofar as their activities do not involve exploitation, this would not be in breach of international law.[25]

The Sahrawi people's legal and economic rights were violated through illegal commercial ventures conducted in Western Sahara.[26] Furthermore, Moroccans have openly exploited the Sahrawi people's natural resources in violation of international law, as corroborated by the UN Under-Secretary-General of Legal Affairs, Hans Correll. In 2002, Corell reaffirmed the ICJ verdict in a legal opinion to the Security Council on the matter of Western Sahara resources. He added that if exploration and exploitation of the oil resources of the territory "were to proceed in disregard of the interests and wishes of the people of Western Sahara, they would be in violation of the international-law principles applicable to mineral resource activities in Non-Self-Governing Territories."[27]

Since their illegal occupation of Western Sahara in 1975, Moroccans, who also seized the portion of the territory that the Mauritanians evacuated in August 1979, perpetrated grave violations of International Humanitarian Law contained in the 1949 Geneva Convention. From October to November 2002, two NGOs, France Libertés and AFASPA, conducted jointly an investigation in Western Sahara[28] that demonstrated the innumerable violations that Moroccans have committed in Western Sahara, which, from a legal point of view (article 73 of UN Charter), still remains under de jure Spanish administration. The most important aspect of the report is that it proves not only that Morocco has attempted genocide against the Sahrawi people even when Spain was still present in the country but also that Spain has partaken in the exploitation of the territory's resources.

After the Moroccan possession of the territory, Sahrawi civilians did not benefit from the protection inscribed in the Geneva Convention. Worse still, the civilian population became "the chosen target of a Moroccan army fully equipped with tanks, fighter-jets, and helicopters." The document *International Mission Investigation* is replete with testimonies from the Sahrawis about the violations of their basic human rights: no rights to equitable trial and reparations, torture—even of pregnant women—mutilations, forced disappearances, arbitrary arrests, and no access to a useful appeals procedure. The investigators discovered that, "not only do the torturers continue to exercise their (official) functions and that they have been promoted, but that they also continue to harass their former victims." The same applies to the area of socioeconomic rights; the study revealed the absolute inequality of the Sahrawis' socioeconomic conditions and that Moroccans repress the defense of economic rights as much as they do civil and political rights of the subjugated population.

The second part of the document highlights the exploitation of Western Sahara by Morocco and how "since the implementation of the 1991 U.N. ceasefire, Morocco embarked on a policy aiming at settling Moroccans in Western Sahara, in addition to some 200,000 members of the Moroccan security forces already stationed in the territory since the beginning of the conflict. This is why today the Sahrawi population is a minority in the territory." This has two implications: The Sahrawis do not benefit from the exploitation of the natural resources, mainly phosphates and fisheries, in their territory; the presence of settlers' colonization has made a free referendum a difficult enterprise.

In addition to phosphates and oil, Morocco has also exploited the fisheries of Western Sahara. Morocco has entered agreements with a number of European countries the latest of which being the four-year Fishing Partnership Agreement (FPA) signed with the European Union in 2006, entered into force on February 28, 2007.[29] That agreement allowed European vessels not only to fish off the coast of Morocco, but also off the coast of Western Sahara.[30] The European Parliament questioned the legality of the FPA.[31]

The uprising in the Western Sahara in 2005[32] and November 2010 confirm, if need be, the dire conditions that the Sahrawis live under and that the benefits accruing from the exploitation of their resources by the Moroccan occupier do not reach them. As K. Jennings put it, "Moroccan settlers tend to have more political freedom and economic power than Sahrawis; much of Moroccan investment in the territory has been oriented towards its soldiers or settlers rather than Sahrawis; and discrimination by settlers against Sahrawis is seemingly commonplace."[33] The Moroccan authorities also sought to divide the Sahrawis, co-opting some tribes through bribes. Keen observer of this conflict A. Theophilopoulo reported that not only has Morocco tried to win the process through overwhelming the Identification Commission with applicants, but it ". . . also proceeded to inject resources into the territory, building up its cities, developing its infrastructure, and providing financial and other incentives to thousands of Moroccans to move there. It tried to divide the Saharans by co-opting certain tribes and giving them privileged positions, while remaining indifferent to the fate of the majority and repressing those who challenged Morocco's presence. It thus created a local constituency of Saharans that expected to benefit in the final settlement, making Morocco's task of compromise with POLISARIO all the more difficult."[34]

The Algerian-Moroccan Arms Race

Although the risk of war between Algeria and Morocco has been quite low since the early 1980s, the nonresolution of the Western Saharan dispute has continued to strain relations between the two countries. One of the consequences of the stalemate has been the arms race they have engaged in since the beginning of the conflict. Even in the absence of the conflict in Western Sahara, the defense policies of the two countries are structured around the threat they perceive from each other. Undoubtedly, Morocco's defense policy rests on the consolidation of its occupation of Western Sahara on the one hand and on the strategic balance with Algeria on the other hand.[35] Since the ceasefire between Morocco and POLISARIO in 1991, and even before, Algeria no longer supplies weapons to POLISARIO combatants. However, the crisis that ravaged Algeria and the quasi arms embargo imposed upon it throughout the 1990s resulted in the necessity to replace its obsolete arsenals with modern ones and restructure its armed forces. A decade of antiterrorist struggle forced Algeria to consider other threats than that emanating from Morocco.

In the 1970s, Morocco relied on its Western allies and on the Gulf monarchies to finance its war against Sahrawi fighters. Between 1975 and 1977, Morocco's defense spending increased from 13 percent to 23 percent of the national budget.[36] The estimates for the cost of the war from the mid-1970s to the late 1980s vary but the most agreed-upon figure is that at the peak of the war, Morocco spent between two and five million dollars per day. However, Saudi Arabia's contribution to the cost of the war through generous loans alleviated Morocco's budgetary burden; indeed, Saudi Arabia provided for a long time one billion dollars per year as loan and later reduced it to $500 million.[37] Owing to its participation in the Gulf War against Iraq in 1991, the Saudis wrote off Morocco's debt. While Saudi Arabia provided the badly needed funds to offset the cost of the war, France and the United States supplied Morocco with the necessary hardware to defeat the Algerian-backed POLISARIO.[38] Even if the conflict was strictly regional, France and the United States approached it through the prism of the Cold War during which Morocco was perceived as a pro-Western ally while Algeria was seen as a close partner of the Soviet Union. Morocco received weapons not only from France and the United States, but also from South Africa, Great Britain, and Israel.[39] These countries not only supplied military equipment, but they also sent advisors to assist the Moroccans in their war against Sahrawis.[40] Although the Soviet Union supplied weapons to Algeria, it did not provide any arms directly to POLISARIO or supported the movement owing to its important commercial interests in Morocco—a major supplier of phosphates to the Soviet Union.[41]

The end of hostilities in Western Sahara did not end the arms race between Algeria and Morocco. This race seems to have intensified in recent years despite the fact that President Abdelaziz Bouteflika had declared in Johannesburg in October 2004 that, "Algeria will never declare war to Morocco because we are peaceful people . . . Western Sahara is not casus belli between Algeria and our brother Morocco."[42] Both Algeria and Morocco purchased massive quantities of modern weapons. However, as shall be shortly seen, Algeria's modernization of its arsenal is not limited to the strategic balance with Morocco. Developments in the Sahel region have also compelled the country to acquire large amounts of equipment from a variety of sources. Nonetheless, some analysts have argued that the acquisitions on both sides have been made to the detriment of socioeconomic development,[43] especially, Morocco, which does not have resources, such as oil and gas, similar to the ones Algeria has. Furthermore, Morocco's public external debt reached more than $20 billion in 2010.[44] The increase in oil prices has allowed Algeria to modernize its armed forces to a much greater extent than Morocco or Libya, for that matter. The data provided by the Stockholm International Peace Research Institute (SIPRI) in 2012 shows continuous increased military expenditures for North Africa, from $3.4 billion in 1988 to $13.9 billion in 2011.[45] The figures from SIPRI show that in 1988 Algeria spent $672 million in constant (2010), amounting to 1.7% of GDP against $8.170 billion in 2011, representing 3.6% of GDP. Morocco spent $1,734 billion in 1988, representing 4.1% of GDP against $3,186 billion in 2011, a proportion of 3.5% of GDP.[46] Both Algeria and Morocco rank third and fifth, respectively, in terms of arms' purchases in the

Arab world. The armament consists of warplanes, tanks, and modern electronic systems (Algeria needed these systems for the war on terrorism).[47]

Given that the modernization of Algeria's armament is not related to the conflict in Western Sahara in particular or to the war against Morocco in general, it is necessary to provide some explanation as to why the country decided to engage in such gigantic military expenditures since 2002. There are several explanations:

1. The quasi arms embargo imposed on Algeria in the 1990s is the primary explanation; throughout the 1990s, Algeria suffered a great deal. The financial distress prevented Algerians from purchasing equipment. They had difficulty in acquiring spare parts for their old, nearly obsolete Soviet equipment; some senior officers traveled to Eastern European countries and other Soviet/Russian clients to get such parts.[48] The replacement of obsolete Soviet weapons was thus necessary. Algeria not only purchased more modern weapons, but it also contracted with new suppliers, namely, South Africa, Turkey, the United States, United Kingdom, Italy, Germany, France, and, of course, Russia, which remains its main supplier.

2. Algeria was in dire need of appropriate equipment for the fight against terrorism, which the country continues to face, albeit at a lower intensity than in the 1990s.

3. Increased revenues for the export of oil allowed the country to allocate a larger portion of the national budget for the purchase of weaponry and the modernization of the armed forces. The positive financial situation resulted in the tripling of the military budget between 2006 and 2009. From 2002 to 2011, Algeria's arms purchases increased by 170 percent whereas Morocco's rose by 42 percent for the same period.[49] In 2011, the Libyan crisis and its repercussions in Mali resulted in a 22-percent increase in the military budget (the national budget was revised in July probably because of those security concerns).[50] Undoubtedly, the conflict in northern Mali will provoke more military spending as Algeria needs equipment adapted to fight in the desert. Algeria will also need to reinforce its military bases near the borders as well as its surveillance of the whole expanse.

4. For regional imperatives, Algeria decided to assert its hegemony in the Maghreb; the return of Libya to the international community following its decision to abandon its Weapons of Mass Destruction Programs in 2003 constituted another incentive because Libya intended on acquiring substantial amounts of conventional weapons that could threaten Algeria's security. Libya too was alarmed by Algeria's large arms purchases especially because Libya too had regional hegemonic ambitions. Libya had begun receiving weapons from Europe in 2004; in 2007 and 2008, it signed major military contracts with France and Russia, respectively. It also was in discussion for purchases from the United States not long before Qaddafi's fall in 2011.

5. The fight against Al Qaeda in the Islamic Maghreb has been a major factor in the acquisition of sophisticated equipment. Even if the majority of the equipment it has acquired is not related to the fight against terrorism, it provides the justification for the military to secure a substantial portion of the national budget for arms procurement. Furthermore, the military has a considerable weight in the political system and can secure such budget without too much justification. There is no civilian control over the armed forces.

As shall be seen in Chapter Seven, although Western powers expressed concern over Algeria's arms purchases, they have not refrained from signing lucrative arms contracts with both Algeria and Morocco.

NOTES

1. This has become part of Moroccan narrative on Western Sahara. For instance, a Moroccan scholar stated that "Algeria dug up a people (in other words, the Sahrawis)" to spoil Morocco's claims, a point of view most Moroccans share today. Abdelkhaleq Berramdane, *Le Sahara Occidental—Enjeu Maghrébin* (Paris: Karthala, 1992).

2. See Stephen Zunes and Jacob Mundy, *Western Sahara: War, Nationalism, and Conflict Irresolution* (Syracuse, NY: Syracuse University Press, 2010).

3. http://www.icj-cij.org/docket/index.php?sum=323&code=sa&p1=3&p2=4&case=61&k=69&p3=5. For a recent in-depth, excellent analysis of the conflict from an international law perspective, see The New York City Bar Association, Committee on the United Nations, "The Legal Issues Involved In The Western Sahara Dispute-The Principle of Self-Determination and the Legal Claims of Morocco" (June 2012), http://www2.nycbar.org/pdf/report/uploads/20072264-WesternSaharaDispute--SelfDeterminationMoroccosLegalClaims.pdf.

4. For a detailed account, see Zunes and Mundy, *Western Sahara: War, Nationalism, and Conflict Irresolution* (Syracuse, NY: Syracuse University Press, 2010); Yahia H. Zoubir, "Stalemate in Western Sahara: Ending International Legality," *Middle East Policy*, 15, 4 (Winter 2007): 158–77.

5. Abdallah Laroui, *L'Algérie et le Sahara Marocain* (Casablanca: Serar, 1976), 91.

6. Cited in Souhail Karam, "Morocco Rejects W. Sahara Partition, Slams Algeria," *Reuters* (Rabat). 20 Feb. 2002

7. For a detailed analysis, see Yahia H. Zoubir, "Algerian-Moroccan Relations and Their Impact on Maghrebi Integration," *Journal of North African Studies*, Vol. 5, No. 3, (2001), 43–74. The arguments the author then discussed have remained the same to this date.

8. Yahia H. Zoubir, "In Search of Hegemony: The Western Sahara in Algerian-Moroccan Relations," *Journal of Algerian Studies* 2, (1997): 43–61.

9. Anthony S. Reyner, "Morocco's International Boundaries: A Factual Background," *Journal of Modern African Studies,* Vol. 1, no. 3 (September 1963): 313–26.

10. Tony Hodges, *Western Sahara: The Roots of a Desert War* (Westport, CT: Laurence Hill, 1983), 85.

11. "Document No. 3, Rapport du Ministre des Liaisons Générales et Communications au Président du Conseil et aux Membres du Gouvernment sur les Relations Algéro-Marocaines I," in *Les Archives de la Révolution Algérienne*, ed. Mohammed Harbi (Alger: Editions Dahlab, 2010), 429–45.

12. Mohamed Sadek Loucif, "Son Premier Ministre Revendique Tindouf-Le Maroc Franchit la Ligne Rouge!" *L'Expression* (Algiers), January 13, 2009, http://www.lexpressiondz.com/actualite/61583-le-maroc-franchit-la-ligne-rouge.html.

13. For an extensive study of Algeria's Africa policy until the 1990s, see Slimane Chikh, *L'Algérie Porte de l'Afrique* (Algiers: Casbah Editions, 1999).

14. Colonel Djamel Bouzghaia, "Politique de Défense de l'Algérie," unpublished paper, February 26, 1995, in Ministère de la Défense Nationale, Institut Supérieur pour les Etudes de Sécurité Nationale, Recueil de Conférences, 1995–2010, 80.

15. John Damis, "The Western Sahara Dispute as a Source of Regional Conflict in North Africa," in *Contemporary North Africa,* ed. Halim Barakat (Washington DC: CCAS, 1985), 139–40.

16. See Yahia H. Zoubir, "Tipping the Balance toward Intra-Maghreb Unity in Light of the Arab Spring," *International Spectator: Italian Journal of International Affairs,* Vol. 46, no. 3 (September 2012): 64–80.

17. Jacob Mundy, "The Morocco-Polisario War for Western Sahara, 1975–1991," in *Conflict and Insurgency in the Contemporary Middle East,* ed. Barry Rubin (London: Routledge, 2009), 209–31.

18. Chad McCoull, "Morocco and Western Sahara," *Journal of ERW and Mine Action,* April 2008, http://maic.jmu.edu/journal/11.2/profiles/mccoull/mccoull.htm.

19. Michael Bhatia, "The Western Sahara Under Polisario Control," *Review of African Political Economy,* 28, 88 (2001): 295; for additional details, see Mundy "The Morocco-Polisario War for Western Sahara, 1975–1991," in *Conflict and Insurgency in the Contemporary Middle East,* ed. Barry Rubin, (London: Routledge, 2009), 221.

20. For a detailed account of Moroccan investments in occupied Western Sahara, see Yahia Zoubir, "Western Sahara Conflict Impedes Maghreb Unity," *Middle East Report,* Vol. 20, issue 163 (March–April 1990): 28–29.

21. Erik Hagen, "Norwegians Shipping Phosphates from Western Sahara," *Norwatch,* June 17, 2007, www.vest-sahara.no/index.php?parse_news=single&cat=49&art=538. See also Western Sahara Resource Watch, http://www.wsrw.org/index.php?parse_news=single&cat=105&art=683.

22. Stefan Armbruster, "Oil: Western Sahara's Future," BBC, March 4, 2003, http://news.bbc.co.uk/2/hi/business/2758829.stm.

23. For detailed analysis of the role of oil companies in Western Sahara, see Philippe Riché, "Le Maroc ouvre le Territoire du Sahara Occidental à L'exploitation Pétrolière," *ARSO,* July 2004, www.arso.org/ressnat3.html; see also "Campaign to Stop Oil Exploration in Western Sahara," *afrol News,* June 30, 2004, www.afrol.com/articles/13488.

24. ONHYM, "List of Companies Partnering with ONHYM at February 12, 2012," http://www.onhym.com/en/HYDROCARBURES/PartenariatetCoop%C3%A9rationP%C3%A9trole/Listedespartenaires/tabid/325/language/en-US/Default.aspx?Cat = 30.

25. New York City Bar Association, Committee on United Nations, *Report on Legal Issues Involved in the Western Sahara Dispute: Use of Natural Resources,* April 2011, http://www.nycbar.org/pdf/report/uploads/20072089-ReportonLegalIssuesInvolvedintheWesternSaharaDispute.pdf, 27.

26. International Mission of Investigation in Western Sahara, January 2003, 50 pages, www.france-libertes.fr.

27. UN Security Council, S/2002/161, "Letter dated 29 January 2002 from the Under Secretary General for Legal Affairs, the Legal Counsel, addressed to the President of the Security Council," February 12, 2002.

28. France Libertés-AFASPA. *International Mission Investigation in Western Sahara du 28 Octobre au 5 Novembre 200-Etat des Droits Civils, Politiques, Socio-Économiques et Culturels des Sahraouis-Etat de L'exploitation Économique de ce Territoire non Autonome,* January 2003, http://www.arso.org/FL101102f.pdf.

29. European Commission, "Recommendation from the Commission to the Council," February 11, 2011, http://eur-ex.europa.eu/SECMonth.do?year=2011&Month=02.

30. Central Intelligence Agency, *The World Factbook: Western Sahara,* updated April 5, 2012, https://www.cia.gov/library/publications/the-world-factbook/geos/wi.html.

31. European Parliament, *Legal Opinion, Proposal for a Council Regulation on the Conclusion of the Fisheries Partnership Agreement between the European Community and the Kingdom of Morocco-Compatibility with the Principles of International Law,* February 20, 2006, http://www.arso.org/LegalopinionUE200206.pdf. For detailed discussion on Morocco's exploitation of the fisheries of Western Sahara, see New York City Bar Association, Committee on United Nations, *Report on Legal Issues Involved in the Western Sahara Dispute: Use of Natural Resources,* April 2011, http://www.nycbar.org/pdf/report/uploads/20072089-ReportonLegalIssuesInvolved intheWesternSaharaDispute.pdf, 16.

32. Maria Stephan and Jacob Mundy, "A Battlefield Transformed: From Guerrilla Resistance to Mass Nonviolent Struggle in the Western Sahara," *Journal of Military and Strategic Studies,* 8, issue 3 (2006): 1–32.

33. Kathleen Jennings, "Western Sahara," *Norwegian Peace Building Center,* Noref Report, March   2009,   http://www.peacebuilding.no/var/ezflow_site/storage/original/application/f1f14a6048ee2c208bda6605496a63ee.pdf.

34. Anna Theofilopoulo, "Morocco's Short-Sighted Politics," *Foreign Policy in Focus,* May 21, 2012, http://www.fpif.org/articles/moroccos_short-sighted_politics.

35. Brahim Saidy, "La Politique de Défense Marocaine: Articulation de L'interne et de L'externe," *Maghreb-Machrek* (Paris), no. 202 (Winter 2009–2010): 131.

36. Mundy, "The Morocco-Polisario War for Western Sahara, 1975–1991," in *Conflict and Insurgency in the Contemporary Middle East,* ed. Barry Rubin (London: Routledge, 2009), 223.

37. John Damis, "King Hassan and the Western Sahara War," *The Maghreb Review,* 25, nos. 1–2 (2000): 13–30.

38. On the United States and France's military assistance to Morocco, on the one hand, and of the Soviet Union to Algeria, on the other hand, during the war, see Daniel Volman, "The Role of Foreign Military Assistance in the Western Sahara War," in *International Dimensions of the Western Sahara Conflict,* ed. Yahia H. Zoubir and Daniel Volman (Westport, CT: Praeger, 1993), 151–68; Daniel Volman, "Foreign Arms Sales and the Military Balance in the Maghreb," in *North Africa in Transition—State, Society, and Economic Transformation in the 1990s,* ed. Yahia H. Zoubir (Gainesville, FL: University Press of Florida, 1999), 212–26.

39. Bhatia, "The Western Sahara under Polisario Control," *Review of African Political Economy,* 28, 88 (2001): 292.

40. Barbara Harrel-Bond, *Struggle for the Western Sahara,* Part II (Hanover, NH: American Universities Field Staff Reports Service, 1981), 12–13; Claudia Wright, "Journey to Marrakech: U.S.-Moroccan Security Relations," *International Security,* 7, 4 (Spring 1983): 167; David J. Dean, The Air Force Role in Low-Intensity Conflict (Maxwell AFB, AL: Air University Press, 1986), 69; Stephen Zunes, 'The United States in the Sahara War: A Case of Low Intensity Intervention," in *International Dimensions of the Western Sahara Conflict,* ed. Zoubir and Volman (Westport, CT: Praeger, 1993), 53–92.

41. Yahia H. Zoubir, "Soviet Policy toward the Western Sahara Conflict," *Africa Today,* Vol. 34, no. 3 (1987): 17–32.

42. "Abdelaziz Bouteflika: l'Algérie ne Déclarera Jamais la Guerre au Maroc," *AP,* October 23, 2004, http://algerie.actudz.com/article93.html. The statement came at a time of high tension between Algeria and Morocco regarding the conflict in Western Sahara and rumors that Algeria was preparing for war against Morocco.

43. Gawdat Bahgat, "Sécurité en Afrique du Nord—La Perception d'une Menace Contre les Intérêts Nationaux et les Revenus Massifs Provenant du Pétrole ont ouvert la Course à L'armement dans la Région," *Idées/Afkar,* 18 (Summer 2008): 43.

44. United States Department of State, "Background Note: Morocco," March 12, 2012, http://www.state.gov/r/pa/ei/bgn/5431.htm.

45. SIPRI Military Expenditures Database 2011, http://milexdata.sipri.org.

46. Other sources give higher percentage of GDP. See the excellent dossier the Algerian *El Watan* published in 2009, M.A.O, "Dossier: L'Algérie et le Maroc Augmentent leur Budget Défense—Maghreb: Les Dessous d'une Course à L'armement," *El Watan,* May 12, 2009, http://www.elwatan.com/archives/article.php?id = 125590. The estimated share of GDP of Morocco's military budget is five percent.

47. For an interesting discussion, see Soufiane Ben Farhat, "La Course au Surarmement au Maghreb—Les Rivalités Internes, la Concurrence Géostratégique et le Spectre d'Al Qaida Expliquent la Frénésie de Surarmement de l'Algérie, du Maroc et de la Libye," *Idées/Afkar,* 18 (Summer 2008): 36–39.

48. Zoubir's interviews in the mid- and late-1990s with senior military officers in the ANP.

49. Gaidi Mohamed Faouzi, interview with Sam Perlo-Freeman, Director of SIPRI Project, "Depuis 2002, l'Algérie a Augmenté ses Dépenses Militaires de 170%," *El Watan,* May 24, 2012, http://www.elwatan.com/actualite/depuis-2002-l-algerie-a-augmente-ses-depenses-militaires-de-170–24–05–2012–171962_109.php. (no longer available online)

50. Gaidi Mohamed Faouzi, interview with Sam Perlo-Freeman, Director of SIPRI Project, "Depuis 2002, l'Algérie a Augmenté ses Dépenses Militaires de 170%," *El Watan,* May 24, 2012, http://www.elwatan.com/actualite/depuis-2002-l-algerie-a-augmente-ses-depenses-militaires-de-170–24–05–2012–171962_109.php. (no longer available online)

CHAPTER 6

Security in the Sahara-Sahel Region: National and Regional Approaches

INTRODUCTION

The Sahel region,[1] which lies at the proximity of the Maghreb States, has become a region of serious security concern for the Maghreb and Sahel states. Although some analysts define the Sahel as a long strip that encompasses 10 countries, in this chapter, we will only consider the limited definition of the Sahel, which includes Algeria, Libya, Mali, Mauritania, and Niger. Because of unfolding developments, Burkina Faso and Nigeria are now being linked to the Sahel, which explains their inclusion, and that of other neighboring states, in this chapter. The Sahara-Sahel region has become a security threat primarily because of the inability of any state, strong or weak, to control it. This immense region has porous borders, which have historically been crossed at will by tradesmen who went through the historic city of Timbuktu in northern Mali, but also by traffickers of all kinds. It would, however, be erroneous to view it simply as an area of trafficking. In reality, it is a zone of interaction between Arab Africa and Black Africa in which all kinds of human, financial, and religious exchanges take place.[2]

In this chapter, we will focus on the main security problems that have arisen in the Sahara-Sahel region. We will review the main legal and military/intelligence instruments that the states in the region have developed at the national and regional levels to address those issues. Considering the recent, still ongoing developments, we will provide a preliminary analysis on the situation in northern Mali and its potential regional and international implications.

THE SAHEL REGION

The Sahel is an eco-climatic zone located on the southern edge of the Sahara desert; this difference has had implications for both the Sahel and the Sahara regions. The structural, perennial problems stemming from this geographical extension have been the oldest forms of tensions in the region. Undoubtedly, the climatic changes in one or the other area could produce long periods of drought that would create food insecurity, which worsens due to the demographic growth. Climate changes in this zone can also produce climate refugees who will inevitably migrate toward the cities—a migration that might result in conflicts. The advance of the desert has progressively pushed nomads to seek lands further south where there is more vegetation. This has resulted in conflicts between nomadic and sedentary populations, exacerbated by racial and ethnic tensions, such as the ones between Moors, Songhais, Arabs, and Tuareg in the northern areas on the one hand, and the Toucouleurs, Sarakolés, Wolof, and Peuls in the southern areas, on the other hand. In addition to these problems, the geographic conditions result in rivalry for access to water and land between the nomadic and sedentary populations—the rivalry aggravated by climatic warming.

THE NEW THREATS

The fragility and failure of the Sahel states has impeded their development, resulting in new threats unknown hitherto. The Sahel states are among the poorest in the world. For instance, more than half the populations of Mali and Niger live under $1.25 a day (72.3% for Mali and 61.4% for Niger) while one-thirds suffer from daily hunger. With respect to human development, they rank 174 and 177, respectively. This poverty and the dire socioeconomic conditions, such as high unemployment, weak educational and social infrastructures, and precarious agricultural resources, have created a propitious terrain for the expansion of illegal trafficking, such as drugs, clandestine immigration, cigarettes, gasoline, medicines, light weapons, vehicles, automobile spare parts, and, more recently, the recruitment of young men by terrorist groups. Given the instability generated by the various factors already enumerated, the Sahel is obviously not favorable for foreign direct investments, which are necessary for industrialization. Paradoxically, although these countries are among the poorest in the world, they are very rich in natural resources. However, the revenues from natural resources, including oil and uranium, are used for militarization and rent redistribution among clans in power, thus exacerbating frustrations and claims by marginalized groups.

The Sahel region has become an unstable, insecure zone precisely because of the fragility—some would say failure—and vulnerability of the states.[3] The failed states[4] have similar characteristics; most of them have experienced domestic struggle between a center that controls political power and the country's wealth and marginalized peripheries seeking to break the status quo—Mali being one of the best illustrations. The internal power struggles within these states have resulted in political destabilization, often in the form of military coups. Mali, which has experienced a coup on March 22, 2012, is a case in point. The states have failed to manage the clannish and tribal orders thus resulting in an accumulation of intrastate crises. Undoubtedly, the colonial domination, which broke or inverted the traditional hierarchies and amalgamated or separated ethnic groups in an arbitrary territorial design, has generated long-lasting structural problems for these states. However, colonial domination alone cannot explain the failure of these states. The bad governance since independence, coupled with the lack of political participation, the great level of corruption, including among the security forces, also account for their failure. The unequal redistribution of the wealth extracted from the exploitation of the natural resources the benefits from which the local populations are excluded is yet another factor in explaining the failure of these states. The Sahel states have been unable to manage the ethnic, tribal, and religious conflicts within their borders.[5] Those conflicts have often generated domestic unrest, leading to repression by security forces who commit grave violations of human rights. These weak states have also faced major problems in guaranteeing their national sovereignty, making them vulnerable to transnational organizations, and even failing to protect their own populations.[6] In sum, these failed states have always been quite vulnerable to the anarchic forces within their borders. These factors have created the propitious terrain not only for the rise of religious radicalism, but also for terrorism both domestic and transnational.[7]

In recent years, the Sahel has also witnessed a rise of religious radicalism[8] that grafted itself into the already complex ethnic distinctions. Traditionally, Islam in the Sahel and in West Africa has been linked to Sufism, a moderate, liberal form of Islamic practice. Sufism is tolerant toward other beliefs and has always ensured the coexistence of populations from different cultures.[9] The recent presence of Salafist preachers has destabilized the traditional balancing role that the religious brotherhoods have played in Sahel societies. The spread of Saudi, Wahhabi Islam through various NGOs, which have built a number of mosques in order to preach their more conservative brand of Islam that denounces Sufi beliefs as contrary to tradition,[10] has contributed to the rise of radicalism. This development, combined with the accumulation of political and economic frustrations for which the incumbent regimes are partly to blame have produced some of the ingredients contributing to the rise of terrorism.

The Rise of Terrorism and Trafficking

The Sahara-Sahel space provides an ideal sanctuary of terrorist groups; this partly explains why Al Qaeda in the Islamic Maghreb has moved most of its operations to this region and made it one of its zones of combat.[11] In fact, Osama Bin Laden had sent the first emissaries to the region (mainly to Kidal and Tessalit in Mali) in 2001; the main objectives were to prepare for the arrival of members of Al Qaeda (Pakistani and Afghani preachers) and establish a base in the region. The jihadist groups that had been weakened by the increasingly effective attacks by security forces in their respective countries (Algeria, Mauritania, Morocco, and Libya) had begun retreating in the Sahel. In fact, the Algerian Salafi Group for Preaching and Combat (GSPC), the Moroccan Group for Preaching and Combatant (GMPC), the Islamic Moroccan Front, and Mauritanian groups were already active there. They were later joined by members of the Libyan Islamic Fighting Group (LIFG) and the Tunisian Islamic Fighting Group (TIFG). Algerian jihadist groups had begun deploying in the Sahara-Sahel in the 1990s; this deployment was motivated by the uncontrolled nature of the region and the relative ease with which they could acquire weapons that they could supply to their associates in Algeria's northern zones.[12]

Given that funding of terrorist groups had become difficult after 9/11, the Sahel provided a golden opportunity for Al Qaeda affiliates to establish a safe haven, particularly in northern Mali. Kidnappings of Westerners, drug smuggling, arms trafficking, and clandestine immigration networks now serve as the main sources of financing of these groups.[13] AQIM raised $360 million through the payment of ransoms by Western governments.[14] Kidnappings have thus become an important source of revenue for AQIM, which explains the frequency of kidnappings of Europeans since 2003. In April 2012, the number of hostages reached 20, including seven Algerian diplomats seized in the Azawad (northern Mali) on April 5—three were freed in summer 2012, while one has apparently been executed. A whole network has been set in place to snatch foreigners who venture in areas where AQIM or its accomplices are active.[15]

Drug Trafficking

Drug trafficking is not a new phenomenon in the Sahel. Traditionally, the Sahara-Sahel area has been an area for the traffic of drugs, especially cannabis, which is produced, consumed, and sold in the region. However, since the 1980s, the region has turned into an important passageway for drug trafficking from Latin America, crossing Guinea Bissau, Mauritania, Morocco, and Algeria, usually en route to Europe. In addition to the antidrug laws, the rising corruption and instability have pushed the traffickers to exploit the cannabis channels. Drug trafficking has resulted in the emergence and growth of criminal organizations in the region that, in some cases, have been willing to help AQIM and other armed political groups obtain weaponry, travel documents, and other materiel. In other instances AQIM and other armed groups have themselves become involved in drug trafficking as a means of obtaining money to fund their operations and activities.[16] In 2008, the United Nations Office on Drugs and Crime reported that 50 tons of cocaine transited through West Africa.[17] Undoubtedly, as the United States succeeded in controlling the use of drug trafficking routes by the criminal cartels based in Latin America (using the Caribbean route to Europe), these cartels found alternative itineraries that allowed them to transport drugs, especially cocaine, through the Trans-Saharan region, via West Africa, to Europe.[18]

Drug smuggling has become a major security concern particularly after clear connections between terrorists and drug traffickers have been confirmed.[19] One of the most significant signals was in late 2009, when a Boeing 727 full of drugs and other illegal products, doubtless weapons, landed in Gao, a remote northeastern area of Mali, where AQIM has been conspicuously present. AQIM, which has sought various sources of funding in order to purchase weapons and invest in some lucrative sectors, established links with drug traffickers as a way of increasing its revenues. Thus, AQIM provides safe passage for the merchandise (cigarettes, cocaine, light weapons, and so on) through the desert in exchange for protection. AQMI has also provided storing facilities of the drugs, also in exchange of payment. In sum, the Sahel has become the principal hub for drugs.[20] Drug trafficking in the Sahel has alarmed not only European countries, which are geographically close to the region (drugs get to Europe through Morocco), but also the United States.[21]

Undoubtedly, though, the massive profits AQIM and other groups gain from the drug trade have been used, as we saw earlier, to fund criminal and violent enterprises in the region, which, coupled with the acquisition of sophisticated weapons, further exacerbates instability and the vulnerability of the states.

MAGHREB-SAHEL STATES' ANTITERRORISM POLICIES

The states in the Maghreb and the Sahel have adopted a variety of instruments, legal and political, to deal with terrorism. They have done so in the hope of deradicalizing extremist movements. In this section, we shall review the legislation that each state has put in place to fight terrorism and other illegal activities; the argument here is that while there has been much focus on legislation, the states have not tackled adequately the conditions (bad governance, lack of democracy, exclusion, and marginalization), which have contributed to the rise of terrorism and the persistence of illicit activities.

Algeria

Soon after the cancellation of the second round of the legislative elections, which the FIS was poised to win, and the implementation of the state of emergency (February 1992), the authorities suspended various institutions and sought to quell the violence not only through repressive measures, but also through reconciliation policies aimed at inducing Islamist armed groups to lay down their weapons.[22] With respect to repressive measures, they issued legislative decree 92-03 of September 30, 1992 on the fight against subversion and terrorism, which was later supplemented by ordinances 95-10 and 95-11 of February 25, 1995, titled "Reform of the Penal Code and the Code of Criminal Procedure." The legislation provided wide latitude for the authorities to arbitrarily interpret any form of opposition as being subversive. However, the government also sought nonrepressive policies. The first such policy was initiated under the presidency of Liamine Zeroual; this was known as the policy of clemency, Rahma, which offered terrorists who decided to repent the possibility of benefiting from reduced sentences and eventually reintegrating society. When the Rahma policy failed, the state responded to the intensity of the rebellion through executive decree no. 97-04 of January 4, 1997, which recognized the right to legitimate self-defense that in essence blurred the distinction between national defense and domestic public order. This blending of the two functions emerged through the concept of civil defense, which received new substance[23] with the use of the concept of subversion, drawn from the penal code, and figures as both a threat to the *Sûreté de l'Etat* (security of the state) and national defense. After more than five years of uninterrupted military campaign against the Islamist guerrillas, the military hierarchy began secret negotiations that resulted in an agreement the terms of which were never revealed but finalized and legalized through *La loi sur la Concorde civile* (Law on Civil Concord), which was to last from July 7, 1999 to January 13, 2000. On the whole, the law ensured the execution of a compromise, a tradeoff between Islamists and the authorities, whereby the former would renounce the use of violence in exchange for judicial advantages. The law was never ended; in fact, in August 2005, Bouteflika launched the Charter for Peace and National Reconciliation in an attempt to end terrorism, which reduced or annulled sentences for terrorists who did not commit blood crimes or rapes. Terrorists who surrender benefit from financial compensation and social and professional reintegration. The families of deceased terrorists also receive financial compensation and so do the families of the disappeared. Thousands of Islamists have benefited from this charter, which has not been limited in time.[24] Pressured by the unfurling Arab Spring, the authorities lifted the state of emergency in February 2011. In reality, the legislation, adopted to remove the state of emergency, was also accompanied by new legislation permitting the armed forces to continue their role, as they did under emergency rules, to fight terrorism and subversion.[25] In addition, a June 2001 order—part of the emergency rules and never made public apparently—has remained in force.

In February 2012, the government decided to strengthen law 05-01 of 2005 related to the prevention and fight against money laundering and the funding of terrorism; this came in the form of ordinance 12-02 related to the same two issues.[26] It became a law in April 2012;[27] the proclaimed objective of the law is to adapt it to the new developments in information technologies and banking systems and the new schemes that terrorists and traffickers resort to in order to fund their operations.

Libya

In the 1990s, the Qaddafi regime, which had resorted to terrorism from the early 1970s to the late 1980s, faced an armed Islamist insurgency; the regime responded with fierce repression and even collective punishment to dissuade Islamist militants from pursuing their fight against the regime.[28] In 1997, the General People's Congress adopted a series of measures to that effect. Following the events of 9/11, Libya became party in 2002 to the 1999 Convention for the Control and Financing of Terrorism. It also acceded to the 1991 Convention on the Marking of Plastic Explosives for the Purpose of Detection. Libya also ratified the 12 international conventions and protocols relating to terrorism. Probably inspired by the policy of national reconciliation in Algeria, Qaddafi released in 2005 and 2006 a few members of the LIFG from jail.[29] The aim was to co-opt Islamists and defuse their opposition potential. The dialogue between the LIFG and the authorities continued until the policy of reconciliation reached its apex when Libya decided in March 2010 to free the leaders of the LIFG who were allowed to reintegrate society as individuals, not as members of a former organization.[30]

Like the other states faced with armed Islamists groups, Libya also produced antiterrorism legislation. Thus, in 2007, Libya enacted a penal code, which stipulated that anyone convicted of acts of terrorism against the state would be sentenced to death (article 207).[31] The legislation is very stringent; thus, the code stated in the same article that, "Any person who owns books, flyers, drawings, slogans or any other material aimed at favoring the aforementioned acts, or favors these acts in any shape or form shall be punishable by imprisonment for life." Given that Libya wished to prove that it had truly abandoned state-sponsored terrorism, the penal code made clear that the legislation would apply to any of its citizens who commit criminal acts abroad. It is doubtful whether the new Libyan Republic would modify this penal code; the leaders' declared intent to use Shari'a Law as the basis for legislation will certainly make punishment for certain crimes even harsher than the current body of laws.

Mali

Mali, which considers terrorism as the gravest threat to human rights, peace, and security, adopted a counterterrorism law on July 23, 2008 (law no. 08-025) that incorporates the offences, such as those related to civil aviation, vessels and fixed platforms, dangerous materials, diplomatic agents, hostage-taking, financing of terrorism, and nuclear terrorism.[32] Until then, Mali's penal code of 2001 did not include specific articles on terrorism although some aspects of the legislation were applicable to acts of terrorism.[33] It should be noted that the counterterrorism law applied life imprisonment or the death sentence to terrorism offenses.

Given the insecurity that prevailed in the northern part of Mali (and still does), the government of Amadou Toumani Touré (also known as ATT), decided in 2010 to launch the Special Program for Peace, Security, and Development in Northern Mali (PSPSDNM) the main objective of which was to inject $63.5 million over a two-year period to develop a region that the authorities have traditionally neglected. The PSPSDNM, whose official execution began in July 2011, rests on eight guidelines to counter the terrorist threat. These include the following: implant at all levels of the administration in the area; assist the population; fight against the illegal trafficking of light weapons, drugs, and organized crime; cooperate with other countries, and coordinate, monitor, and evaluate the strategy to fight insecurity and terrorism. The PSPSDNM is made up of five components: security (to strengthen national security in the northern area); governance (improved governance in the north for better functionality of the state administration and local authorities); development (job creation and development activities that could also help the realization of basic social infrastructure for people in certain strategic sites; communication (to mobilize the population); and, management (which includes the coordination unit of the program and technical support).[34] However, this program came too late. Mali has faced major challenges in the underdeveloped, neglected northern part, where AQIM has established safe haven since 2007; transnational drug and arms traffickers operate in the same area under AQIM's protection. Because of the financial support it provides to the poor Arab, black, and Tuareg communities, and in the absence of an effective presence of the central government, AQIM secured a relatively strong base of support. AQIM has acquired considerable funds not only through its association with transnational organized crime, but also through the payment of ransoms it receives from foreign governments for the hostages to be released.

Until his overthrow on March 22, 2012, Malian President Touré had underplayed the security threat that AQIM posed for Mali, Algeria, Mauritania, and Niger, known together as the countries of the field or core countries (African Union appellation). ATT had paid lip service to the fight against AQIM because he believed that AQIM represented no real menace to the country. He kept tacit agreement with AQIM that the government would not interfere with AQIM's business dealings in the north when the rest of the country did not suffer from its presence, an attitude, which infuriated the other countries of the field. Worse, ATT did not fulfill the pledge made to the Tuareg contained in the

2006 Algiers Accord: state development of the northern region in exchange for dropping their demand for Tuareg autonomy. Fears about the domino effect of the Libyan crisis materialized when on January 17, 2012, the National Movement for the Liberation of Azawad (MNLA) began its conquest of the Azawad. The surprise assaults by the hardened, better prepared Tuareg were no match for the ill-equipped, poorly trained, and dispirited government soldiers. The mutiny within the armed forces and the subsequent military coup on March 22 by Captain Amadou Haya Sanogo weakened Mali further because of the isolation and the threat of sanctions from the Economic Community of Western African States (ECOWAS) and the African Union. In the meantime, however, seizure of the three major cities in northern Mali —Gao, Kidal, and the historic Timbuktu—highlighted the newly acquired power of the Tuareg. The MNLA, which proclaimed the independence of the Azawad on April 6, is not the sole representative of the Tuareg. The Ansar al-Din, a jihadist Tuareg faction led by the Salafi Iyad Ag Ghaly, former Mali's cultural attaché in the Malian Embassy in Riyadh in Saudi Arabia, has been intent on imposing Shari'a Law throughout the country, starting with Tessalit, Aguelhok, Kidal, and Timbuktu, the cities he conquered with the assistance of AQIM. Unlike the MNLA, Ghaly said that he did not seek independence for the Azawad but the establishment of an Islamic state in Mali. Another AQIM dissident group, the Movement for Oneness and Jihad in West Africa (MOJWA), which kidnapped seven Algerian diplomats on April 5, 2012,[35] and, apparently, members of the Nigerian Boko Haram, are now operating in the region—although it is not quite clear whether MOJWA is really a dissident group or is using mere tactics to sow confusion among analysts. In July 2012, because of international pressure and the defeat in May–June of its troops against the combined forces of AQIM, MOJWA, and Ansar El Din, the MNLA rescinded its decision regarding the Azawad's independence and has since favored a political solution, which would grant a large autonomy to the territory. Unlike Ansar El Din, which, in January 2013, reneged on the promises it made to Algeria and Burkina Faso to negotiate a peaceful resolution of the conflict and sought to advance southward with the support of AQIM and MOJWA, the MNLA offered to support France, which intervened militarily to "protect her citizens" and protect the territorial integrity of Mali, one of her closest friends in the African continent.

Mauritania

On July 26, 2005, Mauritania introduced stringent legislation in the form of law no. 2005-047 relating to the fight against terrorism. The law, through article 6, sought to punish any individuals, that is, Islamists, "1) participating in a formed group or an established agreement . . .; 2) receiving training on national territory or abroad in view of committing a terrorist infraction on the national territory or abroad; 3) recruiting or training a person or a group of persons in view of committing a terrorist act inside or outside of the country." This law was enacted for identifying, tracing, freezing, seizing, and forfeiting narcotics-related assets as well as assets derived from or intended for terrorist financing and other serious crimes.[36] Five years later, in July 2010, Mauritania adopted a new antiterrorism law in order to give its security forces greater powers in the fight against AQIM; the law also applies to other terrorism-related acts such as money laundering and computer infractions. Restrictions on searches of homes or eavesdropping by the security forces—previously not allowed due to Islamic laws—were lifted, provided that the judge grants an authorization for that purpose. Under this law, youngsters under 18 can be charged despite Islamic Shari'a Law, which does not apply the same measures on juveniles. In order to encourage terrorists to denounce their associates, the 2010 law grants immunity to those who notify the authorities of intended assaults.[37] The defection of 30 young AQIM combatants in November 2010 inspired the authorities to un-veil initiatives aimed at deradicalizing Islamist militants. One of these programs was to have imams meet with radical Islamist prisoners and preach the correct interpretation of Islam to them. The government also recruited 500 imams to teach moderate Islam in Mauritania's mosques.[38]

In a seminar held in late April 2012, Mauritanian religious scholars, sheikhs, and leaders called on *madares* (religious schools) and mosques to instill in their teachings and sermons the moderate values of Islam—this is particularly aimed at the youth. The initiative for the seminar of religious scholars came from the Ministry of Islamic Affairs in collaboration with the League of Religious Mauritanian Scholars.[39] This initiative was probably prompted by events in northern Mali, where AQIM and other jihadist groups are trying to recruit youngsters for jihad.

Morocco

Although Morocco is not part of the Sahel countries, it needs to be included here because it has experienced similar problems as the Sahel states.

After the Casablanca terrorist attacks on May 16, 2003, which left scores dead and wounded, Morocco adopted an antiterrorist strategy that incorporated an antiterrorism law, social assistance programs, and a reform of the religious sector. Similar to laws adopted by other Maghreb-Sahel countries, the Moroccan legislation gave terrorism a broad definition, allowing the authorities to inflict heavy sentences (a minimum of a 10-year term in prison) and giving security forces wide prerogatives in terms of investigation, seizure of private properties, detention, and control of means of communications. The strong legislation, coupled with better international cooperation, has been relatively successful until the bombing in Marrakech on April 28, 2011 that resulted in the killing of 15 people, 10 of whom were foreign nationals.[40] The legislation, like the ones in the other Maghreb-Sahel countries, has been the subject of harsh criticism from many NGOs, which argued that the law violated individual liberties; the Moroccan government rebuked such criticism, asserting that the absence of attacks was proof of its efficiency. Like Algeria, Morocco has mustered various means, including economic ones, to fight terrorism. Hence, in 2005, the government launched the $1.2 billion National Initiative for Human Development (INDH).[41] This ambitious program aimed at enhancing the use of social and economic infrastructure and services by poor and vulnerable groups to reduce poverty and social exclusion in rural and urban places.[42] Although the authorities argue that poverty caused terrorism, they nonetheless tried to undercut one of the arguments that terrorists have used against the monarchy suggesting that the latter was unable to achieve equal national development.

Religion is yet another instrument the Moroccan authorities have used in the antiterrorist campaign. To undermine the legitimacy of the ideological precepts of the terrorists, the government decided to reform and modernize the national religious corpus. In 2006, the government made one of the most spectacular and publicized decisions: the introduction of the *Mourchidate* (female Muslim clerics),[43] a rather bold decision in the Arab and Muslim world. The feminization of this exclusively masculine milieu was a strong symbolic message to demonstrate that one can be religious and modern at the same time.

Niger

Niger, a country rich in uranium, gold, and oil, has suffered from terrorism, especially from kidnappings of foreign nationals on its territory. In 2006, Niger implemented UN Security Resolution 1373 (2001) through the creation of a committee on the fight against terrorism under the authority of the Minister of Foreign Affairs. One of the objectives of the committee was the creation of a database on antiterrorism measures.[44] Considering that the country's penal code of 1961 and the law 2003-25 of June 13, 2003 that amended it did include some measures on terrorism, the Nigerien authorities adopted the counterterrorism law on June 23, 2008 (law no. 2008-18), which complemented the penal code. This legislation includes severe sentences against terrorist acts, namely, the possession of explosives, crimes linked to civil aviation, vessels and fixed platforms, terrorist bombings, crimes against diplomatic agents, hostage-taking, financing of terrorism as well as nuclear terrorism.[45] As early as 2002, Niger had contracted regulation no. 14/2002/CM/UEMOA of the West African Economic and Monetary Union (WAEMU/UEMOA) on the freezing of funds linked to terrorist activities. The same year, Niger also adopted directive no. 07/2002/CM/UEMOA on the fight against money laundering; the directive also calls for the institution of a Financial Intelligence Unit (FIU), which Niger has adhered to through the acceptance of decree no. 2004-262/

PRN/ME/F of September 14, 2004 (S/2003/631).[46] However, Niger is a poor country with limited means. Niger, similar to the other Sahel states, has inadequate operational and strategic capabilities in the broader security, law enforcement, and judicial sectors to control its territory or prevent and respond to the many security threats. The central authority to fight terrorism is still to be established.[47]

Nigeria

Like Morocco, Nigeria is not part of the Sahel; however, it needs to be included in this chapter not only because of its membership in the Sahara-Sahel counterterrorism partnership, but also because of the potential connection that might have developed between AQIM and the Nigerian terrorist organization Boko Haram.[48] In 2002, Nigerian law provided a broad definition of terrorism,[49] which was updated as an antiterrorism bill on February 22, 2011 by Nigeria's House of Representatives (An Act to Provide for Measures to Combat Terrorism and for Related Matters).[50] The Nigerian legislation defines terrorism as any act that can damage seriously a country or an organization, intimidate a population, destabilize or destroy the fundamental political, constitutional, economic and social structures, or cause bodily harms and 'death (article no. 2). Anyone who attempts, facilitates, threatens to commit, or does not prevent such an act is considered as terrorist (part 1, article 1). All governmental agencies are involved in the counterterrorism campaign: the Defense Intelligence Agency, Department of State Services, the Economic and Financial Crimes Commission, the National Agency for the Prohibition of Persons, the National Drug Law Enforcement Agency, the National Intelligence Agency, Nigerian Immigration Services, Nigerian Customs Services, and the Nigerian Police Force (part IV, article no. 33). These agencies have broad powers to investigate terrorist activities.[51] For instance, properties and funds can be seized if suspected to be for terrorism purposes (part II, article no. 1). A security intelligence officer may enter and search any place, person, or vehicle without a warrant if he has reason to suspect that an offense is being committed. He can also search and detain any person suspected of having committed or likely to commit a terrorist act (part IV, article no. 23). A senior security officer has the authority to order the detention of a terrorism suspect for 48 hours without that suspect having access to anyone, including his attorney (part IV, article no. 26). Despite criticism against this legislation, many of whose articles are in violation of human rights and individual liberties, Nigeria's national assembly decided in January 2012 to strengthen the law "so it can be more effectively used to checkmate the activities of the rampaging Islamic sect Boko Haram."[52]

Boko Haram ("Western education is sinful" in Hausa language) has attracted much attention because of the particularly brutal methods it has used against Muslim clerics who reject its ideology and against Christians. The apparent growing links between this organization and other jihadist groups, such as Al-Shabaab in Somalia or AQIM in northern Mali, have caused concerns among regional and international security officials. Reports have indicated that members of Boko Haram were among those jihadists who seized the city of Gao in April 2012.[53]

Tunisia

Tunisia, a neighbor of the Sahara-Sahel states (Algeria and Libya), has also faced acts of terrorism, notably the April 2002 bombing of the synagogue in Jerba and the confrontation between jihadists and security forces in December 2006 and January 2007. However, already in the late 1980s, the authorities had raised the specter of extremist Islamist activities to justify security and antiterrorist procedures to eliminate any opposition to Ben Ali's dictatorial regime; in fact, the intent was to persecute members of the unauthorized, moderate Islamist Ennahda party, led by Rashed Ghannoushi, who was forced into exile in the late 1980s. Soon after the bombing in Jerba, which resulted in the killing of dozens of people, mostly German tourists, the authorities developed legislation against terrorism and money laundering, promulgated in December 2003.[54] According to article 4 of that legislation, "is considered as terrorist any offense, whatever the motives, in relation to an individual or collective activity that might terrorize a person or group of people, spread terror among the population, with the aim of influencing state policy . . ., to disturb public order, peace or international security. . . ."[55] Given that Tunisia does not have the death penalty, the maximum sentence is life imprisonment while the minimum is 30 years (article no. 7). Under the rather broad definition of terrorism, any person who encourages, discusses or plans to commit a terrorist act can be prosecuted (article no. 11). The law demands that individuals inform security forces of any terrorist attempt they may be aware of, even if they must violate professional secrecy (article no. 22). The law (article no. 26) demonstrates leniency toward any member of a terrorist organization who decides to inform the authorities of an act of terrorism prior to its being committed. The individual will not be charged with a crime; the court may, however, place the accused under administrative supervision or forbid him to stay in certain places for a period not to exceed five years. As to money laundering, any suspected financial operation can be immediately interrupted and the funds frozen (article no. 86). This penal code has been severely criticized because the Ben Ali regime used it to violate civil liberties and human rights.[56] However, the transition government that was formed in the post-Ben Ali era has yet to annul the 2003 Penal Code, which some judges continue to use in prosecuting individuals.[57] Tunisia is expected to create a new legislative framework to bring antiterrorism efforts in line with international legal standards.

Table 6.1 provides a summary of the various measures the Maghreb-Sahel countries have taken in the fight against terrorism.

Table 6.1 Maghreb Antiterrorist Legislation

	Extended Definition of Terrorism	Security Prerogatives	Death Penalty	Appeasement Policy	Use of Religious Sanction	Influence of 9/11 and Regional Threats
Algeria	Yes	Strengthened, even after Lifting of State of Emergency	Included in the Law but not Applied	Conditional Amnesty, Financial Compensation	Yes	No
Libya	Yes	Strengthened	Included in the Law but not Applied	Dialogue, Release of Terrorists	Yes	Yes
Mali	Yes	Strengthened	Included in the Law	Program for Peace, Security, and Development in Northern Mali	Yes	Yes
Mauritania	Yes	Strengthened	Suspended	Deradicalization Policy through Religious Teaching	Yes	Yes
Morocco	Yes	Strengthened	Included in the Law but not Applied	Reconciliation, Social Assistance	Yes	No
Niger	Yes	Strengthened but Still Weak	Suspended	-	-	Yes
Nigeria	Yes	Strengthened	Applied	-	No	Partially
Tunisia	Yes	Strengthened	Abolished	-	No	Yes

The Maghreb states have adopted different approaches to either secure economic gains (Morocco) or to emphasize security (Algeria). Algeria, Libya (under Qaddafi), and Morocco have used the Sahel as an area of competition to achieve their geopolitical interests.[58]

Morocco: Economic Diplomacy

Like for Algeria and Libya, the Sahel region is at the core of Morocco's interests. The monarchy considers part of the Sahel as its natural zone of influence and the natural extension of occupied Western Sahara, which it deems as being an integral part of its southern provinces. Morocco has resorted to soft power to spread its influence in the Sahel region: investments, trade, and cooperation in educational programs. The Moroccan offensive toward the Sahara-Sahel countries was made easier owing to the monarchy's abandonment of the dogmatic diplomacy of the past, which had consisted of boycotting the countries that recognized the Sahrawi Arab Democratic Republic (SADR), proclaimed on February 27, 1976, following the withdrawal of Spain, the former colonial power. Instead of severing all ties with those states, Morocco has launched instead an active economic diplomacy to make them more amenable to its position through increasing investments. This was a way of making Moroccan companies' economic presence essential and more profitable for those countries than support to the Sahrawi cause.[59] This strategic shift is evident in the growth of Moroccan exports, which have more than doubled since 1990.[60] In 2009, Morocco's pragmatic strategy was perceptible during the launch of the Conference of African States Bordering the Atlantic. The conference focused on dialogue with the objective of confronting collectively the threats facing these countries and exploiting the opportunities that this region offers. The participants adopted an action plan based on a "progressive and solidarity approach in the fields of economic and human development, security, and political dialogue and environment issues."[61] In the same vein, Morocco had in 2002 signed in Rabat a trade and investment agreement with the member countries of the West African Monetary and Economic Union (also known as UEMOA in its French acronym). Morocco is a member of the UMA, the Community of Sahel-Saharan States (CEN-SAD), the Common Market for Eastern and Southern Africa (COMESA), and holds an observer status in ECOWAS. It has concluded agreements of non-double taxation with almost all the Sahara-Sahel countries in addition to accords to promote and protect mutual investments.[62] In 2000, Morocco cancelled the debt of the poorest African countries and exonerated their products of any taxation. In addition to emergency aid programs, Morocco granted around $300 million a year to its African partners in the Official Development Assistance (ODA) program; this represented 10 percent of the total exchanges with Africa.[63] Morocco has sought to increase its trade with sub-Saharan countries as the following table demonstrates. It has adopted an action plan that includes standard trade agreements or preferential agreements with Niger, Mali, and Nigeria. This plan has also consisted in creating networks through which Moroccan and Saharan entrepreneurs can interact, organize business trips for Moroccan businesspeople, open national consultancy offices, and provide business prospection studies on some African markets to assist Moroccan businesspeople.[64] The result has been rather positive since Moroccan exports have multiplied sixfold from 1990 to 2008.

Table 6.2   Moroccan Trade with Saharan Countries in 2011

	Imports	Exports
Mali	21,073	380,090
Mauritania	6,936	679,535
Niger	116	64,998
Nigeria	1,664,499	295,328

Value in Thousands of Dirhams
100 Moroccan Dirhams (MAD) = $11.95

Source: Moroccan Ministry of Trade, Industry and New Technologies, Department of Foreign Trade, http://www.mce.gov.ma/statistiques/Echanges_com_pays.asp.

Investments

Telecommunications account for 25 percent of the global amount of Moroccan Foreign Direct Investments in Africa. Maroc-Telecom is the major shareholder of the Mauritanian operator Mauritel and, since June 2009, has held 51 percent of the Malian operator.[65] As regard banking and finance investments, Attijariwafa and BMCE Banks are the leading Moroccan banks in the African markets. In the Sahel, Attijariwafa Bank is present in Mali, with a buyout of 51 percent of the shares of Banque Internationale du Mali, which cost around 60 million euros. With a market share of 13.8 percent of Moroccan FDI, investment holding is in the third position. Ynna Holding Group is involved in Mali, in the construction of a cotton-spinning mill factory, crushing and production of cement.[66] As to the mining and energy sectors, ONA, through its mining subsidiary Managem, holds many iron ore deposits in Mali and Niger. Morocco has concluded several bilateral agreements with Saharan countries, notably, Mauritania, in civil aviation, security of airports, safety, and training.[67] The two countries also cooperate in various socioeconomic areas, such as literacy development, the fight against locust, water sanitation, transportation, and health.[68]

Unlike Morocco, Algeria has sought to protect its national security interests through a collective approach. Algeria shares long borders with three Sahara-Sahel states, Libya (982 km), Mali (1,376 km), and Niger (956 km), with the latter two states being weak states. The border with Mauritania is relatively smaller with 463 kilometers.

Algeria: Collective Security Approach

In addition to the usually close bilateral relations that they have developed with one another (Algerian-Malian Commission, Algerian-Nigerien Commission, Great Mixed Algerian-Mauritanian Commission), the Sahel states have sought to cooperate collectively—under the leadership of Algeria, the most powerful state in the region. Three main reasons enticed the Sahel states to increase their cooperation and eventually formalize that regional partnership through regional institutions: The increased presence of terrorist groups in the Sahel (arms trafficking, hostage-taking, and so on); The threat that the separatist Nigerien Movement for Justice (MNJ) and Tuareg rebels posed to the Nigerien government; and the Tuareg rebellion in Kidal, Mali, and, the menace that the obscure jihadist group, Ansar al Islam in the Sahara, represented for Mauritania (the group operates in the southwest region). All these factors persuaded these countries to work together. Both Niger and Mali had solicited Algeria, by far the most important military power in the region to assist them, either militarily or through mediation (for example, between the Malian central government and the Tuareg, most significantly, in 1996 and again in 2006) in resolving these issues.[69] This cooperation coincided with the creation in 2007 of the U.S. Command for Africa (AFRICOM); many countries also responded to the influence of the United States, which brought these countries and other African and European nations into a wider antiterrorism cooperation through annual joint maneuvers (Flintlock since 2005). In fact, it was the apprehension about an imposing U.S. presence in the region through AFRICOM that persuaded the regional actors to cooperate more closely and adopt a common security policy in the Sahel region.[70] It was thus not surprising that this idea emerged in October 2007, soon after the creation of AFRICOM. In November 2008, the foreign ministers of seven Sahel countries, Algeria, Burkina Faso, Chad, Libya Mali, Niger, and Mauritania met in Bamako in an attempt to address collectively the various security issues plaguing the Sahel-Sahara region, most importantly the problem of terrorism, and develop a multifaceted cooperation to ensure "security, stability, and development."[71] The Bamako Forum, as it came to be known, set the stage for the forum held in Algiers in March 2010.

The most concrete example of the cooperation among the four Sahel countries (Algeria, Mali, Mauritania, and Niger)[72] took place in April 2009, when the Algerian Air Force decided to use unmanned aircraft to establish surveillance over the whole area and interdict the movement of terrorists.[73] In fact, military cooperation among Algeria, Mali, and Niger increased considerably because, as Mali's president at the time Amadou Toumane Touré put it, "all the threats (in the Sahara-Sahel) are trans-border threats and no country can alone find the solution to confront them."[74] The intelligence services of these countries also sought to coordinate their efforts to thwart terrorists from their continued abductions of foreign nationals, mostly Western tourists, in the region. Some military and intelligence officials from the Sahel countries met in Niger in May 2009 to discuss the security situation in the Sahara-Sahel. This coordination was made all the more necessary because the European countries were also coordinating their forces and decided to intervene directly in and/or from the countries where they have had a military and intelligence presence, notably, in Mali, Chad, and Senegal.[75]

In August 2009, an important meeting of senior military and intelligence officers from Algeria, Mali, Mauritania, and Niger took place in Tamanrasset, the headquarters of Algeria's Sixth Military Region, located in the Deep South.[76] Particularly noteworthy was the absence of Libya from that meeting, probably because of disagreements and the struggle between Algerians and Libyans for leadership in the region.[77] The objective of the meeting was to prepare for a common offensive to fight transborder criminality in general and terrorism in particular. A month later, the heads of the chiefs of staffs of the four countries met in Algiers to set up joint patrols along the borders in what would be considered common territory, meaning the possibility of hot pursuit, chasing terrorists inside each other's territory without first obtaining permission. The meeting also aimed at preparing a joint offensive against AQIM.[78]

The Sahel countries had opposed, at least publicly, until France military invasion in Mali in January 2013, any foreign interference. They were also apprehensive about foreign intervention owing to the repeated kidnappings in the region. Although Western countries, with the exception of Great Britain, had paid ransoms to free their hostages, officials from the Sahel feared that Western countries would decide to intervene directly to free their hostages or preempt the abduction of their citizens in those states. The uneasiness of the regional states transpired even more clearly during the Algiers conference on the Sahel-Sahara security, held in March 2010, which brought together the representatives, at the ministerial levels, from Algeria, Burkina Faso, Chad, Libya, Mali, Mauritania, and Niger. The countries agreed on a number of political, economic, and security measures to be executed collectively to counter the threat of terrorism. This conference took place at a time when terrorist activities in the region had increased considerably, and also when major disagreements among the states regarding the payment of ransoms had become apparent. Another difficulty was to secure agreement on a common vision and strategy, abided by all the neighbors, to fight terrorism. The strategy consisted of strengthening bilateral and regional cooperation and securing international cooperation at various levels, including legislation with respect to the payment of ransoms and the forms of financing of terrorism. However, though the states felt that international cooperation was important, they agreed that the responsibility for security of the region was national and regional to avoid any extra-regional interference. The countries seemed to agree that bringing development to the region was critical to thwart the recruitment of terrorists because the lack of human development constitutes the best breeding ground for such recruitment. Furthermore, there was also general consensus that the local populations, the primary victims of terrorism, should be made part of this multifaceted fight against terrorism and illicit trafficking of all kinds.[79] In order to demonstrate that the seven states were serious about securing the region and that the decisions made at the Algiers conference would be executed, a secret conclave of the heads of intelligence services was held in Algiers on April 5, 2010;[80] there is no doubt that the objective of the meeting was not only to share information among the military intelligence of these countries, but also to create a certain level of trust among them and avoid the Sahel area becoming the arena of struggle among Western intelligence services.[81]

A week after the conclave of the chiefs of intelligence services and in application of the resolution of the Algiers conference of foreign ministers held in March 2010, the heads of the chiefs of staffs of the armed forces of the seven countries convened in Algiers on April 13.[82] The urgency and the frequency of the meetings demonstrated, if need be, that the security situation in the Sahel had become worrisome. More importantly, it aimed at demonstrating that the countries of the region could handle the security and stability of the region on their own. This meeting, held in Tamanrasset, and the one that preceded it resulted in the creation on April 21, 2010 of the Comité d'état-major opérationnel conjoint (General Staff Joint-Operations Committee, CEMOC) limited to four Sahara-Sahel countries: Algeria, Mali, Mauritania, and Niger, whose center of operations is based in Tamanrasset.[83] The main objective of CEMOC, which has a rotating command in an alphabetical order, has been to consolidate the military and security relations among the four countries. CEMOC's main mission is to oversee the coordination of intelligence and military operations in all matters relating to counterterrorism and the management of possible military missions and operations against AQIM. Missions were assigned to each country; thus, Algeria is in charge of the air force, Mali of the ground forces, Mauritania of transmissions, Niger of logistics, while Burkina Faso has an observer role.[84] According to Algerian military public sources, CEMOC's theater of operations covers a space of desert of 1,956 kilometers in length and a depth of 933 kilometers.[85]

Soon after its creation CEMOC gave the impression of being an ineffective organization owing to the decision of Mauritania, a member of CEMOC, to call, in July 2010, on France to assist Mauritanian troops in a military operation against AQIM in northern Mali, thus undermining the whole notion of regional self-reliance and extra-regional noninterference. The Mauritanians did not inform their partners in CEMOC of the planned operation; the French-Mauritanian raid failed to free the French hostage, Michel Germaneau, who had either been dead or was later executed by AQIM.[86]

As seen earlier, the payment of ransoms to free hostages abducted by AQIM has provided the organization with funds that help it to purchase weapons. In 2012, the funds garnered through the ransoms had reached $360 million,[87] which is more than Mali's defense budget of $183 million. Such financing has incited the core countries to hold a secret meeting of the chiefs of their armed forces to create a joint intelligence cell to trace the activities of AQIM, particularly to avert the spending of the ransom money to purchase weapons or finance the network of informers and corrupt officials.[88] The collapse of the Libyan regime and the instability that prevailed in that country resulted in the dispersion of weapons making it possible for AQIM to acquire all-terrain (4×4) vehicles and sophisticated missiles;[89] and so did the Tuareg, who eventually conquered the Azawad.[90]

The chiefs of staffs held a second, emergency meeting on September 26, 2010; events in the region were alarming, especially with the kidnapping of five French citizens in Niger. The meeting also aimed at assessing the deterioration of the situation and producing the most effective joint approach to deal with the problem. This was also yet another opportunity to remind the partner countries about the commitments they had made since the Tamanrasset gathering in August 2009 and to iron out any differences or misunderstandings.[91]

In order to assist the chiefs of staffs, the four countries announced the creation of an Algiers-based Joint Intelligence Center (CRC, French acronym), inaugurated by the chiefs of intelligence of the four states on September 29, 2010. The mission of the Joint Intelligence Center, known as the Unity of Fusion and Liaison (UFL), is to collect information on terrorism in the Sahel region and make it available to the military operations center in Tamanrasset. It seems that Mali was reluctant to see the establishment of such institution, arguing that the common fight against terrorism should be purely military, not involve intelligence elements, a farfetched argument, which aggravated suspicions about some Malian officials' acquaintances with AQIM and narco-traffickers.[92] According to Algerian security officials, contrary to Niger, the reluctance of Mali to play the game loyally, at least until December 2010, had been one of the main impediments to a more effective fight against AQIM and its connections in the Sahara-Sahel.[93] Considering that Mali shares information with France, it is conceivable that Malian officials did not feel the necessity of participating in a regional intelligence institution. In 2009, Algerian officials complained to the head of AFRICOM, General William Ward, that Malians were not resolute in their cooperation on terrorism.[94] In December 2011, Nigeria, faced with the threat of the terrorist organization Boko Haram, decided to join the UFL.[95] Curiously, the UFL's building is within the same compound as the African Union's African Center for the Study and Research on Terrorism (ACSRT, also known as CAERT)—created in 2004 with the purpose of developing a strategy in the fight against terrorism, analyzing, diffusing information on terrorism, and providing advice to the African Union on the implementation of legal instruments in the fight against terrorism.

Regional cooperation took on more concrete steps with the decision to deploy joint Malian-Mauritanian patrols in northern Mali, where most of AQIM's forces operate.[96] Owing to increasingly more effective attacks conducted by Algerian security forces against AQIM militants, AQIM's fighters had had no choice but to move to northern Mali or northern Mauritania. These tangible regional actions, albeit insufficient, reflected the countries' concerns about the ongoing, worsening developments in the Sahara-Sahel. More worrisome were the developments taking place in Libya, which coincided with a period when the members of CEMOC were seeking to consolidate their coordination and mend their differences. The Malian authorities decided to take the regional threat more seriously; the new foreign minister, Soumeylou Boubeye Maïga, who had in the past served as defense minister and as head of intelligence, respectively, contributed a great deal to the reconciliation of his country with Algeria, Mauritania, and Niger. Thus, in April 2011, Bamako hosted the CEMOC meeting whose main objective was not only to increase regional military cooperation, but also to focus on the new threat emerging from the destabilization of Libya, whose borders were no longer secured, thus allowing the transfer of heavy weapons into other Sahel states.[97] One of the major objectives that followed the meeting in Bamako was to unify the political command of the four countries: that is, ensuring that all share the same objectives and pursue concerted policies in securing the stability of the region. The reconciliation resulted in the holding, in Bamako on May 20, 2011, of a conference of foreign ministers under the theme of "Security and Development." Again, the aim of this conference was to strengthen political coordination among the four Sahel states, increasingly worried about the unstable situation in Libya and its consequences for the Sahara-Sahel region. Considering accusations that CEMOC was an empty shell, precisely because it was not operational many months after its creation, officials began advancing the idea for the four core countries to set up a joint military force of 25,000–75,000.[98] Although such a force was never formed, the reconciliation between Algeria and Mali resulted in greater action on the ground. Thus, Algerian military instructors were deployed in northern Mali in late December 2011 to train and assist their Malian counterparts.[99] This improved cooperation among the countries in the region has been prompted not only by the circulation of weapons coming from Libya and the increase in the number of kidnappings of Westerners, but also by the return of armed groups from Libya to their countries of origin. Indeed, pro-Qaddafi Tuareg had begun returning to northern Mali and northern Niger in July 2011–August 2011, thus posing a serious threat to those governments.[100] That threat proved real as deadly combats opposed Tuareg militants of the MNLA to Malian troops, particularly in January 2012.[101] The well-seasoned Tuareg of the MNLA easily defeated the unprepared, dispirited Malian government troops, a debacle that provided the excuse for a group of Malian officers under Captain Amadou Haya Sanogo to overthrow the civilian government on March 22, barely five weeks before presidential elections were to take place.

The four Sahel countries had yet another major challenge to face: the collusion between the Nigerian terrorist organization, Boko Haram, which committed a series of bomb attacks against Christians in Nigeria, and AQIM. The links between the two organizations prompted the core countries to invite Nigeria to their midst. Thus, on January 24–25, 2012 the foreign ministers of the four Sahel countries and Nigeria met in the Mauritanian capital Nouakchott to evaluate their cooperation at the security and development levels and assess the links between Boko Haram and AQIM. The conference was attended by members of UFL to provide an intelligence assessment of the situation on the ground and representatives of CEMOC on the coordination among the armed forces of the Sahel countries.[102] One outcome of the meeting was the creation of two instruments to strengthen the existing mechanisms of cooperation of the countries of the field: a political committee to supervise the implementation of the actions decided by the ministries of foreign affairs, the ministries of defense, or the presidencies; and a technical committee to coordinate the various developments projects, such as the infrastructure and other "projects aiming at improving the lives of the inhabitants of the region."[103] Also important was a deliberation during that meeting on the collaboration that these countries will have with the United States and the European Union, keeping in mind that initiatives from outside the region should come as complement not as substitute to the actions of the core countries.[104] This objective was shattered with France's intervention in Mali on January 11, 2013 which received the backing of the United States, the EU, and the African Union. In February 2013, the US government decided to establish a drone base in Niger; unarmed Predator aircraft to monitor the movements of terrorist groups in the area.

THE SECURITY CONSEQUENCES OF THE COLLAPSE OF THE QADDAFI REGIME: THE NEW TUAREG QUAGMIRE AND THE CRISIS IN MALI

Historically, the Tuareg in Libya, Mali, and Niger, and those in Algeria have shared some common characteristics. Colonial France's redrawing of the borders in Africa resulted in the scattering of the Tuareg population throughout the Maghreb and the Sahel regions. However, despite their dispersion the Tuareg succeeded in maintaining links owing to the seasonal movements across borders throughout the region.[105]

In Algeria, it was not until the late 1960s, under President Boumediene's rule, that the government recognized some of the Tuareg's rights. In Libya, King Idris Senussi granted privileges to the Tuareg soon after the country's independence in 1951. Colonel Qaddafi, who overthrew the king in September 1969, maintained those privileges primarily because the Tuareg had supported the military coup that brought him to power.[106] Unlike the Algerian authorities who had been reluctant for a while to recognize the right of the Tuareg to use their own language, the Libyan government acted with more tolerance toward them; in fact, Qaddafi went further than the king by making possible the political representation of this social category into the popular committees,[107] the equivalent of parliament in Qaddafi's Jamahiriya (republic of the masses). This political representation was however less consequential than their involvement in the security apparatus in which the Tuareg acted forcefully in the repression campaign that the Libyan government had launched against the Islamists in the 1990s and, more recently, alongside Qaddafi's forces against the rebellion that ended with the fall of the Qaddafi regime in October 2011.[108]

Encouraging the political and social promotion of the Tuareg was part of Qaddafi's strategy of promoting a Targui (singular of Tuareg) state, comprised of the Tuareg from Algeria, Mali, and Niger, under Libyan influence. Thus, Qaddafi tolerated the creation of training camps and encouraged the emergence of a Targui independent movement, which was a way of exerting leverage over the rival actors, especially Algeria.[109] The Libyan regime enrolled the Tuareg in his war against the Chadian regime in the disputed Aouzou strip from 1983 onward while others had been sent to support the Palestinian movement in Lebanon.[110] Pushing his logic further, Qaddafi called for the creation of the great united state of the Sahara; this paralleled his call in 1980 for the creation of a state for the Tuareg. This is the inspiration that has recently driven movements, like the MNLA, to seek the creation their own state.

The fall of the Qaddafi regime has and will undoubtedly have serious implications for the Tuareg issue. One of the direct consequences of regime change in Libya has been the almost immediate resurgence of the old ethno-tribal claims and the militarization on a large scale of Libyan society. One of the major spawns of events in Libya was the massive return in August 2011 of the Tuareg based in Libya to Mali and Niger. When it became apparent that the Libyan rebels, with consequential NATO support, were winning the war, entire armed Tuareg units who had served alongside Qaddafi's loyalist troops had begun leaving Libya en route to their home in the Azawad. The first group, under the leadership of the late Brahim Ag Bahanga, who had fled Mali in 2009 after the failed rebellion he had commanded in 2007–2009, began its journey in July 2011. Although Bahanga died in August under mysterious circumstances, there was consensus among most of the returning Tuareg to create a movement for the liberation of the Azawad. A Targui chieftain, Aïssa Ag Akli, revealed in an interview, that 3,000 Malians had returned from Libya, equipped with heavy weaponry and 600 all-terrain vehicles.[111] In November, they founded the MNLA, a secular movement led by Billal Ag Achérif. This has seriously impacted the security of Algeria since the management of the Tuareg question remains one of the pillars of Algeria's strategy in the region;

fear of a spillover of secessionist sentiments among the Tuareg in southern Algeria is strong.

Resolving the Tuareg Question and Preventing a Spillover Effect

The Tuareg' aspiration for statehood has been of great concern to Algeria as the dissemination of this population throughout the North African and Sahel countries renders its management more complicated. Algerian security officials viewed suspiciously the Tuareg claims, especially in 1963–1964 when the first rebellion broke out. This explains why Algerian president Ahmed Ben Bella granted permission to Malian troops to pursue the rebels who had crossed into Algerian territory. This episode and others (such as Biafra's in the early 1970s) highlights Algerian policy makers' attitude toward attempts at secession: they mistrust any political, social, or ethnic category whose claims could jeopardize the national unity and territorial integrity of a state and violate the OAU and AU charter on the inviolability of borders.

In spite of the attitude the regime adopted in the first years of independence with respect to the Tuareg question, the position gradually changed under Houari Boumediene who decided to grant some rights to the Algerian Tuareg. The government incorporated the Tuareg into the political scene through the appointment of some Tuareg notables in parliament and in the ruling party FLN. The regime came to the conclusion that the best approach to dissuade the Tuareg from seeking autonomy was to integrate them socially and politically. Algerian authorities were, and still are to this date, very cautious about any cross-borders solidarity among the Tuareg that could have a negative impact on the efforts made to integrate the Tuareg living in southern Algeria. In order to prevent any escalation of the Tuareg problem, Algerian authorities undertook a number of measures. They treated the Tuareg community as part of the Berber National identity; they have tried to help the Tuareg settle in the southern cities by providing them with modern means to improve their basic living conditions. The Algerian government has also always been swift in brokering peace agreements between the Tuareg rebels and the central governments in Mali and Niger.[112] One of the recent such agreements between Mali and the Tuareg was brokered by Algeria in 2006. In fact, it was partly the noncompliance of Mali's president Touré that resulted in the events of early 2012. The last point highlights the regional dimension of the Tuareg question and how difficult it is to contain this problem within its national dimension. The outbreak of the conflict in northern Mali in 1992 confirms this hypothesis. The issue is very sensitive for Algeria's national security, and the enduring status quo will render the management and the resolution of this conflict quite complicated. Algerian mediation in the 1990s and the one in 2012 to resolve the Tuareg problem shows how important securing the country's southern borders is for

Algeria's national security. Algerian authorities fear that the return to the status quo of the pre-1990s could jeopardize the efforts made since the beginning of the last decade to secure the southern borders. Mediating the conflict opposing the Tuareg rebellion to the Malian government rests on a strategy derived from the necessity to prevent a spillover effect of this conflict onto Algeria's internal territory. The presence of Tuareg populations in Algerian departments (Tamanrasset, Adrar, and I'n Salah) is one of the key elements of this equation: Algerians fear that the success of Malian and Nigerien Tuareg to create their own political entity could encourage those living in Algerian departments to make the same demand. Avoiding such domino effect is thus of paramount strategic importance for Algeria. The agreement signed in Algiers in 2006 between the Malian government and the Tuareg rebels in northern Mali was conceived in such a way as to inhibit any secessionist temptation. It did that by promoting decentralization as a mode of governance. The measures contained in this agreement have not been fully implemented. Failure of the Malian government to fulfill the commitment contained in the agreement of 2006 is one of the main reasons why the MNLA resumed hostilities. Algeria's mediation efforts, which had arranged a meeting in Algiers in February 2012 failed to produce any tangible results. Also, what made matters really worse in reaching agreement among the contending parties was the military coup in Mali on March 22, 2012 that Captain Sanogo orchestrated.

What matters most for Algeria is to avoid a domino effect of the Azawad's independence in northern Mali on the other Tuareg populations scattered in Mali, Niger, Libya, and Algeria. The political change in Libya resulted in the extension of the arc of crisis in the region. Sharing 980 kilometers of borders with Libya and 1,376 kilometers with Mali, Algeria's capacity to protect itself against the consequences of the instability in Mali and Libya has no doubt been weakened. Thousands of Malians fled to Algeria to escape the fighting and seek refuge. The capture of three major cities in northern Mali—Gao, Kidal, and Timbuktu—by the MNLA, Ansar Edin, and other armed groups, coupled with the severe food crisis, has provoked an even greater exodus from Mali to Algeria—as of January 2013, 30,000 Malians had found refuge in southern Algeria. To this, one should add other fears that relate to the stimulation of autonomous tendencies among Algerian Tuareg and the proliferation of small arms. Algeria sought to persuade both the MNLA and Ansar El Din to distance themselves from the terrorist and narco-trafficking groups. Ansar El Din's attempt to conquer southern Mali in January 2013 undermined Algeria's efforts to resolve the crisis and resulted in France's decision to intervene militarily. Despite Ansar El Din's volte-face, Algeria's strategy will obviously consist in breaking any links that exist between the Tuareg, who have legitimate socioeconomic and political claims, and terrorist organizations that seek to create safe haven inside Mali. Obtaining the Tuareg' support against AQIM and other terrorist organizations in the region has been one of the pillars of Algeria's strategy.

NOTES

1. The Sahel region is an ecoclimate zone located on the southern edge of the Sahara desert; it is practically a transition zone between the Sahara, the greatest desert in the world where it is hardly possible to cultivate the land, and the Savannah, which boasts some agriculture, albeit a rudimentary one, due to a relatively good rainfall.

2. Ali Bensaâd, "Aux Marges du Maghreb, des Tribus Mondialisées—Réseaux Tribaux et Réseaux Diasporiques Commerciaux Maures," *Méditerranée,* no. 116 (2011): 25–34.

3. For a good analysis, see Lothar Brock, Hans-Henrik Holm, Georg Sørensen, and Michael Stohl, *Fragile States-Violence and the Failure of Intervention* (Cambridge, UK: Polity, 2012).

4. For a theoretical discussion of the concept, see Charles T. Call, "Beyond the 'Failed State': Toward Conceptual Alternatives," *European Journal of International Relations,* Vol. XX, no. 10 (April 2010): 1–24.

5. Rasheed Draman, "Managing Chaos in the West African Sub-Region: Assessing the Role of ECOMOG in Liberia," *Journal of Military and Strategic Studies,* Vol. 6, issue 2 (Fall 2003): 1–31.

6. Susanna Wing, "The Coup in Mali Is Only the Beginning," *Foreign Affairs/Snapshot* (April 11, 2012), http://www.foreignaffairs.com/articles/137398/susanna-wing/the-coup-in-mali-is-only-the-beginning?cid = nlc-this_week_on_foreignaffairs_co-041212-the_coup_in_mali_is_only_the_b_2–041212.

7. Joseph Siegel, "Stabilizing Fragile States," *Global Dialogue,* Vol. 13, no. 1 (Winter/Spring 2011), http://africacenter.org/wp-content/uploads/2011/07/Stabilizing_Fragile_States_Global_Dialogue.pdf.

8. See Stephen A. Harmon, "Radical Islam in the Sahel: Implications for U.S. Policy and Regional Stability," in *The United States and West Africa: Interactions and Relations,* ed. Alusine Jalloh and Toyin Falola (Rochester, NY: University of Rochester Press, 2008), 396–422; Murad Batal al-Shishani, "Salafi-Jihadis in Mauritania at the Center of al-Qaeda's Strategy," *Terrorism Monitor,* Vol. 8, issue 12 (March 26, 2010), http://www.jamestown.org/programs/gta/single/?tx_ttnews%5Btt_news%5D=36196&cHash=25a3c17d07; Garba Bala Muhammad and Muhammad Sani Umar, "Religion and the Pan-African Ideal: The Experience of Salafi Islam in the West African Sub-Region," *International Journal of African Affairs,* Vol. 5, nos. 1 and 2 (2002): 141–60.

9. The popular Malian preacher Ousmane Madani Chérif Haïdara epitomizes this form of tolerant Islam; see "Mali: Cherif Haïdara, le Prédicateur Qui Dit non à 'la Charia de Iyad' Ag Ghali," *Jeune Afrique* (April 10, 2012), http://www.jeuneafrique.com/Articleimp_ART JAWEB20120410130736_mali-cherif-haidara-le-predicateur-qui-dit-non-a-la-charia-de-iyad-ag-ghali.html.

10. Hussein D. Hassan, "Islam in Africa," *Congressional Research Service*, Washington, DC (May 9, 2008), http://www.fas.org/sgp/crs/row/RS22873.pdf.

11. On the developments that gave rise to AQIM, see Stephen Harmon, "From GSPC to AQIM: The evolution of an Algerian Islamist Terrorist Group into an Al-Qaʻida Affiliate and its Implications for the Sahara-Sahel region," *Bulletin of the Africa Concerned Scholars,* N°85 (Spring 2010): 12–29; see also Jean-Pierre Filiu, "The Local and Global Jihad of Al-Qaʻida in the Islamic Maghrib," *Middle East Journal,* Vol. 63, no. 2 (Spring 2009): 213–26.

12. Lakhdar Benchiba, "Sahel: Nouvelles Menaces et Vieux Problèmes," *Afkar/Idées* (Fall 2009): 21.

13. For details on AQIM's activities in the area, see Ricardo René Larémont, "Al Qaeda in the Islamic Maghreb: Terrorism and Counterterrorism in the Sahel," *African Security,* 4 (2011): 242–68.

14. See, "Selon le Directeur du CAERT, La Situation au Mali Menace la Stabilité des Pays Voisins," *Le Soir d'Algérie* (Avril 10, 2012), http://www.lesoirdalgerie.com/articles/2012/04/10/article.php?sid=132706&cid=2.

15. Mohamed Mokeddem, *Al-Qaïda au Maghreb Islamique-Contrebande au Nom de L'islam* (Algiers: Casbah Editions, 2010), 37–68.

16. Mokeddem, *Al-Qaïda au Maghreb Islamique-Contrebande au nom de L'islam* (Algiers: Casbah Editions, 2010), 116–21.

17. United Nations Office on Drugs and Crime, "Drug Trafficking as a Security Threat in West Africa," (November 2008), http://www.unodc.org/documents/data-and-analysis/Studies/Drug-Trafficking-WestAfrica-English.pdf.

18. Jamie Doward, "Drug seizures in West Africa Prompt Fears of Terrorist Links: Al-Qaida is Thought to Have Gained Control of the Cocaine Trade Flourishing in Guinea and Mali," *The Observer* (November 29, 2009),http://www.guardian.co.uk/world/2009/nov/29/drugs-cocaine-africa-al-qaida.

19. Zoubir's interviews with African security officials in Algiers, Dakar, Tunis (2011–2012); see also Mokeddem, *Al-Qaïda au Maghreb Islamique-Contrebande au Nom de L'islam* (Algiers: Casbah Editions, 2010), 119.

20. "Al-Qaeda in the Islamic Maghreb and the Africa-to-Europe Narco-Trafficking Connection," *The Jamestown Foundation* (November 24, 2010), http://www.unhcr.org/refworld/country, THE_JF,,DZA,,4cf4da682,0.html.

21. See, for instance, the statement of Senator Russ Feingold, "Hearing on Confronting Drug Trafficking in West Africa," Senate Foreign Relations Africa Subcommittee (June 23, 2009), http://www.foreign.senate.gov/hearings/confronting-drug-trafficking-in-west-africa. See also the testimony of Assistant Secretary of State for African Affairs Johnnie Carson, "Hearing on Confronting Drug-trafficking in West Africa," Senate Foreign Relations Subcommittee on African Affairs (June 23, 2009), http://www.foreign.senate.gov/hearings/confronting-drug-trafficking-in-west-africa.

22. For detailed treatment of deradicalization in Algeria, see Omar Ashour, *The De-Radicalization of Jihadists-Transforming Islamist Movements* (London and New York: Routledge, 2009), 110–35; see also Zine Mohamed Barka, "The Causes of Radicalization in Algeria," in *Islamist Radicalizaion in North Africa-Politics and Process,* ed. George Joffé (London and New York: Routledge, 2012), 95–113; and George Joffé, "Trajectories of Radicalization, Algeria 1989–1999," in *Islamist Radicalizaion in North Africa-Politics and Process,* ed. George Joffé (London and New York: Routledge, 2012),114–37.

23. See Walid Laggoune, "Ordre Public et Défense Nationale: Fondements et Limites d'une Distinction," in *Actes des Premières Journées Parlementaires sur la Défense Nationale-Pour un Débat Citoyen sur la Défense Nationale,* Vol. 1 (Algiers: Editions ANEP, 2003), 71.

24. Souhil B., "Bilan de la Réconciliation Nationale-7500 Terroristes ont Bénéficié des Dispositions de la Charte," *ElWatan,* October 4, 2010, http://www.elwatan.com/actualite/7500-terroristes-ont-beneficie-des-dispositions-de-la-charte-04–10–2010-93047_109.php. (no longer accessible online)

25. See "Ordonnance no. 11-03 Modifiant et Complétant la Loi no. 91-23 du 6 Décembre 1991 Relative à la Participation de L'armée Nationale Populaire à des Missions de Sauvegarde de L'ordre Public Hors les Situations D'exception"; "Décret Présidentiel no. 11-90 Relatif

à la Mise en Œuvre et à L'engagement de L'armée Nationale Populaire dans le Cadre de la Lutte Contre le Terrorisme et la Subversion," published in the *JORADP,* Vol. 50, no. 12, February 23, 2011, 4–5, http://www.joradp.dz/HFR/Index.htm.

26. "Ordonnance no. 12-02, Relative à la Prévention et à la Lutte Contre le Blanchiment D'argent et le Financement du terrorisme: Un Arsenal Renforcé," *El Moudjahid,* March 14, 2012, http://www.elmoudjahid.com/fr/actualites/25269/print.

27. "Loi n° 12-10 du 26 mars 2012 Portant Approbation de L'ordonnance n° 12-02 du 2013 Février 2012 Modifiant et Complétant la loi n° 05-01 du 6 Février 2005 Relative à la Prévention et à la Lutte Contre le Blanchiment D'argent et le Financement du Terrorisme," *JORADP,* April 1, 2012, http://www.joradp.dz/FTP/JO-FRANCAIS/2012/F2012019.pdf.

28. Yahia H. Zoubir, "Contestation Islamiste et Lutte Antiterroriste en Libye, 1990–2007," *L'Année du Maghreb 2008* (Paris: CNRS Editions, 2008), 267–77.

29. Zoubir, "Contestation Islamiste et Lutte Antiterroriste en Libye, 1990–2007," *L'Année du Maghreb 2008* (Paris: CNRS Editions, 2008), 267–77.

30. Omar Ashour, "Deradicalizing Jihadists, the Libyan Way," *The Daily Star,* April 26, 2010, http://www.dailystar.com.lb/Opinion/Commentary/Apr/26/Deradicalizing-jihadists-the-Libyan-way.ashx#axzz1kNpxgrKG.

31. Excerpts of the penal code in English are available on the website of the UN Office on Drugs and Crime, https://www.unodc.org/tldb/browse_country.html?country=LIB.

32. The law is available onhttps://www.unodc.org/tldb/browse_country.html?country= MLI.

33. Secrétariat Général du Gouvernement, République du Mali, Communiqué du Conseil des Ministres (Projet de loi Portant Répression du Terrorisme), September 5, 2007, . http://www.peinedemort.org/document.php?choix=2502.

34. Chahana Takiou, "La Situation Politique et Sécuritaire au Nord: Pour la Paix, la Sécurité et le Développement au Nord Mali: ATT a Concocté un Programme Spécial de 32 Milliards," *Mali Web,* September 22, 2010, http://www.maliweb.net/news/la-situation-politique-et-securitaire-au-nord/2010/11/01/article,1051.html.

35. In July 2012, MOJWA released three of those hostages. No reliable information has transpired regarding the conditions of their release. It is doubtful however whether Algeria paid any ransom demanded by the MOJWA for their release.

36. UN Office on Drugs and Crimes, Terrorism Prevention Branch, "A Review of the Legal Regime against Terrorism in West and Central Africa," October 2008, http://www.unodc.org/documents/terrorism/Publications/Review_West_African_CT_Legal_Regime/A_Review_of_the_Legal_Regime_Ag_Terr_in_W_and_C_Africa_V09837531.pdf.

37. "Mauritania Adopts new Anti-Terrorism Law," *Reuters,* July 9, 2010, http://af.reuters.com/article/topNews/idAFJOE66802520100709.

38. Cédric Jourde, "Mauritania 2010: Between Individual Willpower and Institutional Inertia," *IPRIS Maghreb Review,* March 2011.

39. Jemal Omar, "Mauritanian Sheikhs Review Mahdharas Role," *Magharebia,* May 1, 2012, http://www.magharebia.com/cocoon/awi/xhtml1/en_GB/features/awi/features/2012/05/01/feature-02.

40. "Morocco: Marrakesh Bomb Strikes Djemaa el-Fna Square," BBC News Africa, April 28, 2011, http://www.bbc.co.uk/news/world-africa-13226117.

41. Jack Kalpakian, "Current Moroccan Anti-Terrorism Policy," *Real instituto Elcano,* WP 89/2011, May 13, 2011, http://www.realinstitutoelcano.org/wps/portal/rielcano_eng/Content?WCM_GLOBAL_CONTEXT = /elcano/elcano_in/zonas_in/ari89–2011.

42. See "*Initiative Nationale pour le Développement Humain, Programme 2006–2010*http://www.indh.gov.ma/fr/programme_2006-2010.asp.

43. Margaret Rausch, "Women Spiritual Guides (*Mourchidate* in Morocco): Agents of Change," Work in Progress 2008 and 2009, http://www.yale.edu/macmillan/africadissent/rausch.pdf.

44. République du Niger, Ministère des Affaires Etrangères, de la Coopération, et de l'Intégration Africaine, Arrêté No. 6/MAE/C/IA du 24 Octobre 2006 Portant Création du Comité Contre le Terrorisme, https://www.unodc.org/tldb/pdf/Niger_arrete_creationcomite terrorisme.pdf.

45. See République du Niger, Loi No. 2008–18 du 23 Juin 2008, https://www.unodc.org/tldb/pdf/Niger%20Loi%20contre%20le%20terrorisme_23%20juin%202008.pdf.

46. *UN Office on Drugs and Crimes, Terrorism Prevention Branch,* "A Review of the Legal Regime Against Terrorism in West and Central Africa," October 2008, http://www.unodc.org/documents/terrorism/Publications/Review_West_African_CT_Legal_Regime/A_Review_of_ the_Legal_Regime_Ag_Terr_in_W_and_C_Africa_V09837531.pdf, 133.

47. European Union External Action Service, "Strategy for Security and Development in the Sahel," September 21, 2011, http://eeas.europa.eu/africa/docs/sahel_strategy_en.pdf.

48. Gabe Joselow, "Boko Haram Seen Linked to Other African Terror Groups," VOA, December 27, 2011, http://www.voanews.com/content/boko-haram-seen-linked-to-other-african-terror-groups--136260858/150015.html.

49. *UNODC, Terrorism Prevention Branch,* "A Review of the Legal Regime against Terrorism in West and Central Africa," October 2008, http://www.unodc.org/documents/terrorism/Publications/Review_West_African_CT_Legal_Regime/A_Review_of_the_Legal_Regime_ Ag_Terr_in_W_and_C_Africa_V09837531.pdf, 138.

50. "A Bill for an Act to Provide Measures to Combat Terrorism and for other Related Matters," https://www.unodc.org/tldb/showDocument.do?documentUid=10164.

51. Mathias Vermeulen, "Nigeria: Senate, House Approve Anti-Terrorism Bill," *The Lift,* February 27, 2011, http://legalift.wordpress.com/2011/02/27/nigeria-senate-house-approve-anti-terrorism-bill/.

52. "Nigeria Boko Haram: Nigerian legislature to strengthen Anti-terrorism Act," *Afrique en Ligne,* January 24, 2012, http://www.afriquejet.com/nigeria-boko-haram-nigerian-legislature-to-strengthen-anti-terrorism-act-2012012432036.html.

53. "Dozens of Boko Haram in Mali's Rebel-Seized Gao: Sources," Agence France Presse (AFP), reprinted in Yahoo News, April 9, 2012, http://www.google.com/hostednews/afp/article/ALeqM5jja3wkqRG-4HgkkwIh58wADYHnpQ?docId=CNG.a75736e328 fa24c63b13df0aba476481.41.

54. "Loi 2003 Contre le Terrorisme et le Blanchiment de l'Argent," https://www.unodc.org/tldb/showDocument.do?documentUid = 1836&country = TUN&language = FRE.

55. "Loi 2003 Contre le Terrorisme et le Blanchiment de l'Argent," https://www.unodc.org/tldb/showDocument.do?documentUid=1836&country=TUN&language=FRE.

56. Amnesty International, "Tunisia: New Draft 'Anti-Terrorism' Law Will Further Undermine Human Rights," *Briefing Note to the European Union EU-Tunisia Association Council 30 September 2003,* http://www.amnesty.org/fr/library/asset/MDE30/021/2003/fr/0283d281-d689–11dd-ab95-a13b602c0642/mde300212003en.html. (no longer accessible online)

57. United Nations Human Rights, "Counter-Terrorism: UN Human Rights Expert Concludes Follow up Mission to Tunisia," *Office of the High Commissioner for Human Rights,*

May 26, 2011, http://www.ohchr.org/EN/NewsEvents/Pages/DisplayNews.aspx?NewsID = 11066&LangID = E.

58. Yahia H. Zoubir, "Tilting the Balance Towards Intra-Maghreb Unity in Light of the Arab Spring," *International Spectator,* Vol. 47, no. 3 (September 2012): 64–80.

59. M.A.M., "Forum de Rabat: Le Maroc à la Conquête de l'Afrique, *L'Economiste* (Rabat), no. 3707, January 26, 2012, http://www.leconomiste.com/article/890728-forum-de-rabat-le-maroc-la-conqu-te-de-l-afrique. Fahd Iraqi, "Business: Le Maroc à la Con-quête de l'Afrique," *TelQuel,* no. 257 (January 2006), http://www.telquel-nline.com/257/economie1_257.shtml. (no longer accessible online)

60. "Le Maroc à la Conquête de l'Afrique: Le Sahara est-il Soluble dans le Business," *Jeune Afrique,* November 10, 2009, http://www.jeuneafrique.com/Articles/Dossier/ARTJAJA2547p063.xml0/afrique-diplomatie-maroc-mohammed-vile-sahara-est-il-soluble-dans-le-business.html.

61. "Second Conference of African States Bordering the Atlantic opens in Rabat," *Agence Maghreb Arabe Presse* (*MAP*), November 15, 2010, reprinted in the Free Library, http://www.thefreelibrary.com/Second+Conference+of+African+States+Bordering+the+Atlantic+opens+in . . .-a0242563387.

62. "Le Positionnement du Maroc en Afrique. Bilan et Perspectives," *Ministère des Finances et de la Privatisation, Direction des Etudes et des Prévisions Financières,* July 2006, 9, http://www.ilo.org/public/french/region/afpro/algiers/download/maroc_ecoafrique.pdf.

63. Ministry of Economy and Finance, "A Status Report of Morocco's Relations with Sub-Saharan African Countries," Department of Economic Studies and Financial Forecast, April 2010, 4, http://www.finances.gov.ma/portal/page?_pageid=93,17858036&_dad=portal&_schema=PORTAL&id=67&lang=n

64. Ministry of Economy and Finance, "A Status Report of Morocco's Relations with Sub-Saharan African Countries," Department of Economic Studies and Financial Forecast, April 2010, 3.

65. "A Status Report of Morocco's Relations with Sub-Saharan African Countries," Depart-ment of Economic Studies and Financial Forecast, April 2010, 9, http://www.finances.gov.ma/portal/page?_pageid=93,17858036&_dad=portal&_schema=PORTAL&id=67&lang=En.

66. "A Status Report of Morocco's Relations with Sub-Saharan African Countries," Department of Economic Studies and Financial Forecast, April 2010, 10.

67. "Le Maroc et la Mauritanie Renforcent leur Coopération en Matière D'aviation Civile," *PANA,* March 16, 2011, http://www.panapress.com/Le-Maroc-et-la-Mauritanie-renforcent-leur-cooperation-en-matiere-d-aviation-civile—12–764162–11-lang1-index.html.

68. "Maroc-Mauritanie, Cinq Accords de Coopération," *Le Matin,* March 9, 2005, http://www.maghress.com/fr/lematin/51471.

69. Ali Titouche, "Les Pays du Sahel Coordonnent leurs Actions, " *L'Expression* (Algiers), August 5, 2007, http://www.lexpressiondz.com/actualite/44257-Les-pays-du-Sahel-coordon nent-leurs-actions.html.

70. Hassan Moali, "Les Pays de la Bande Sahélo-Saharienne en Conclave-Les USA Per-dent L'initiative des Opérations," *El Watan,* October 2007,http://www.elwatan.com/archives/article.php?id=78558.

71. Algeria's Minister of Cooperation and Maghrebi Affairs, Abdelkader Messahel, cited in B. Mokhtaria, "Pays du Sahel: L'Algérie pour un Dispositif Opérationnel contre le Terrorisme," *Le Quotidien d'Oran* (Algeria), November 13, 2008.

72. Burkina Faso, Chad and Libya, for complex reasons which go beyond the scope of this chapter, did not remain in the group.

73. "Des Avions de Reconnaissance sans Pilotes pour Surveiller les Terroristes au Sud," *El Khabar*, Avril 4, 2009, reprinted in *Algeria-Watch,* http://www.algeria-watch.org/fr/article/pol/geopolitique/avions_sud.htm.

74. Cited in, Mahrez Ilies, "Lutte Antiterroriste au Sahel: L'axe Alger-Bamako-Niamey se Précise," Le Quotidien d'Oran, May 7, 2009, http://www.lequotidien-oran.com/index.php?news = 5120474&archive_date = 2009–05–07.

75. "L'Algérie y Participe et la France Installe Deux Forces Spéciales au Mali," *El Khabar,* May 18, 2009.

76. Salima Tlemçani, "Réunion entre l'Algérie, le Niger, la Mauritanie et le Mali—Des chefs Militaires des Etats du Sahel à Tamanrasset," *El Watan,* August 13, 2009,http://www.elwatan.com/archives/article.php?id=134525.

77. Most officials Zoubir interviewed have given vague reasons as to why Libya did not join. However, a plausible explanation has to do with Libya's seeking to prevent Algeria from playing a leadership role while Libya controlled the Tripoli-based CEN-SAD. Algeria never joined CEN-SAD although it was Algerians who initially came up with the idea of forming an organization regrouping Sahel states. See Ministère des Affaires Etrangères de Côte d'Ivoire, "La CEN-SAD," http://www.diplomatie.gouv.ci/politique_afrique.php. Algerians saw CEN-SAD as a parallel Qaddafi-dominated African Union and a rival to other similar regional organizations, such as the Arab Maghreb Union, ECOWAS, among others.

78. Zine Cherfaoui, "Algérie-Pays du Sahel: Offensive Commune contre le Terrorisme," *El Watan,* September 10, 2009, reprinted in: http://www.algerie-dz.com/forums/archive/index.php/t-140410.html.

79. A good summary of the points raised during the conference can be found in Selima Tlemçani, "Conférence Ministérielle d'Alger contre le Terrorisme—Éloigner Toute Ingérence dans la Région du Sahel," *El Watan,* March 18, 2010, http://www.elwatan.com/archives/article.php?id=154125.

80. Atef Kedadra, "Elle Intervient après la Rencontre des Ministres des Affaires Etrangères-Réunion Secrète des Chefs des Renseignements de 7 Pays du Sahel à Alger," *El Khabar,* April 6, 2010, reprinted in http://www.algeria-watch.de/fr/article/pol/geopolitique/reunion_secrete.htm.

81. Ikram Ghioua, "Réunion des Sept Pays du Sahel à Alger—Les Services de Renseignements s'en Mêlent, " *L'Expression* (Algiers), April 7, 2010, http://www.lexpressiondz.com/actualite/76633-les-services-de-renseignements-s'en-mêlent.html.

82. Synthèse R.N., "Les Chefs D'état-Major de la Région Sahélo-Saharienne Accordent leurs Violons: Démenti aux Velléités D'intervention Etrangère," *Le Quotidien d'Oran,* April 14, 2010, http://www.lequotidien-oran.com/index.php?news = 5136817&archive_date = 2010–04–14.

83. Djamel Belaïfa, "Algérie, Mali, Mauritanie et Niger: Un Etat-Major Opérationnel Installé, Aujourd'hui, à Tamanrasset, " *Le Quotidien d'Oran,* April 21, 2010, http://www.lequotidienoran.com/index.php?news = 5137121&archive_date = 2010–04–21 (no longer accessible online). It remains a mystery as to why Libya never joined CEMOC. An official of CEN-SAD told Zoubir that Qaddafi would not have wanted to enter an organization dominated by Algeria. Zoubir's interview with CEN-SAD official, Tunis (April 29, 2012).

84. Selima Tlemçani, "Comité D'état-Major de Tamanrasset: Une Mission Plus Formelle Qu'active," *El Watan,* July 25, 2010, http://www-front.elwatan.com/actualite/comite-d-etat-major-de-tamanrasset-une-mission-plus-formelle-qu-active-25-07-2010-84696_109.php.

85. "Création du Comité D'état-Major Opérationnel Conjoint: le Fruit d'une Vision Commune," *El-Djeich* (Magazine of the Algerian Armed Forces), no. 579 (October 2011), 18.

86. "Enlèvement de Michel Germaneau-Pourquoi Nicolas Sarkozy est Passé à L'action," *Le Point* (Paris), July 27, 2010, http://www.lepoint.fr/chroniqueurs-du-point/jean-guisnel/enlevement-de-michel-germaneau-pourquoi-nicolas-sarkozy-est-passe-a-l-action-26-07-2010-1218757_53.php.

87. C.B., "Selon le Directeur du CAERT, la Situation au Mali Menace la Stabilité des Pays Voisins," *Le Soir d'Algérie,* April 10, 2012, http://www.lesoirdalgerie.com/articles/2012/04/10/article.php?sid=132706&cid=2.

88. A.R., "Réunion Secrète des Chefs Militaires des Pays du Sahel à Alger," *Le Temps d'Algérie,* September 15, 2010, in http://www.algeria-watch.org/fr/article/pol/geopolitique/chefs_militaires_reunion.htm.

89. Thierry Oberlé, "La Montée en Puissance d'AQMI," *Le Figaro* (Paris), September 11, 2011, http://www.lefigaro.fr/international/2011/09/04/01003–20110904ARTFIG00247-la-montee-en-puissance-de-l-aqmi.php. (no longer accessible online)

90. See, the interview of Lamine Ag Billal, a Tuareg captain in the MNLA, in *El Watan,* April 21, 2012, http://www-front.elwatan.com/international/3000-touareg-sont-morts-en-libye-et-3000-autres-sont-rentres-au-mali-21–04–2012–167628_112.php. (no longer accessible online)

91. Selima Tlemçani, "Une Réunion pour Lever les Divergences," *El Watan,* September 27, 2010, http://www.elwatan.com/actualite/une-reunion-pour-lever-les-divergences-27–09–2010–92024_109.php. (no longer accessible online)

92. Ikram Ghioua, "Face au Jeu Trouble du Mali dans la Région, l'Algérie Mobilise ses Forces Spéciales," *L'Expression,* October 7, 2010, http://www.lexpressiondz.com/actualite/83032-L%E2%80%99Alg%C3%A9rie-mobilise-ses-forces-sp%C3%A9ciales.html.

93. Zoubir's interviews with Algerian officials, Ministry of Defense, January and September 2011.

94. Wikileaks, Viewing cable 09ALGIERS948, "Algeria says Bamako Summit Key to Regional," http://wikileaks.org/cable/2009/10/09ALGIERS948.html.

95. Djilali Benyoub, "Lutte Antiterroriste au Sahel-Le Nigeria Rejoint l'UFL," *Liberté,* December 19, 2011, http://www.algeria-watch.org/fr/article/pol/geopolitique/nigeria_rejoint_ufl.htm.

96. "Un Pas de Plus dans la Lutte Contre AQMI," *Jeune Afrique,* November 8, 2010, http://www.jeuneafrique.com/Article/ARTJAWEB20101108120616/mali-mauritanie-cooperation-terrorismeun-pas-de-plus-dans-la-cooperation-contre-aqmi.html.

97. R.P., "Sécurisation du Sahel en Débat à Bamako-Réunion des Chefs des Armées de Quatre Pays du Sahel," *El Watan,* April 30, 2011, http://elwatan.com/actualite/reunion-des-chefs-des-armees-de-quatre-pays-du-sahel-30–04–2011–122582_109.php. (no longer accessible)

98. Zine Cherfaoui, "Armes Libyennes aux Mains d'Al Qaïda-Les Pays du Sahel en Etat D'alerte Maximum," *El Watan,* May 21, 2011, http://elwatan.com/actualite/les-pays-du-sahel-en-etat-d-alerte-maximum-21–05–2011–125295_109.php. (no longer accessible)

99. "Reprise Effective de la Coopération Militaire Entre le Mali et l'Algérie dans la Lutte Contre le Terrorisme," *Radio France Internationale, RFI,* December 21, 2011, http://www.rfi.fr/afrique/20111221--cooperation-militaire-mali-algerie-lutte-aqmi-sahel-terrorisme-bamko-alger.

100. "Le Retour des Touareg pro Kadhafi Inquiète le Mali," *Agence France Presse* (*AFP*), reprinted in Radio Nederland Wereldomroep, August 30, 2011, http://www.rnw.nl/afrique/article/le-retour-des-touareg-pro-kadhafi-inqui%C3%A8te-le-mali; Djilali Benyoub, "Les

Pays du Champ s'engagent dans un Défi Sécuritaire et de Développement: La Sécurisation de l'espace Sahélien en Toile de Fond," *Liberté,* December 29, 2011, http://www.liberte-algerie. com/actualite/la-securisation-de-l-espace-sahelien-en-toile-de-fond-les-pays-du-champ-s-engagent-dans-un-defi-securitaire-et-de-developpement-168918.

101. "Reprise des Combats entre L'armée Malienne et des Rebelles Touaregs," *Le Monde* (Paris), January 26, 2012, http://www.lemonde.fr/afrique/article/2012/01/26/reprise--des-combats-entre-l-armee-malienne-et-des-rebelles-touaregs_1634975_3212.html.

102. "Réunion des Pays du Champ à Nouakchott: Une Rencontre pour Faire le Bilan de la Coopération Sécuritaire," *El-Moudjahid* (Algiers), January 24, 2012, http://www.elmoudja hid.com/fr/actualites/22821.

103. "Création d'un Comité Politique et d'un Comité Technique des Pays du Champ," *Algerian Ministry of Foreign Affairs,* January 24, 2012, http://www.mae.dz/ma_fr/stories. php?story = 12/01/25/8051736.

104. Abdelkader Messahel, Minister Delegate in Charge of Maghreb and African Affairs, cited in, "M. Messahel Pour des Initiatives Complémentaires et non Substitutives à la Démarche des Pays du Champ," *Algerian Ministry of Foreign Affairs,* January 24, 2012, http:// www.mae.dz/ma_fr/stories.php?story = 12/01/25/8036653.

105. Badi Dadi, "Les Relations des Touarègues aux Etats: Le Cas de l'Algérie et de la Libye," *Notes de l'IFRI,* Paris, 2010. 23 pages.

106. Badi Dadi, "Les Relations des Touarègues aux Etats: Le Cas de l'Algérie et de la Libye," *Notes de l'IFRI,* Paris, 2010. 23 pages.

107. Badi Dadi, "Les Relations des Touarègues aux Etats: Le Cas de l'Algérie et de la Libye," *Notes de l'IFRI,* Paris, 2010. 23 pages.

108. Yahia H. Zoubir and Erzsébet Rózsa, "The End of the Libyan Dictatorship: The Uncertain Transition," *Third World Quarterly,* 33, 7 (June 2012): 1269–85.

109. Yahia H. Zoubir, "Tilting the Balance toward Intra-Maghreb Unity in Light of the Arab Spring," *International Spectator,* 47, 3 (September 2012): 64–80.

110. Yahia H. Zoubir, "Tilting the Balance toward Intra-Maghreb Unity in Light of the Arab Spring," *International Spectator,* 47, 3 (September 2012): 64–80.

111. See his interview with Selima Tlemçani in, "Nous Devons Resserrer les Rangs et Eviter Toute Confrontation qui Diviserait le Mouvement," *El Watan* (Algiers), April 9, 2012, http://www.elwatan.com/international/nous-devons-resserrer-les-rangs-et-eviter-toute-confrontation-qui-diviserait-le-mouvement-09–04–2012–166075_112.php. (no longer accessible online)

112. Belkacem Iratni, *The Strategic Interests of the Maghreb States,* NDC Forum Paper 4 (Rome: NATO Defense College, 2008), 37.

PART III

Maghreb Security in the International Context: Source of Tensions or Stability Providers?

CHAPTER 7

The Maghreb in Extra-Regional Great Powers Security

THE MAGHREB IN INTERNATIONAL RELATIONS

Although it never was strategic to United States and Soviet security during the Cold War era, the Maghreb was not of marginal interest to the superpowers either.[1] One of the main reasons is that the Maghreb sits astride Europe and sub-Saharan Africa and may also be considered a subsystem of the wider Middle East. Nominally nonaligned, the Maghreb states had nonetheless ideological and political proclivity with one or the other superpower. For historic reasons, each of the Maghreb states proclaimed its preference soon after independence.

In this chapter, although economic issues are important, we shall focus solely on the political and security relations between the Maghreb states and the major powers. The analysis demonstrates that regardless of its limited strategic importance as a region, outside powers maintained important bilateral patron-client relations[2] with their respective allies in the Maghreb. The Maghreb countries made security choices, which brought them at loggerheads ideologically, especially in the 1960s and 1970s at the peak of the Cold War. The end of the Cold War, however, did not end the rivalry between the Maghreb states, and their foreign policies remained relatively consistent with the ones they had established following their independence. Although a historical perspective is necessary, this chapter will concentrate on the more recent relations. We will review and analyze the political and security bilateral relations that the Maghreb states developed with the external powers: the United States, the Soviet Union/Russia, Europe, and China.

THE MAGHREB IN U.S. POLICY: MARGINAL AREA OR NEW REGION TO CONQUER?[3]

In recent times the Maghreb has acquired greater strategic significance. Not only has the search for energy become a paramount objective, but the events of 9/11 and their aftermath have also played a critical factor in persuading U.S. policy makers to ascertain a presence in the Maghreb and its neighboring Sahel region. The expansion of the Al Qaeda network into the Maghreb-Sahel region in 2007 enticed the United States to devise a number of security measures to counter the perceived threats emanating from the sizable, vastly barren, not fully controlled Sahara-Sahel expanse. More concretely, the United States has instituted many security and military arrangements with the local governments to achieve its objectives: arrangements that have served the interests of the authoritarian governments in the Maghreb-Sahel. What has heightened interest in the Maghreb were the events of 9/11, not least because members of the Al Qaeda terrorist network, the Arab Afghans, are of North African origin. In spite of the initial optimism pertaining to the economic potential of the Maghreb as an integrated entity, tensions in Algerian-Moroccan relations, primarily because of the protracted conflict in Western Sahara, have dimmed that optimism. Thus, American economic interests center on the energy sectors, particularly oil and gas, in Algeria and Libya. Given the contrasted history of the bilateral relations between the United States and the Maghreb states, providing an analysis of the relations that each country had developed with the United States will shed light on the complexity of U.S. security relations with those states.

Morocco and the United States: The Enduring Alliance

In spite of the close military and security ties that have developed between Algeria and the United States since 9/11, Morocco remains without a doubt the main ally of the United States in the Maghreb. The United States considers Morocco as a friend and a major non-NATO ally—a designation President George W. Bush bestowed upon it in 2004. Formal U.S. relations with Morocco date from 1787, when the two nations negotiated a Treaty of Peace and Friendship (Treaty of Marrakech), which has remained the oldest unbroken treaty in U.S. foreign relations. A chapter alone will barely do justice to the intensity of U.S.-Moroccan ties. We can only highlight some of the key factors that have created such strong relations and made Morocco today a valuable ally of the United States in the Middle East and North Africa.

Even though Morocco is a country producing neither oil nor natural gas, the kingdom boasts important mineral resources.[4]

No matter the geopolitical transformations, the strategic significance of Morocco has experienced minor attenuation because, since its independence, Morocco has played a key role in support of the United States in various areas.

This is why Morocco has, since the late 1950s, received more U.S. aid than any other Arab country, except for Egypt and Israel, which have a particular deal with the United States. Following the war in Western Sahara, which Morocco invaded in 1975, Morocco had obtained by 1990 more than one-fifth of all U.S. aid to Africa, totaling more than one billion dollars in military assistance alone whereas economic assistance amounted to $1.3 billion.[5] That figure has tripled since. In fact, it is primarily the support from the United States (and France) that allowed Morocco to reverse the war over Western Sahara in Morocco's favor through large-scale economic and military assistance, military advisors, and logistical support. In 1978, when war in Western Sahara was raging, U.S. military aid to Morocco was multiplied twentyfold to reach more than $99.8 million from a mere $4.1 million in 1974.[6] With the end of the Cold War, American economic and military assistance had considerably decreased due to congressional budget restrictions. However, Morocco managed to regain shortly afterward its position as an important ally. In terms of aid, one can cite a few recent figures. In 2002, Morocco received 72 percent of the total U.S. assistance to the three Maghreb countries whereas in 2005 the figure amounted to 81 percent, that is, $58 million.[7] The May 2003 jihadist attacks in Casablanca increased U.S. determination to protect Morocco.[8] For its part, Morocco used the opportunity to try to convince U.S. policymakers that an independent Western Sahara would be a threat for U.S. interests and that the Polisario Front was linked to terrorism—an accusation the United States has not adhered to.

In 2006, military aid rose to $20 million in order to help Morocco not only to stop clandestine immigration but also, and above all, to be able to protect its borders and continue the fight against terrorism. In the fiscal year 2007, the department of state authorized the export to Morocco of defense articles and services valued at $87,475,761.[9] The two countries have maintained an extensive military and security cooperation since the 1950s; the sale of U.S. weapons has allowed Morocco to maintain its illegal occupation of Western Sahara. In 2002, the two countries established the U.S.-Morocco Defense Consultative Committee. For years, they have conducted annual joint maneuvers; the latest, the Saharan Express and Phoenix Express took place in May 2012 in southern Morocco. As seen in Chapter Five, in 2004, Morocco entered an armed race with Algeria, which prompted it to continue acquiring more equipment from the United States. Morocco has purchased helicopters CH-47D and, more importantly, 24 F-16s ordered in 2007 (instead of the French Raffale), costing two billion dollars, as well as over $300 million for a T-6 training aircraft. Under the Obama administration, aid extended to other allocations, such as the Trans-Saharan Counterterrorism Partnership (TSCTP), through which Morocco receives military and security assistance. In late December 2009, Lockheed Martin (with Washington's support) secured an $841.9 million contract to finalize production of 24 new F-16 fighters for the Kingdom of Morocco, as well as for electronic-warfare gear and support equipment. The contract builds on a preliminary $233 million award Lockheed obtained in June 2008 to start off the construction of the airplane.[10] In 2010, security assistance amounted to $35,296 million. The congressional budget request for fiscal year 2011 was set at $42,500 million.

In June 2012, Morocco requested upgrades for 200 M1A1 Abrams tanks and associated parts, equipment, logistical support, and training worth more than one billion dollars funded by the United States. Between 30 and 50 officers are sent annually to the United States for training. In 2011, Morocco received close to two million dollars from the International Military Education and Training allocation.

This continuous aid to Morocco can be explained by the support Morocco provided to U.S. strategic planning during the Cold War. Morocco also served as an important surrogate for U.S. interests in Africa and the Middle East, even dispatching its troops to troubled countries and giving the CIA and NSA wide latitude to operate. King Hassan II had established solid contacts not only with U.S. officials at all levels, such as Henry Kissinger or Vernon Walters, but also with Israeli officials. Even though Morocco sided with the Arabs, and even sent troops during the 1967 and 1973 wars, the king took advantage of Kissinger's tour of the region in late 1973, which incidentally began in Morocco, to seek a role in Middle Eastern diplomatic negotiations. His real objective was to eventually obtain U.S. support for his own designs over Western Sahara; playing the Israeli card would obviously facilitate the execution of such a plan. Unlike Algeria, for instance, Morocco has mostly supported U.S. foreign policy objectives in the Middle East by promoting the Arab-Israeli peace process. Hassan II was the first Arab leader to receive a visit by an Israeli prime minister; he secretly met Yitzhak Rabin in Rabat in October 1976. The following year, he, again secretly, invited Egyptian and Israeli officials to the kingdom for direct discussions that eventually paved the way for Egyptian president Anwar Sadat's November 1977 visit to Jerusalem.[11] In 1991, for instance, Morocco sent troops to the Persian Gulf to force Iraq out of Kuwait.

Undoubtedly, the issue of Western Sahara, which served the monarchy at a time when its survival was at stake domestically, led to greater U.S. interest and presence in the Maghreb region.[12] From 1976 to the late 1980s, U.S.-Moroccan relations were dominated by that conflict; while the United States provided the necessary support for Morocco to maintain its conquest of the territory, Morocco served U.S. interests in Africa and the Middle East.[13] Like France, the United States has since the inception of the conflict not only sided with Morocco, but was also instrumental in Morocco's colonization of the territory.[14] A close associate of Kissinger apparently suggested to Hassan II to undertake the Green March, during which 350,000 carefully selected Moroccans, many of whom soldiers in civilian clothing, invaded peacefully the former Spanish colony.[15] At the height of the Cold War, the United States feared Soviet expansion into sub-Saharan

Africa. Despite the fact that the Soviets never supported the Sahrawi nationalist movement,[16] Washington worried about the potential emergence of a pro-Soviet state in the Maghreb region. Throughout the Cold War, American preoccupation with the survival of the pro-Western monarchy—as guarantor of U.S. and Western presence in the area—overrode other regional concerns. In August 2004, James Baker corroborated this point by stating that U.S. support for Morocco was justified because "in the days of the Cold War (. . .) the POLISARIO Front was aligned with Cuba and Libya and some other enemies of the United States, and Morocco was very close to the United States."[17]

Today, Morocco continues to be perceived as an ally in the war on terror and as a bulwark against radical forces in the region. It is also seen as an important player in the fight against drug trafficking and illegal migration to Europe. Since 2002, Morocco has been a member of the U.S.-funded Pan-Sahel Initiative and its successor, the TSCTP. Morocco has also engaged in U.N. peacekeeping activities and has sent troops to assist friendly countries, such as Côte d'Ivoire and the Democratic Republic of the Congo.

American concern with the survival of the pro-Western, moderate monarchy—as guarantor of the U.S. and Western interests in the area—has overridden other regional concerns. The emergence of the Global War on Terror after 9/11 bolstered Morocco's standing in U.S. policy, even though neighboring Algeria, whose security and military cooperation has been very effective, is now a strategic partner of the United States in the region. One cannot understand U.S. support for Morocco, which has continued under the Obama administration, without comprehending the historic centrality of Morocco in the U.S. policy toward the Maghreb.

Algeria and the United States: Cautious Partnership

Looking at U.S.-Algerian relations today, one would hardly guess that the two countries were at loggerheads for decades. Unlike relations with the Moroccan and Tunisian neighbors, U.S. relations with Algeria are more complex and, even though they have witnessed incredible progress, they are still marked by fundamental disagreements on a variety of issues. The primary reason for the disagreements derives from the determinants of Algeria's foreign policy, which have been shaped by the geopolitical (regional) context, the country's historical experience, ideological imperatives, as well as the economic choices imposed by the postcolonial conditions.[18] Algerians have more often than not gauged their relations with any country against the position taken by that country regarding Algerian national interests of prime importance. Thus, cooperation or conflict always depend on how the outsider acts toward what Algerian policymakers believe is favorable or unfavorable to the country's national interests.

Therefore, following the country's independence the country's elites felt that they owed a moral and ideological debt toward those who either supported them or were under colonial domination and played a leading role in organizations, such as the Organization of African Unity (OAU) or the Nonaligned Movement (NAM), which supported independence and self-determination. Algeria's support for national liberation movements was genuine; the country committed resources to those anticolonial struggles by providing military, political, and financial support.

Algerian-U.S. security and military relations had a bad start. The problems between the two countries were exacerbated as a result of the role that the United States played during the Moroccan-Algerian conflict in fall 1963.[19] Moroccan irredentism was the cause of the war, but the confrontation took the form of an ideological clash between a country closely associated with the West, the United States in particular, and one proud of being revolutionary, albeit nonaligned, and antagonistic to what it saw as imperialistic ploys in the region. Although the exact U.S. role in the border conflict is not known, Algerians had evidence that the United States provided at the very least logistical support to the Moroccans.[20] Furthermore, Algerian leaders were persuaded that the United States was intent on rolling back their revolution and preventing that experience from being emulated in other Third World countries. The refusal of the United States to sell them, that very same year, badly needed military equipment for the ill-equipped National Popular Army (ANP),[21] helped confirm Algerian suspicions vis-à-vis U.S. intentions despite the economic assistance that President John F. Kennedy was seeking to provide to Algeria. In contrast to the United States, the Soviets agreed in November 1963 to supply modern military equipment to Algeria:[22] a decision that irritated the United States.[23] The mutual distrust led to a closer political and military relationship between the Soviet Union and Algeria—an association that has continued with Russia today. However, because of their staunch nationalism and nonalignment, Algerians firmly refused to grant the Soviets any military or naval bases.[24]

Regardless of Algeria's pragmatism, nonalignment, and its guarded ties with Moscow, Americans still perceived, quite mistakenly, Algeria as a pro-Soviet, radical state. This image of Algeria[25] persisted well into the 1990s, despite the shifts that Algerian foreign policy underwent in the 1980s.[26] Conflict in Western Sahara worsened relations between Algeria and the United States because though the conflict was of a regional nature, the United States inscribed it in the frame of the East–West confrontation. The United States, which, according to Henry Kissinger, could not allow another Angola on the Atlantic, put pressure on the Spaniards to cede the former colony to the Moroccans and in fact gave the green light for the latter to invade the territory.[27] Thus, promises of betterment in relations even under President Jimmy Carter were short-lived due to the U.S. pro-Moroccan position on the Western Sahara.[28] The conflict brought the United States and Morocco closer, especially in the area of military and political cooperation. The greatest blow to the Algerians was the U.S. decision to sell offensive weapons to Morocco. Due to the Soviet invasion of Afghanistan, the Carter administration had shifted its position from a regionalist approach to the Middle East and Africa to a globalist course. This became even more pronounced under the Reagan administration, obsessed with forging a strategic consensus in the Middle East to contain what was perceived as a global Soviet threat. Algeria's pivotal part in helping release the American hostages in Iran did nothing to persuade Americans to change their attitude toward Algeria. Even if some officials did not necessarily view Algeria as a Soviet client state, they nonetheless believed that all-out support should be given to Morocco. The overwhelming perception was—and still exists—that Morocco is a stable kingdom and a reliable friend of the United States. Regardless of the change of regime in Algeria, following Boumediene's death in December 1978, and the emergence of a more pragmatic Algerian foreign policy, the Reagan administration showed no particular predisposition toward Algeria, whose image as a radical state and a Soviet ally remained as strong as ever. Insensitive to the positive mediating role Algerians played in resolving the Iranian hostage crisis, the United States showed no particular gratitude. The U.S. decision, under strong support from Secretary of State Alexander Haig to sell 108 M-60A3 tanks to Morocco,[29] in spite of proclaimed U.S. neutrality in the Western Sahara conflict, worsened Algerians' distrust toward Americans.

Although they today collaborate on fighting terrorism, the United States and Algeria still hold differing positions on what constitutes terrorism. Where Algerians differentiate between legitimate armed struggle and revolutionary violence against foreign occupation, the United States, tend practically to lump all groups under the same designation. Algerians, who fought a revolutionary war against the French, would never characterize the PLO and its armed branch Fatah as a terrorist organization, and neither would they demonize Hamas because the group is seen as a movement of resistance, its Islamist orientation notwithstanding. For Algerians, these organizations have not only the legitimate right to fight occupation, like the Algerian wartime FLN did, but they must do so to free themselves through whatever means, similar to the armed struggle Algerian nationalists waged against France. This explains why, although Algerians support an international convention on terrorism, they warn against "any position or proviso which would undermine the legitimate peoples' struggle to recover their freedom or to discredit a particular religious community."[30]

In the 1990s, the Algerian government, faced with an internal armed Islamist uprising, was rather perplexed by the position the U.S. government adopted vis-à-vis the Islamic Salvation Front (FIS), which it did not consider as a radical party but as a legitimate contender for power.[31] Although there existed no consensus in Washington on how to address the Algerian crisis, the escalation of violence, coupled with European fears regarding the potential spillover of that violence into Europe and the potential wave of immigrants, led Washington to provide minimum, conditional support to the Algerian regime, which included among other things political and economic reforms and the inclusion of moderate Islamists into the government. The policy of reconciliation and the promise of reforms the newly elected president Abdelaziz Bouteflika proclaimed had a positive echo in Washington, resulting in improvement in relations. Indubitably, 9/11 and the subsequent global war on terrorism are the main factors that set off U.S.-Algerian relations on a new course at all levels although signs of a new development was apparent shortly before 9/11, the best illustration being Bouteflika's official visit to the United States in July 2001.

The 9/11 attacks heightened U.S.-Algerian security cooperation. Soon after the attacks, Algerian authorities joined the U.S.-led international coalition against terrorism, sharing information on terrorists on the run in Europe and the United States and offering assistance in security and intelligence matters. With respect to the fight on terrorism, the CIA, FBI, and NSA sought and obtained assistance from their Algerian counterparts who have acquired significant experience in this area. In 2002, though reluctant to sell lethal weapons to Algeria, to avoid upsetting the military balance with Morocco, the United States decided to provide Algerian security forces with equipment used in the fight against terrorism.[32] Secretary of State Colin Powell paid a visit to Algeria—during his tour of the region—to discuss issues of military cooperation and economic exchanges. This was a reversal of the policy in the 1990s, when the United States like other Western nations refused to supply weapons to Algeria. Indeed, a quasi-arms embargo had been imposed upon Algeria, forcing the country to seek alternative suppliers, such as Spain, Turkey, the former Eastern Bloc, South Africa, and to a lesser degree France.[33]

The security relations had begun at the multilateral level with Algeria's adherence to NATO's Mediterranean Dialogue in 2000; Bouteflika himself paid visits in 2001 and 2002 to NATO's headquarters in Belgium. Algeria has since participated in numerous joint military, mostly naval, exercises, such as "Active Endeavor" in the high seas. Algeria has also been drawn into a regional security arrangement, which includes not only the Maghreb countries (Algeria, Mauritania, Morocco, and Tunisia—Libya was not formally part of it), but also the Sahel states, such as Chad, Mali, Senegal, Niger, and even Nigeria. Under the pretext that thousands of Al Qaeda troops had moved to the desert astride the Maghreb-Sahel region, the United States launched in 2002 the Pan-Sahel Initiative, replaced in 2004 by the Trans-Saharan Counterterrorism Partnership, which has brought together these countries to combat terrorism in a region that has now been dubbed by *The Economist* magazine as Afrighanistan. Thus, the armed forces of the Maghreb-Sahel countries participate in military maneuvers, known as "Flintlock" every two years.

Obviously, terrorism and the need to identify its components and eradicate them is what brought together the security services of the two countries. The bilateral military cooperation has become evident on the ground as U.S. and Algerian troops work closely together in the Algerian desert.[34] Yet, the amount of U.S. military assistance to Algeria remains insignificant. In 2007, the United States provided Algeria with $806,000 within the International Military Education and Training (IMET) program and a mere $731,000 in counterterrorism assistance.[35] In 2009 the United States provided Algeria with a modest $870,000 within the IMET program ($950,000 in FY 2010) for training military personnel in the United States and a mere $400,000 in counterterrorism assistance although the request for 2010 doubled this amount.[36] The budget request for allocation to the IMET program has increased to $1.3 million.[37] The figures are low; however, considering that Algeria is a relatively rich country, external funding is not really needed.

Clearly, security relations between Algeria and the United States are stronger than imagined. There has been much speculation regarding U.S. supplies of weapons to Algeria. However, except for some sophisticated night-vision equipment and specific types of radar, Algeria showed little interest in large purchases from the United States.

Despite the undeniably close cooperation with the United States, two points need to be made: 1) Algerians are unwilling to have too close a military cooperation with the United States that is conducted on U.S. terms;[38] and 2) Algeria is not inclined to become dependent on the United States, or any other power for that matter, for its military hardware, which explains the diversification of its arms purchases from Russia, China, France, Germany, Italy, South Africa, the United States, the former Communist bloc, and Turkey. Furthermore, United States's close alliance with Morocco, Algeria's immediate challenger in the region, perpetuates Algeria's suspicion vis-à-vis the United States.

The United States and Libya: Perpetual Insecurity

For a long time, United States officials regarded Libya as a Soviet satellite and Qaddafi as a Soviet puppet.[39] Ideological differences between the United States and Libya were such that the Libyan leader supported governments and movements of national liberation who were on Washington's blacklist whereas the United States repeatedly sought to undermine the Libyan regime.[40] Hostile relations between Libya and the United States reached their apex in the 1980s, mainly during the Ronald Reagan administration, which espoused the rollback approach—later renamed the "Reagan Doctrine"—aimed at forcing change on Third World states. Either covertly or openly, the United States endorsed regime change coups, and even conflicts, where these would weaken the Soviet Bloc.[41] In the case of Libya, not only did the United States seek to overthrow Qaddafi, but it also attempted to assassinate him.[42] The Clinton administration treated Libya as a rogue state,[43] which represented a threat not only to U.S. security because rogue states were said to develop weapons of mass destruction (WMD), but also to the security of U.S. allies, such as Egypt or Tunisia.

The resolution of the Lockerbie case whereby Libya paid $2.7 billion to the families of the victims and Libya's abandonment of its WMD program facilitated complete normalization between the United States and Libya, which ended four decades of strife.[44] The normalization process had begun in 1999, and although contentious issues were not completely resolved until 2008, the two countries had cooperated on security issues before, and more closely, after 9/11.

A major interest of the United States vis-à-vis Libya related to the latter's role in the Global War on Terrorism (GWOT).[45] The Bush administration was alarmed about the activities of the LIFG and, like the Obama administration that succeeded it, about the consolidation of the AQIM across Sub-Saharan Africa.[46] As indicated earlier, even before 9/11, Libya had developed cooperation with the United States on issues of terrorism.[47] Libya itself had faced a genuine threat from Islamist groups, both moderate and radical.[48] A month after the 9/11 attacks, the United States asked Libya not only to abandon its WMD but also to assist in the fight against terrorism.[49] Cooperation between the two countries deepened in important ways[50] until the armed uprising that eventually toppled the Qaddafi regime in October 2011. In acknowledging the strategic importance of Libya's cooperation, the United States sought to co-opt it into the security network across the Maghreb-Sahel region.[51] Indeed, classified cables released through Wikileaks corroborate that the United States encouraged Libya to enlist in the TSCTP.[52] In April 2005, General Charles Kip Wald, deputy chief of the United States European Command (EUCOM), argued that the reestablishment of military relations with Libya would improve political stability across North Africa.[53] Despite U.S. inducement, Libya refused to join the TSCTP, "because it duplicated CEN-SAD's efforts,"[54] according to Libyan officials. Nevertheless, Libya maintained contacts at the highest levels—General William Kip Ward visited Libya twice in 2009—and even requested military equipment[55] and training. More importantly, Libya, along with 10 other African countries, participated in AFRICOM's Operation Enduring Freedom Trans Sahara (OEF-TS), which provides military support to the TSCTP program.[56]

When all the bilateral issues had been resolved, military cooperation between the two countries became possible. Hence, in January 2009, the United States and Libya signed the "Defense Contacts and Cooperation Memorandum of Understanding."[57] The nonbinding agreement, the two delegations signed at the Pentagon, revealed that the two countries now had military-to-military relations and planned on working together in areas, such as peacekeeping, maritime security, counterterrorism, and African security/stability. As a result of the MOU, foreign military sales to Libya were to follow, as disclosed by Theresa Whelan, deputy assistant secretary of defense for African affairs.[58] Evidently, Libya and the United States were eager to restart the military and security cooperation they had maintained until 1970. In fact, the justification for the IMET funding to Libya ($350,000 in FY 2010 and 2011) was to "creat(e) vital linkages with Libyan officers after a 35-year break in contact."[59] For 2011, the Obama administration requested foreign assistance funds for a variety of programs, including $250,000 in Foreign Military Financing (FMF), $350,000 for IMET, and $275,000 in counterterrorism and border security assistance (Nonproliferation, Antiterrorism, Demining, and Related Programs Account, NADR). There is more. The Obama administration disclosed that it would seek out "additional NADR funding for Libya through the Trans-Saharan Counterterrorism Program for antiterrorism assistance, counterterrorism finance, terrorist interdiction, and de-legitimizing terrorist ideology through educational, cultural, and information programming."[60] Qaddafi's Libya was interested in purchasing an assortment of military articles, including Humvees and Hercules C-130 transport carriers. The FMF that the Obama administration requested aimed at offering assistance to the Libyan Air Force in developing its air transport capabilities "in order to facilitate an increase of Libya's participation in peacekeeping and humanitarian operations." It also planned to provide assistance to the Libyan Coast Guard to improve Libya's coastal patrol and search and rescue operations. FMF was also to finance Libya's participation in the C-130 working group.[61] In 2011, the administration requested $1,650 million to be allocated to Libya in fiscal year 2012, broken down into $1,050 million for NADR, $350,000 for IMET, and $250,000 for FMF.[62]

One can safely surmise that had it not been for the unexpected armed uprising, military and security cooperation between the United States and Libya would have strengthened. The necessity to fight terrorism in the volatile Sahel region made necessary Libya's participation in that fight. The new Libya will remain obliged to U.S. role in the overthrow of Qaddafi. Military and security relations will certainly develop at a fast pace especially because the Libyan armed forces have to be built anew.

The United States and Tunisia: Protecting a Small Ally

Owing to its structural vulnerability, Tunisia has always sought to play a mediation role within its regional environment where competing, stronger powers—Algeria, Morocco, and Libya—pursue hegemonic policies. Mindful of their vulnerability to the threats and ambitions of external, mainly regional, powers, Tunisians have developed a moderate foreign policy the main goal of which is to decrease their geopolitical and security weaknesses.[63] Given that the mediation role is not sufficient to contain the potential threats from its more powerful neighbors, Tunisia has established solid relations with the West, the United States in particular, without however entering into formal security arrangements.

Tunisia's moderation, lack of regional ambitions, as well as the nonexistence of any durable conflict, such as the one that has characterized Algerian-Moroccan relations for decades and has forced the two countries to demand assistance from the superpowers, are the main factors that have allowed this nation to deal with the United States from a secure position, with rare ephemeral setbacks. Indeed, the main characteristic of U.S.-Tunisia relations is constancy. Whenever events, such as the 1985 Israeli bombing of the PLO headquarters, the Israeli assassination of PLO official Abu-Jihad in his home in Tunis, or the Gulf War in 1991, affect the serenity of U.S.-Tunisian ties, both sides are quick to repair them, thus highlighting the importance of the reciprocal attachment of the two governments.

Owing to its weaknesses, the Tunisian leadership devised a foreign policy, which allowed it to transform its "geopolitical weakness into a strategic asset."[64] Like Morocco, Tunisia was seen in Washington as a pole of stability in the Maghreb, which needed to be protected against the threat from the Libyan rogue state. Tunisia should also be shielded against the potential spillover emanating from the civil unrest in Algeria, which pitched security forces against Islamists throughout the 1990s.[65] Therefore, arms sales to Tunisia continued to flow, half from the United States.[66] Obviously, the Tunisian regime used the situation in Algeria as a scarecrow against potential internal opponents and for justification of its crackdown on its own Islamists even though the latter were quite peaceful compared to the radicals that threatened the existence of the state in Algeria.

Tunisia's partnership with the United States strengthened further after the 9/11 events; Tunisia was quick to join the U.S.-led GWOT. The security relationship is paramount; the United States has consolidated its military cooperation with Tunisia, whose armed forces are majorly (more than 70%) equipped with U.S. weaponry. In 2005, the United States authorized the export of defense articles and services worth $25,397,490 to Tunisia.[67] During his visit to Tunisia in February 2006, Secretary of Defense Donald Rumsfeld announced that the United States and Tunisia were "working on a Status of Forces Agreement, a SOFA, and that's moving along, and that would create a situation where we would be able to do more things, exercises and that type of thing."[68] The SOFA usually specifies the terms under which the foreign military operates in a given country. Tunisia hosts U.S. training facilities as well as landing rights in Tunisia. The United States also maintains this cooperation through Tunisia's participation in NATO's Mediterranean Dialogue, which Tunisia joined soon after its creation in 1995. In FY 2007, the United States committed "to help Tunisia to enhance and modernize its military counterterrorism program by providing individual monitoring equipment (night vision capabilities) and modern communication and surveillance systems, in addition to assisting with mobility and systemic maintenance and logistical shortfalls . . . (to) enhance its (Tunisian military's) capabilities to apprehend and defeat indigenous and transnational terrorist elements and combat trafficking by increasing border monitoring using a combination of air support assets, maritime patrol and tactical ground surveillance and response capabilities, furthering Tunisia's value as an ally in the global war on terrorism."[69] In 2009 Tunisia received $12 million in foreign military financing, which increased to $15 million in 2010, while the IMET program also increased from $1.7 million to $1.9 million.[70] Tunisia also receives funding through other interagency programs. The United States has trained 4,000 Tunisian soldiers from 2002 to 2012.[71] In fiscal year 2011, the United States committed to assist Tunisia in countering the threat of Al Qaeda in the Islamic Maghreb and collaborate with the country in strengthening its counterterrorism and border security capabilities.

From the abdication of Ben Ali on January 14, 2011 to April 2012, the United States had given Tunisia $32 million in military assistance. While military assistance in 2011 reached more than $25 million, the budget request for 2013 amounts to $36.6 million.[72] This, of course, does not take into account the other grants that the United States extended to Tunisia to ensure a smooth transition of the country following the fall of the dictator. Undoubtedly, the United States will continue ensuring Tunisia's security, especially at a time when rapid changes are taking place in the region. It will also support the moderate Islamist regime that succeeded Ben Ali's as long as it does not threaten the interests of the United States. The Tunisian military, which has close ties with the United States, will certainly guarantee that Tunisia's military and security relationship with the United States will outlast any type of regime in power. On July 29, 2012, Secretary of Defense, Leon Panetta declared unequivocally that "The United States continues to support efforts to strengthen Tunisia's democracy, and DOD (Department of Defense) will play an important role in that effort."[73]

EUROPE AND THE MAGHREB, SO CLOSE, YET SO FAR: ILLEGAL MIGRATION, TERRORISM, AND ENERGY SECURITY

Although European security is framed within the context of the Mediterranean, the Maghreb region is the most vital, especially for the southern Mediterranean countries, namely, France, Italy, and Spain. Economic relations between the two shores of the Mediterranean are very important; the Maghreb's dependency on Europe is part of the colonial legacy—France having established its dominance for 132 years in Algeria, 44 years in Morocco, and 74 years in Tunisia. Italy's brutal colonization of Libya lasted for 32 years (1911–1943). Western Sahara suffered from Spanish colonization for 92 years; Spain also has important interests in northern Morocco, where it holds two strategic enclaves. Therefore, it is no surprise that the bulk of the Maghreb's trade is with Europe.

The Maghreb volume of trade with Europe (primarily France, Italy, and Spain) is considerable: it amounts to around two-thirds of the total trade for Morocco (63%), Algeria (64%) and Tunisia (72%). In 2009, the EU absorbed 75 percent of Tunisia's exports; Ninety percent of money transfers by Tunisian expatriates came from Europe. Eighty-three percent of tourism revenue and 73 percent of

FDI were also from Europe. This is similar for Morocco; approximately 60 percent of its exports are geared toward the EU markets. Likewise, 80 percent of the kingdom's tourism revenues and 90 percent of the expatriate money transfers are from the European Union. With respect to Algeria, a sizable share of its imports comes from Europe, which is also an important destination for Algeria's gas exports. The gas is transported to Europe through Medgaz (via Spain), Transmed via Italy, and via the Galsi to Sardinia. Trade between the European Union and the Maghreb states reached 110 billion euros in 2010.[74]

The European Union has initiated a number of actions in its relations with the Southern Mediterranean region. The Euro-Mediterranean Partnership is aimed at creating a region of shared peace, prosperity, and stability in the Mediterranean basin. The European Union sought to approach the perceived threats from the Southern Mediterranean through economic liberalization and cooperation, which would guarantee European security. Indeed, fears of spillovers of the problems in the Southern Mediterranean into Europe prompted Europe—in addition to the bilateral agreements its members entered with the southern states—to devise cooperation arrangements to thwart the perceived dangers emanating from the southern shores, including labor migration. The socioeconomic problems in the southern shores, coupled with problems of governance, lack of democracy, and authoritarianism, provided the main drivers of this illegal migration. While until the 1990s the EU member states dealt individually with migration issues through bilateral negotiations, by the mid-1990s it became evident that the problems were such that they had to be addressed at the supranational level.[75] In appearance, unlike the United States, which has enormous military power and does not hesitate to use it, Europe has sought to portray itself as a normative power—power that rests on values, such as peace, prosperity, good governance, rule of law, respect for individual rights, and freedoms. However, as a keen analyst of EU relations with the Maghreb put it:

> The normative objective, of course, concealed the real purpose of the policy, which was to apply the principles of soft security to enhancing European security along its southern periphery. The soft security objectives were to be achieved primarily by stimulating economic development in South Mediterranean countries in order to minimize labor migration into Europe, seen at the time as a major source of internal social, political, and economic tension in both Europe and the countries concerned, given the demographic pressures they faced.[76]

The European Union hoped that economic development in the Maghreb, with the help of the instruments that the European Union had devised as well as southern market integration, migration would not be necessary because the dynamic process of development in the southern shores would result in higher employment.[77]

In spite of the rhetoric, however, when terrorism became a reality and security paramount, especially after 9/11, the EU's "normative objectives were either marginalized or mobilized as part of the subsequent securitization process."[78] Evidently, the authoritarian regimes in the Maghreb welcomed Europe's securitization process because this entailed the collaboration of the authoritarian regimes in the fight against illegal migration and against terrorism. The necessity to have the collaboration of those regimes on stemming migration to Europe and combating terrorism meant that the European Union would waive the conditionality it sought to impose on regimes that did not subscribe to its normative values. Thus, progressively, democracy promotion and human rights were no longer the sine qua non for its relations with the southern regimes. In other words, the European Union shared the security agenda with the authoritarian regimes, rhetoric on norms notwithstanding. Security cooperation with the Maghreb regimes was particularly important owing to the fact that "the majority of the arrested (Islamist terrorist) suspects was born in Algeria, Morocco and Tunisia and had loose affiliations to North African terrorist groups."[79]

The European Union collaborated with its southern European partners on drugs and human smuggling, terrorism, international crime, migration through a multitude of instruments, such as the Justice and Home Affairs (JHA) programs, COTER, SitCen, the Neighborhood Action Plan, FRONTEX (Union border agency), and Europol. Of course, this did not exclude the bilateral cooperation between European states and their counterparts in the South Mediterranean— quite the contrary. Bilateral cooperation in the area of terrorism and illegal migration was reinforced.

Not only did the events of 9/11 but also the terrorist attacks in Madrid in 2004 and in London in 2005 compel the European Union to adopt new counterterrorism legislation and establish cooperation with the Maghreb governments. In this context, European states provided the Maghreb governments with sophisticated communications equipment and monitoring electronic systems for airports, railway stations and inner city zones, and along land borders.[80] The European Union funded a number of projects, such as the Management of Border Control in Morocco or Support to the Reform of Justice in Algeria.[81]

The Maghreb countries cooperated with the European Union on migration issues. Algeria, for instance, criminalized illegal migration. Morocco and Libya played an important role with respect to border and migration management. Both readmitted illegal immigrants who had landed in Spain and Italy. In June 2005, the EU Council of Ministers adopted concrete measures to cooperate with Libya against illegal immigration. Libya, which had been under embargo for almost a decade received the favors of the European Union soon after the United Nations suspended the sanctions against Libya in 1999. From 2004 onward, Libya purchased light weapons, electronic equipment, as well as frigates to monitor the Jamahiriya's coastline to protect Europe against illegal migration coming from Africa. For European countries, Qaddafi's Libya was a strategic player in the fight against illegal migration. This is why the European Union had repeatedly called on Libya for help in fighting illegal immigration. Libya, which has long sea border (1,770 kilometers) and land border (5,000 kilometers), has often been a transit point for Africans seeking to enter Europe illegally through the Mediterranean. Given that border patrols and coastal radars have facilitated better control by Spaniards and Moroccans, the influx of illegal migrants now concentrated on Libya as the transit route to reach Europe. In 2008 alone, close to 70,000 people crossed the Mediterranean Sea (with half of them landing in Malta and Italy). Following the uprisings in Tunisia and Libya, the wave of immigrants had risen further, creating more problems for Italy, in particular. Between January and June 2011, 25,800 Tunisians had migrated to Italy.[82] While Qaddafi's Libya was willing to assist the European Union in stemming the waves of illegal migrants, it requested financial and technical assistance from the European Union to fight that influx. In February 2009, the European Union granted Libya 20 million euros—a figure that from the Libyan perspective was insufficient to stop the flow of immigrants. Libya asked for more funding but also for more logistical instruments for the surveillance of its border with Niger. The European Commission has also sought to co-opt Libya into joining FRONTEX (the European agency for the control of external borders) patrols in the central Mediterranean. Although Libya refused to participate, the agreement it reached with Italy to execute joint maritime patrols in Libyan waters had in effect brought Libya closer to participating in FRONTEX operations.[83]

The underlying rationale for the Libyan Treaty of Friendship, Cooperation, and Partnership signed with Italy in August 2008, in addition to energy security, had much to do with the problem of migration. Unsurprisingly, Italy agreed to pay $500 million for the supply and installation of electronic equipment along the Libyan coast.[84] Silvio Berlusconi summed up the purpose of the treaty for Italy as "less illegal immigrants and more oil."[85]

Europe's Arms Sales to the Maghreb States

Cooperation with the Maghreb countries also included important arms sales. Libya, which had traditionally received most of its weapons from the Soviet Union, offered a lucrative market for European weaponry following the suspension of sanctions in 1999. In October 2004, for instance, the European Union granted export licenses for 834.5 million euros of arms exports to the Jamahiriya. In 2009, European arms transfers to Libya amounted to 343.7 million euros. Libya received ammunition, small arms, automatic weapons, tear gas, electronic equipment, including radar devices and jamming devices, antitank missiles, helicopters, and military planes from Italy, France, the United Kingdom, Germany, and other European countries.[86] It should be pointed out that because of the sanctions and economic difficulties, Libya's arms purchases in the period 1986–2009, had declined considerably.[87]

In November 2004, President Jacques Chirac went to Tripoli, the first visit by a French head of state since Libya's independence in 1951, to develop bilateral relations. Two months after this visit the Minister of Defence, Michele Alliot-Marie signed a letter of intent for military cooperation and the purchase of weapons by Libya. France was clearly hoping to secure contracts as important as those it signed with Libya in the 1970s. To achieve this, France had, among other things, counted on its arms industry. Negotiations on the acquisition of the Rafale aircraft from the Dassault group (never sold outside of France), helicopters, patrol boats, and many other types of armaments, in addition to the contract for the modernization of 12 Libyan Mirage F1 bombers and the purchase of many Airbus passenger planes, could correct the balance of trade between the two countries. In 2006, Libya had become a priority market for British export of arms equipment.[88] In late 2007, France announced an initial accord with Libya of a armaments package worth over 4.5 billion euros, comprising 10–14 Rafale fighters, two Gowind corvettes, and eight to 12 Tiger attack helicopters, among many more items. Reportedly, Paris had delivered 100 MILAN-3 antitank missiles to Tripoli in 2009, worth 168 million euros. Dassault was apparently working on the overhaul of Mirage fighter aircraft. France is said to have offered a package worth $5.8 billion that included overhaul, armored vehicles, and helicopters.[89] The United Kingdom, meanwhile, was looking to provide security training and counterterrorism support. However, the biggest military-related deal was the 2009 agreement valued at 300 million euros with Italy's Finmeccanica. Finmeccanica and AgustaWestland—each for 25 percent—have created the joint venture Libyan Italian Advanced Technology Company (LIATEC) with the Libyan Company for Aviation Industry; the objective was to win orders from the Libyan air force. LIATEC had already upgraded at least three Chinook helicopters owned by Libya. The Spanish company ITP signed a contract with the Libyan authorities to service and repair Libya's U.S.-made C-130 Hercules transport aircraft. Starting in 2007, the United Kingdom had dispensed arms export licenses to Libya, including among many other items water cannons for riot control and internal security.[90] Many of the weapons supplied to the Qaddafi regime were used during the civil war.[91]

Morocco has acquired considerable military equipment from Europe, mostly from Spain, France, Belgium, the Netherlands, and Italy. The Moroccan Royal Navy procured an $875 million purchase of three multi-mission frigates from Schelde Naval Shipbuilding of the Netherlands. Although Morocco did not purchase the Rafale aircraft, disappointing France, it nevertheless purchased a FREMM frigate from DCNS for $710 million.[92] In 2008, the Moroccan government ordered three Sigma-class frigates from Damen Schelde Naval Shipbuilding in the Netherlands; the export license amounted to 550 million euros. The first frigate was delivered in 2010, the second in March 2012, and the third in July 2012. Purportedly, the vessels are to be used for patrol and coast guard tasks and to permit joint operations with NATO navies. However, armaments that include MICA and Exocet missiles (both of which furnished by European missile maker MBDA) and a 76 mm Oto Melara canon indicate these frigates also offensive capabilities.[93] Morocco concluded other important arms deals with other European country, notably, with France.

Algeria, too, which has been a traditional client of the Soviet Union/Russia, has acquired military hardware from European countries, such as Italy, Germany, and the United Kingdom. Algeria signed an important deal with the Anglo-Italian helicopter manufacturer AgustaWestland, which reportedly will equip Algeria with up to 100 helicopters, worth up to five billion dollars, to meet the country's battlefield and internal security requirements.[94] Some European shipyards will deliver four stealth frigates to Algeria. In October 2009, the U.K. government signed a military cooperation accord for the sale of more helicopters and ships.[95] Between 2008 and 2011, France supplied 20 patrol boats to the Algerian Coast Guards. Algeria has also concluded an agreement valued at $2.5 billion with the German TKMS for the delivery of two corvettes Meko armed with missiles made by the Swedish company Saab Bofors.[96]

In addition to the United States, by far its main arms supplier, Tunisia purchases its military equipment from the Czech Republic, Belgium, Italy, France, Portugal, and Spain. In 2008, Tunisia purchased almost $1.5 million worth of military equipment from Portugal. In 2006 and 2007, Tunisia's purchases from the Czech Republic amounted to 4,171,000 euros and 3,078,000 euros, respectively. In 2005, Germany negotiated an arms accord valued at 34 million euros with Tunisia, which also imported from the Netherlands 1,040,000 euros in military electronics.[97] Spain and the United Kingdom were also among the suppliers of weapons to Tunisia.

The Maghreb is not only a lucrative market for European arms sales, but it is also an important supplier of energy to Europe. The Maghreb is without a doubt vital for Europe's energy security. The European Union imports 15 percent of its oil needs from the Maghreb, mainly Algeria and Libya.[98] Algeria, the world's fifth largest exporter of gas (pipeline and LNG exports combined) provides 13.8 percent of the gas consumed in the 27-country European Union.[99] Europe's imports of oil and natural gas from the Maghreb increased exponentially in the period 1999–2008.[100] The search for energy security partly explains why the European Union could not pursue its normative policy in a consistent way.

The Maghreb states are also involved with other organizations, such as NATO's Mediterranean Dialogue. An informal organization, with no structure, the 5 + 5 Dialogue, revived in 2001 after a decade of inactivity, has brought together five northern Mediterranean countries (France, Italy, Malta, Spain, and Portugal) and five Maghreb countries (Algeria, Libya, Mauritania, Morocco, and Tunisia), which have met regularly since 2003 to cooperate on a number of issues, including, regional security, migration, energy, protection of the environment, and development.[101]

RUSSIA AND CHINA IN THE MAGHREB: CHALLENGERS TO EUROPEAN AND U.S. INFLUENCE OR INEXORABLE KEY PLAYERS?

The common comment in the media and political circles is that Russia and China are coming to the Maghreb. In reality, these two states have been present in the Maghreb for a long time. It is true, however, that since it emerged as a major economic power, China has garnered important commercial deals, particularly in Algeria and Libya. China has been a major player in infrastructural works (housing, highways . . .) and in the energy sector.[102] However, China's presence has caused unease in Europe, which has considered the Maghreb as its chasse gardée (private preserve). The United States, too, has shown signs of concern about China's presence in some oil and mineral producing countries in the Maghreb and Sahel region. In fact, it has been argued that the underlying goal of the creation of AFRICOM was to thwart China's expansion in the area. Daniel Volman, for instance, has observed, the United States is "making (Africa) into another front in its Global War on Terrorism, maintaining and extending access to energy supplies and other strategic raw material, and competing with China and other rising economic powers for control over the continent's resources."[103] Although there are no reliable data on China's sales of weaponry to the Maghreb states, it is certain that it does supply important quantities to Algeria. Recently, China, to the experts' surprise, signed a deal with Algeria for the construction of three corvettes.[104] Although China has not been a major supplier of weapons, it is possible that it will become a player in that field in the future. What is certain, however, is that China is concerned about the security situation in the Sahel and about the uprisings in the Maghreb, which might threaten its interests.[105] The unexpected change of regime in Libya has demonstrated that China's political risks in the region require a new set of policies and a more watchful presence.

Russia and Libya: The Lost Deal

Unlike China, Russia has been a major supplier of weapons to the Maghreb, mainly to Algeria and Libya, but also to Morocco. In the period 1970 to 1991, SIPRI revealed that the Soviet Union accounted for 90 percent of Algeria's importations of major conventional weapons and 78 percent of Libyan arms imports. In that same period, Libya stood as the fourth largest beneficiary of Soviet armaments exports, accounting for eight percent of transfers whereas Algeria

ranked as the eighth largest recipient, with four percent.[106] Still according to
SIPRI, Algeria, Libya, Morocco, and Tunisia accounted for approximately three
percent of global arms imports for the period 2005–2009; the size of key conventional weapons transfers to North Africa in 2005–2009 had increased by
62 percent in comparison with the period 2000–2004. Algeria alone accounted
for close to 89 percent of transfers to the Maghreb during this time, advancing
from 18th to ninth largest receiver of major conventional weapons worldwide.
Morocco, too, had placed substantial orders in 2008 and 2009. Between 2005
and 2008, Russia struck a deal with Morocco worth $250 million for developing
Tunguska mobile air defense systems, a transaction, which included at least 300
surface-to-air missiles.[107]

Libya in the 1990s was the subject of an international arms embargo. In mid-
2000, the Russian manufacturer Promeksport began the execution of contracts
inked in 1999 and 2000 to sell ammunition to Libya and overhaul its Soviet-
supplied armored vehicles and air defense systems.[108] However, Moscow's desire
to reconquer the Libyan arms and energy market only began after the international arms embargo on Libya was lifted in 2004. Yet, there was no major break-
through owing to the nonresolution of Libya's debt to Moscow. The debt issue
of $4.6 billion was finally resolved in 2008, when Vladimir Putin, who visited
Libya, decided to write off $4.5 billion of the debt (the remaining $100 million
was dropped to fulfill Libya's financial claim against Russia) with the purpose
of resolving the debt issue and catching up with the West, primarily Europe,
which had benefited from the end of the isolation of the Libyan regime.[109] Putin
and Qaddafi had agreed on a number of commercial and military deals. Reportedly, the Libyans had agreed to purchase military equipment worth
$2.5 billion, comprising aircraft, antiaircraft missile systems, naval and army weap-
onry: -300PMU2 Favorit; about 20 Tor M1 and Buk M1-2 antiaircraft missile
systems; two aircraft squadrons—one Mikoyan MiG-29 SMT and one Sukhoi
Su-30 MK; several dozens Mil Mi-17, Mi-35, and Kamov Ka-52 helicopters.[110]
In early 2010, Russian Prime Minister Putin announced a deal worth $1.8 bil-
lion with Tripoli, reportedly including 12–20 Sukhoi fighter aircraft, six Yak-130
light combat aircraft, S-300 air defense systems, and a Kalashnikov manufacturing facility. However, the deal never materialized owing to the UN arms embargo
on Libya following the uprising in February 2011. The Russians claim that they
have lost contracts worth four billion dollars with Libya and that they were in
discussions with the new Libyan authorities for the contracts to be honored.[111]

Russia and Algeria: The Strategic Partnership

Algeria's relations with the Soviet Union/Russia developed during the Algerian
War of Independence. As mentioned earlier, the postindependence rapprochement with Soviet Russia was partly the consequence of the suspicions between

the United States and Algeria that resulted from the role that the United States played during the Moroccan-Algerian conflict in fall 1963.[112] The close political and military relationship between the Soviet Union and Algeria then began; that association continued well onto the late 1980s and, though it receded in the 1990s because of Russia's domestic problems, the ties have been renewed and reinvigorated since 2001.[113] Although Algerians have consistently sought to minimize their dependence on Soviet armaments through diversification of their suppliers, they could not find a reliable substitute owing to the lower cost of Russian weaponry, which was (and still is) quite competitive. The terms of credit are also more favorable. Between 1978 and 1987, Algeria received Soviet weapons amounting to $5.7 billion;[114] in doing so, they cumulated a relatively high debt vis-à-vis the USSR. In 1987, Algeria purchased Soviet military equipment worth $2.5 billion, which indicated that notwithstanding the relative improvement of relations with Washington, this did not adversely affect Soviet-Algerian relations.[115] From its independence in 1962 to 1989, Algeria has reportedly purchased Soviet/Russian military equipment valued at more than $11 billion.[116] In spite of the diversification of supplies, Algerians had made in 1996 the decision to develop strategic cooperation with Russia[117] in order to modernize the ANP's mostly obsolete military equipment. The Russians, who complained about Algeria's repayment of the debt incurred under Soviet Russia, were troubled by Algeria's arms purchases from Russia's competitors—the Ukraine and Belarus. Apparently, Algerians used this transaction with Russia's competitors as a bargaining chip to force the Russians to reduce prices.[118] In the 1990s, Russian arms sales to Algeria had dropped significantly from what they were in the 1980s. They plummeted from an annual average of $580 million to approximately $170 million on annual average between 1991 and 2000.[119]

From a Russian perspective, the Maghreb constitutes a potentially lucrative market not only in terms of arms sales—a considerable market for the Russians—but also for big industrial and infrastructural projects. Although Europeans, Americans, Chinese, Indians, and others are present in the Maghreb, Russia strives to be a key competing player. The Russians have been cognizant of the fact that France no longer enjoys the influence it once did in the Maghreb—witness the tense Franco-Algerian relations—and of the United States increased presence in the Maghreb-Sahel region.[120] Thus, regaining presence in the North African region is a way of reaffirming Russia's image as a superpower with global interests, which would now disallow the United States from establishing unilateral domination.

In the late 1990s, Algeria had not only begun to come out of its diplomatic isolation, but its finances, due to the gradual rise in oil prices, had also improved considerably. One of the country's priorities was to modernize the ANP, whose equipment had become virtually obsolete. Following a flurry of bilateral visits, Bouteflika made a trip to Moscow in April 2001, which represented a watershed in Algerian-Russian relations. During that visit, Bouteflika and Putin signed a "Strategic Partnership Agreement," making Algeria the first Arab and African country and the second state after India to sign such partnership. The document signed by the two states aimed at strengthening political, economic, and military relations. Without surprise, the main share of the accord involved the supply of military equipment and expertise to Algeria. The military equipment amounted to three billion dollars.[121] A month later, the Russians agreed to sell the ANP 22 SU-24 MKs and six IL-78 tanker aircraft for refueling, which had been commissioned the year before for $120 million.[122] In May 2002, military strongman General Major Mohamed Lamari visited Moscow to procure more modern weapons (22 more Sokhoi-24s, the ANP having already received 24 of them in late 2001) and the federal state arms factories Rosoboronexport, Mig-ABC, and Topaz. Between 2002 and 2004, the Algerian Air Force acquired 42 additional Mi-171Sh.[123] Unavoidably, Algeria's modernization of the armed forces, which involved the purchase of Russian equipment worth $2.5 billion, generated concerns regionally and internationally. This is why Lamari declared to outsiders, mainly Morocco, that Algeria had no belligerent intentions:

> The capabilities that we acquire from Russia will not result in any strategic imbalance in the region (. . .); the capabilities that we have and will modernize and (those) that we will acquire are intended for the defense of the integrity of our territory . . .[124]

The security dilemma proved real as Morocco, too, began an overhaul of its own armed forces, acquiring sophisticated equipment. In 2008, Morocco submitted a large order for arms worth $2.4 billion from the United States, which included an $841 million contract for 24 F-16Cs Block 50/52 strike jets;[125] the F16Cs were delivered in August 2011.[126] The regional arms race,[127] mainly between Algeria and Morocco, accelerated.

In 2006, Algeria and Russia signed a major arms agreement bringing the value of total contracts for delivery of Russian military equipment to $7.5 billion. Given the preparatory work that was conducted throughout 2005, the two parties had found a solution to the debt contracted in the 1960s and 1970s. Russia agreed to cancel debts incurred by Algeria to Soviet Russia, which amounted to $4.7 billion, an amount that represented 29 percent of Algeria's total foreign debt of the time.[128] Reports indicated that Russia was to sell up to 100 of the most modern combat aircraft to Algeria, including MIG-29 SMT fighter planes, together with sophisticated antimissile air defenses. The deal was that Algeria would benefit from debt exemption of one billion dollars for each one billion dollar purchase of Russian equipment. In other words, Algeria's debt would be totally expunged if it purchased equipment in an amount equivalent or superior to the debt. In the agreement between the two sides, Algeria put forth an order for military hardware valued at $7.5 billion. The amount consisted for the most part in the purchase of brand new materiel; the rest related to revamping or repairing previously bought equipment. The agreement pertained to the delivery of 34 MiG-29 SMT, 28 Su-30 MKI fighters, and 14 Yak-130 jet trainers (for a total of $3.5 billion). The agreement reached also provided for the delivery of 300 tanks T-90S for one billion dollars, eight missile systems S-300 PMU-2 (air defense divisions) for one billion dollars, which, apparently Russia had refused to sell to other countries,[129] 30 aircraft batteries (Tunguska) worth nearly half a billion dollars, two submarines, the modernization of 250 tanks (T-72) for over $200 million, delivery of Kornet and Metis antitank missiles, and repair of Algerian naval forces ships.[130] This was, according to many sources, the largest single contract in military-technical cooperation in Russia's post–Soviet history.

Algeria's determination to diversify its suppliers has overall been quite consistent and, no matter the huge amounts spent to purchase Russian equipment, other suppliers were solicited to provide the most appropriate materiel, high cost notwithstanding because Algeria's revenues from hydrocarbons have made such purchases possible. In July 2011, Algeria opted for some German materiel in the amount of $14 billion (10 billion euros) over a 10-year period. The contract, the largest ever signed with a Western country, rests on the construction of armored vehicles in Algeria, the sale of frigates, an electronic system for border protection, and training of Algerian military personnel. The tender had been launched in 2007; a multitude of international groups had submitted bids for obtaining the contract. Bouteflika's state visit in December 2010 to Germany, with which Algeria has sought to strengthen economic cooperation in recent years, tilted the balance in favor of the German groups. According to a report, Rheinmetall and MAN will build Fuchs armored transport vehicles with their joint venture RMMV whereas Daimler will sell trucks and off-road vehicles. ThyssenKrupp will be in charge of building frigates and training the Algerian navy.[131] The electronic system for border protection is an important security issue for Algeria, especially in view of the instability in its border due to the civil war in Libya and the volatile situation in the Sahara-Sahel region. Algeria had for years sought to obtain the most sophisticated system to secure its huge land borders and its maritime shores.

In summer 2011, Algeria received two Russian 636 Improved Kilo class submarines it had ordered in 2006;[132] they joined the two repaired and modernized ones that Algeria acquired in the 1980s. Additionally, Algeria ordered two Tiger corvettes for its navy,[133] as well as Yak130 training aircraft. In order to demonstrate once again that this decision is based on a commercial basis, Algeria ordered, just a month later, a landing and logistical support vessel from Italy. It is believed that this is a San Giorgio class amphibious transport ship, which can carry a battalion of troops with the capacity to carry 36 armored vehicles or 30 tanks, three landing aircraft and many helicopters, which can fly out from a carrier-style flight deck.[134] Algeria has faced smuggling and other criminal activities emanating from its 620-mile seashore, which explains why it has ordered more vessels for its navy.

In spite of the diversification of its suppliers (purchases from the United Kingdom, Italy, and Germany are considerable), Russia remains by far Algeria's main arms provider; hence, in 2011, Algeria represented 13 percent of Russia's arms market. The arms purchases will continue owing to the instability in the Sahel but also to the uncertainty in Libya and the irresolution of the conflict in Western Sahara. Though from an Algerian perspective these are rational reasons, they have unavoidably resulted in an unprecedented arms race with Morocco.

NOTES

1. There are few writings on this subject; however, the following provide some insight into North Africa's relations with the superpowers during the Cold War period: Yahia Zoubir, "U.S. and Soviet Policies Towards France's Struggle with Anticolonial Nationalism in North Africa," *Canadian Journal of History,* Vol. 30, no. 3 (December 1995); Jack Perry, "Soviet Policy toward French North Africa," Unpublished Dissertation (New York, 1972); Egya Sangmuah, "Sultan Mohammed ben Youssef's American Strategy and the Diplomacy of North African Liberation, 1943–61," *Journal of Contemporary History,* 27 (1992): 129–48; Mohieddine Hadhri, *L'URSS et le Maghreb: De la Révolution d'octobre á l'indépendance de l'Algérie, 1917–1962* (Paris, 1985); L. Carl Brown, "The United States and the Maghrib," *Middle East Journal,* 30, 3 (February 1976); Charles F. Gallagher, *The United States and North Africa: Morocco, Algeria, and Tunisia* (Harvard University Press, 1963).

2. David Lake, *Hierarchy in International Relations* (Ithaca, NY: Cornell University Press, 2009).

3. This section draws from Yahia H. Zoubir, "The United States and Morocco: The Long-Lasting Alliance," in *Handbook of US–Middle East Relations: Formative Factors and Regional Perspectives,* ed. Robert E. Looney (London and New York: Routledge, 2009), 237–48; Yahia H. Zoubir, "The US and Tunisia: Model of Stable Relations," in *Handbook of US–Middle East Relations: Formative Factors and Regional Perspectives,* ed. Robert E. Looney (London and New York: Routledge, 2009), 249–61; "The United States and Algeria: Hostility, Pragmatism, and Partnership," in *Handbook on US Middle East Relations,* ed. Robert Looney (London & New York: Routledge, 2009), 219–36.

4. Morocco produces phosphates, iron ore, manganese, lead, zinc, fish, and salt. Nearly half of the world's known phosphate reserves—an important source for fertilizer which may be in short supply in coming decades—comes from Morocco. With the assistance of U.S. companies, Morocco began to develop its vast oil shale deposits, some of which in the disputed Western Sahara, which it has occupied since 1975. There are also deposits of antimony, zinc, lead, coal, and at least some oil.

5. Stephen Zunes, "Morocco and Western Sahara," 3, 42 (December 1998), http://www.fpif.net/briefs/vol3/v3n42mor.html; see also John Damis, "Morocco and the Western Sahara," *Current History* (April 1990).

6. The *New York Times*, July 7, 1979, cited in Stephen Zunes, "The United States in the Saharan War: A Case of Low-Intensity Intervention," in *International Dimensions of the Western Sahara Conflict,* ed. Yahia H. Zoubir and Daniel Volman (Westport, CT: Praeger, 1993), 55.

7. These figures were calculated from the statistics provided by the U.S. Department of State Congressional Budget Justification for Foreign Operations, Fiscal Years 2004 and 2005.

8. Press Conference, Ambassador William J. Burns, Assistant Secretary of State for Near Eastern Affairs at Villa America Rabat, Morocco, October 28, 2003, http://usembassy-israel. org.il/publish/press/2003/november/110402.html.

9. U.S. Department of State, "Morocco: Security Assistance," October 20, 2008, http:// www.state.gov/t/pm/64727.htm.

10. Tony Capaccio, "Lockheed Martin to Sell Morocco 24 New F-16s for $841 Million," *Bloomberg,* December 22, 2009, http://www.bloomberg.com/apps/news?pid=newsarchive &sid=aaF5gcH2t8H8.; see also, "Royal Moroccan Air Force," *Global Security,* http://www. globalsecurity.org/military/world/morocco/air-force.htm.

11. James Phillips, "King Hassan's Morocco: A Valuable U.S. Ally," *The Heritage Foundation,* Paper 1023, March 13, 1995.

12. Stephen Zunes, "The United States in the Saharan War: A Case of Low-Intensity Intervention," in *International Dimensions of the Western Sahara Conflict,* ed. Yahia H. Zoubir and Daniel Volman (Westport, CT: Praeger, 1993), 53–92.

13. For an extensive account of U.S. policy toward the conflict in Western Sahara, see Stephen Zunes and Jacob Mundy, *Western Sahara: War, Nationalism, and Conflict Irresolution* (Syracuse, New York: Syracuse University Press, 2010).

14. Jacob Mundy, "Neutrality or Complicity? The United States and the 1975 Moroccan Takeover of the Spanish Sahara," *The Journal of North African Studies,* Vol. 11, no. 3 (September 2006): 275–306.

15. Ignace Dalle, *Les Trois Rois—La Monarchie Marocaine de L'indépendance à nos Jours* (The Three Kings—The Moroccan Monarchy since Independence) (Paris: Fayard, 2004), 427.

16. Yahia H. Zoubir, "Soviet Policy toward the Western Sahara Conflict," *Africa Today,* Vol. 34, no. 3 (1987): 17–32.

17. "Former U.S. Secretary of State, and former Personal Envoy of the U.N. Secretary General to Western Sahara, James A. Baker III, discusses the protracted conflict in Western Sahara with host Mishal Husain" PBS TV, August 19, 2004. http://www.pbs.org/wnet/wide angle/shows/sahara/transcript.html.

18. Seghir Rahmani, "Algerian-American Relations (1962–1985): The Study of Algeria's Anti-Imperialist Foreign Policy and its Impact on Algerian-American Relations," PhD Dissertation, Georgetown University, 1985, 3.

19. Senior Algerian diplomats interviewed by Y. Zoubir insisted that they had proof that the United States provided logistical and military assistance to the Moroccan Armed Forces.

20. Nicole Grimaud, *La Politique Extérieure de l'Algérie, 1962–1978* (Paris: Karthala, 1984),147; William B. Quandt, "Can We Do Business with Radical Nationalists? Algeria, Yes," *Foreign Policy,* 7 (Summer 1972): 115.

21. David and Marina Ottaway, *Algeria: The Politics of a Socialist Revolution* (Berkeley and Los Angeles, CA: University of California Press, 1970), 158. In fact, the U.S. decision not to offer Algeria Military Assistance Program (MAP) was made the previous year. American policy makers were of the opinion that Algeria should address its request to France and, if the latter refused, "We should urge them (Algerians) to limit their military program to one oriented toward civic action, progressive reduction of armed forces, and internal security, and offer to help them along these lines," National Security Action Memorandum, no. 211, December 14, 1962.

22. M.J.V. Bell, "Military Assistance to Independent African States," *Adelphi Papers,* 15 (December 1964), 8. The major deliveries, however, did not begin until 1964 and 1966.

23. See Secretary of State Dean Rusk's statement in his news conference of November 8, 1963, *Department of State Bulletin,* hereinafter as *DSB,* November 25, 1963, 817.

24. See Yahia H. Zoubir, "Soviet Policy toward the Maghreb," *Arab Studies Quarterly,* 9, 4 (Fall 1987).

25. On the concept of image as applied to Algeria, see Azzedine Layachi, *The United States and North Africa: A Cognitive Approach to Foreign Policy* (Westport, CT: Praeger, 1990).

26. Nicole Grimaud, "La Diplomatie sous Chadli ou la Politique du Possible," *Annuaire de l'Afrique du Nord,* Vol. 30 (Paris: Editions du CNRS, 1994).

27. See Jacob Mundy, "Neutrality or Complicity? The United States and the 1975 Moroccan Takeover of the Spanish Sahara," *The Journal of North African Studies,* Vol. 11, 3 (September 2006): 275–306.

28. For detailed analyses of U.S. policy toward the Western Sahara conflict, see Yahia H. Zoubir, "Stalemate in Western Sahara: Ending International Legality," *Middle East Policy,* Vol. 14, no. 4 (Winter 2007–2008): 158–77; Yahia H. Zoubir and Daniel Volman, "The United States and Conflict in the Maghreb," *Journal of North African Studies,* Vol. 2, no. 3 (1998): 10–24. Stephen Zunes, "The United States in the Saharan War: A Case of Low-Intensity Intervention" and Richard B. Parker, "US Strategic Interests and the War in the Western Sahara," in *International Dimensions of the Western Sahara Conflict,* ed. Yahia H. Zoubir and Daniel Volman (Westport, CT: Praeger, 1993). See also Claudia Wright, "Journey to Marrakesh: US-Moroccan Security Relations," *International Security,* 7, 4 (Spring 1983).

29. Harold Nelson, ed., *Morocco: A Country Study* (Washington, DC: US GPO, 1985), 354.

30. Yasmine Djaber, "L'Algérie Plaide Pour une Convention Générale de Lutte contre le Terrorisme," Toutsurlalgerie, September, 2008, http://www.tsa-algerie.com/diplomatie/l-algerie-plaide-pour-une-convention-generale-de-lutte-contre-le-terrorisme_4948.html.

31. For detailed analysis, see Yahia H. Zoubir, "Algeria and U.S. Interests: Containing Radical Islamism and Promoting Democracy," *Middle East Policy,* Vol. 9 (March 1, 2002): 64–81.

32. H. B., "W. J. Burns se Prononce sur la Prochaine Présidentielle," *Le Jeune Indépendant* (Algiers), October 26, 2003.

33. See, Daniel Volman, "Foreign Arms Sales and the Military Balance in the Maghreb," in *North Africa in Transition: State, Society, and Economic Transformations in the 1990s,* ed. Yahia H. Zoubir (Gainesville, FL: University Press of Florida, 1999). Algeria's arms imports had decreased by 50 percent in the 1990s due not only to the embargo but also to Algeria's near-bankruptcy.

34. See Robert D. Kaplan, *Hog Pilots, Blue Water Grunts-The American Military in the Air, Sea, and on the Ground* (New York: Random House, 2007).

35. These figures are taken from FY 2009 International Affairs (Function 150) Congressional Budget Justification, http://www.state.gov/f/releases/iab/fy2009cbj/.

36. These figures are taken from U.S. Department of State, "FY 2011 Foreign Operations, Congressional Budget Justification," Vol. 2, www.state.gov/documents/organization/137936.pdf.

37. U.S. Department of State*, Congressional Budget Justification, Foreign Assistance, Summary Table, Fiscal Year 2012,* Released March and April 2011, http://www.state.gov/documents/organization/158269.pdf.

38. Zoubir's Interview with high-ranking Algerian officer, December 2006.

39. Mahmoud G. El Warfally, *Imagery and Ideology in US Policy Toward Libya, 1969–1982* (Pittsburgh: University of Pittsburgh Press, 1988), 155.

40. Dirk Vandewalle, *Libya since Independence* (London: I.B. Tauris, 1998), 121.

41. Thomas Bodenheimer and Robert Gould, *Rollback! Right-wing Power in US Foreign Policy* (Boston, MA: South End Press, 1989).

42. For more on this see Joseph T. Stanik, *El Dorado Canyon: Reagan's Undeclared War with Qaddafi* (Annapolis, MD: Naval Institute Press, 2003); Bob Woodward, "CIA Anti-Qaddafi Plan Backed," *The Washington Post,* November 3, 1985, A19. Seymour M. Hersh, "Target Qaddafi," *The New York Times Magazine,* February 22, 1987, 74.

43. William Clinton, "American Security in a Changing World" in Remarks at George Washington University, Washington, DC, August 5, 1996, *US Department of State Dispatch,* Vol. 7. no. 32, 401–5.

44. For detailed analysis of the normalization process between the two countries, see Yahia H. Zoubir, "The United States and Libya: the Limits of Coercive Diplomacy," *The Journal of North African Studies,* Vol. 16, no. 2 (June 2011): 275–97.

45. Ronald Bruce St. John, "Libya Is Not Iraq": Preemptive Strikes, WMD and Diplomacy" in *The Middle East Journal,* Vol. 58, no. 3 (July 2004): 386–402.

46. Yahia H. Zoubir, "Contestation Islamiste et Lutte Antiterroriste en Libye, 1990–2007," *L'Année du Maghreb 2008* (Paris: CNRS Editions, 2008), 267–77.

47. Carlos Echeverria Jesús, "Radical Islam in the Maghreb," *Orbis* (Spring 2004), 7. See also Moncef Djaziri, "La Libye: les Élites Politiques, la Stratégie de 'Sortie' de Crise et la Réinsertion dans le Système International," *Annuaire de l'Afrique du Nord 1999,* Vol. 38 (Paris: CNRS, 2002).

48. Alison Pargeter, "Localism and Radicalization in North Africa: Local Factors and the Development of Political Islam in Morocco, Tunisia and Libya," in *International Affairs,* 85, 5 (2009): 1031–44.

49. Ron Suskind, "The Tyrant Who Came In From the Cold," *The Washington Monthly,* Vol. 38, no. 10, October 1, 2006.

50. Chistopher Blanchard, *Libya: Background and US Relations,* Congressional Research Service, CRS Report for Congress August 2009, http://www.fas.org/sgp/crs/mideast/RL33142.pdf.

51. Yahia H. Zoubir, "The United States and Maghreb-Sahel Security," *International Affairs,* Vol. 85, no. 5 (September 2009): 977–95.

52. The Telegraph, *Encouraging CEN-SAD to Cooperate with TSCTP and Africom Tripoli* 00000371 001.2 of 002, January 31, 2011, http://www.telegraph.co.uk/news/wikileaks-files/libya-wikileaks/8294557/ENCOURAGING-CEN-SAD-TO-COOPERATE-WITH-TSCTP-AND-AFRICOM-TRIPOLI-00000371–001.2-OF-002.html.

53. Robert Burns, "General: US Gains from Ties with Libya," *Associated Press,* April 21, 2005.

54. The Telegraph, *Encouraging CEN-SAD to cooperate with TSCTP and Africom Tripoli* 00000371 001.2 of 002, January 31, 2011, http://www.telegraph.co.uk/news/wikileaks-files/libya-wikileaks/8294557/ENCOURAGING-CEN-SAD-TO-COOPERATE-WITH-TSCTP-AND-AFRICOM-TRIPOLI-00000371–001.2-OF-002.html.

55. WikiLeaks-Viewing cable 08TRIPOLI992, Libya Interested in U.S. Weapons, More Ambivalent on Other Military Cooperation, http://wikileaks.org/cable/2008/12/08TRIPOLI992.html. It seems that Libya wished to make U.S. sales of military equipment, both lethal and nonlethal, and security guarantees as a litmus test of U.S. real intentions toward Libya. The Community of Sahel-Saharan States, CEN-SAD, was the creation of Qaddafi, who wished to integrate the African continent. The organization started with six countries; it now regroups 28 countries. Algeria never adhered to CEN-SAD.

56. U.S. Africa Command, *The Trans-Saharan Counter-Terrorism Partnership,* http://www.africom.mil/tsctp.asp.

57. U.S. Department of State, *Background Note on Libya,* November 17, 2010, http://www.state.gov/r/pa/ei/bgn/5425.htm.

58. J. Peter Pham, "United States, Libya, Sign Historic Pact on Military Cooperation," *DefendDemocracy*, March 5, 2009, http://www.defenddemocracy.org/index.php?option = com_content&task = view&id = 11784842&Itemid = 0.

59. U.S. Department of State, *Congressional Budget Justification, Foreign Operations, Fiscal Year 2010*, Vol. 2, *Request by Region*, 441, http://www.state.gov/documents/organization/124072.pdf.

60. U.S. Department of State, *Congressional Budget Justification, Foreign Operations, Annex: Regional Perspectives, Fiscal Year 2011*, 497.

61. U.S. Department of State, *Congressional Budget Justification, Foreign Operations*, Congressional Budget Requests for fiscal years 2010 and 2011.

62. U.S. Department of State, *Congressional Budget Justification, Foreign Assistance, Summary Table, Fiscal Year 2012,* Released March and April 2011, http://www.state.gov/documents/organization/158269.pdf.

63. For a similar point, see Emma Murphy, "The Foreign Policy of Tunisia," in, *The Foreign Policies of Middle East States,* ed. Raymond Hinnebusch and Anoushiravan Ehteshami (Boulder, CO: Lynne Reinner Publishers, 2002), 235; Nicole Grimaud's *La Tunisie à la Recherche de sa Sécurité* (Paris: Presse Universitaire de France, 1995) provides the best account of Tunisia's conception of security.

64. Abdennour Benantar, "Etats-Unis et Tunisie: Singularité Tunisienne," in, *Les Etats-Unis et le Maghreb: Regain d'intérêt?* ed. Abdennour Benantar (Algiers: CREAD, 2007),180.

65. Yahia H. Zoubir, "Algeria and U.S. Interests: Containing Radical Islamism and Promoting Democracy," *Middle East Policy,* Vol. 9 (March 1, 2002): 64–81.

66. See Daniel Volman, "Foreign Arms Sales and the Military Balance in the Maghreb," in *North Africa in Transition: State, Society, and Economic Transformations in the 1990s,* ed. Yahia H. Zoubir (Gainesville, FL: University Press of Florida, 1999), 224.

67. http://www.state.gov/t/pm/64779.htm.

68. Al Pessin, Rumsfeld, "Discusses Expanding Military Ties with Tunisia," February 11, 2006, http://www.globalsecurity.org/military/library/news/2006/02/mil-060211-voa03.htm.

69. "Congressional Budget Justification 2007," http://www.state.gov/documents/organization/60641.pdf.

70. See U.S. Department of State, *Congressional Budget Justification, Foreign Operations, Annex: Regional Perspectives, Fiscal Year 2011* (Washington, DC: March 2010), www.state.gov/documents/organization/137937.pdf.

71. "U.S. Gave Tunisia $32 million in Military Aid: General," Defense News, April 24, 2012, http://www.defensenews.com/article/20120424/DEFREG04/304240005/.

72. U.S. Department of State, *Congressional Budget Justification, Fiscal Year 2013, Foreign Operations,* Vol. 2, 510, http://www.state.gov/documents/organization/185014.pdf.

73. Jim Garamone, "Secretary Begins Trip to North Africa, Middle East," American Forces Press Service, July 29, 2012, http://www.globalsecurity.org/military/library/news/2012/07/mil-120729-afps01.htm?_m = 3n%2e002a%2e567%2epd0ao00kra%2eihw.

74. Jiří Holík, "European Policy towards the Maghreb: Learning from the Past?" *Global Europe,* April 18, 2012, http://www.global-europe.org/detail-articles.php?articles=0000000025.

75. Federica Bicci, "The European Origins of Euro-Mediterranean Practices," Working Paper AY0406-12, University of Berkeley, Institute of European Studies, June 12, 2004, 6, http://escholarship.org/uc/item/8c44c395#page-1.

76. George Joffé, "The European Union and the Maghreb in the 1990s," in *North Africa: Politics, Region, and the Limits of Transformation,* ed. Yahia H. Zoubir and Haizam Amirah-Fernández, (London and New York: Routledge, 2008), 311.

77. See George Joffé, "The European Union, Democracy, and Counter-Terrorism in the Maghreb," *Journal of Common Market Studies,* 46, 1 (2008): 154.

78. See George Joffé, "The European Union, Democracy, and Counter-Terrorism in the Maghreb," *Journal of Common Market Studies,* 46, 1 (2008): 154.

79. EUROPOL, *EU Terrorism Situation and Trend Report 2007* (The Hague: Europol, March), 5, https://www.europol.europa.eu/sites/default/files/publications/tesat2007.pdf.

80. See, for instance, Achira Mammeri, "Algeria Goes High-Tech to Confront Organized Crime," *Magharebia,* May 20, 2008, http://magharebia.com/cocoon/awi/xhtml1/en_GB/features/awi/features/2008/05/20/feature-01.

81. Verónica Martins, "Externalization of Cross-Pillar Approach: the EU-Maghreb Case," Paper presented at The Pan European International Relations Conference 2010; "Politics in Hard Times: International Relations Responses to the Financial Crisis," Stockholm, September 10, 2010, 18.

82. Souhayma Ben Achour and Monia Ben Jemia, "Révolution Tunisienne et Migration Clandestine vers l'Europe: Réactions Européennes et Tunisiennes," *CARIM Analytic and Synthetic Notes,* 2011/65, Robert Schuman Center for Advanced Studies, http://cadmus.eui.eu/handle/1814/18977.

83. M. Kananen, "Externalization of Migration Management—the Libyan Case," *Newropeans Magazine,* February 27, http://www.newropeans-magazine.org/content/view/8957/1/.

84. Yahia H. Zoubir, "Libya and Europe: Economic Realism at the Rescue of the Qaddafi Authoritarian Regime," *Journal of Contemporary European Studies,* Vol. 17, no. 3 (December 2009): 410.

85. Cited in Claudia Gazzini, "Assessing Italy's Grande Gesto to Libya," *Middle East Report Online,* March 16, 2009, . http://www.merip.org/mero/mero031609.

86. Jiří Holík, "European Policy towards the Maghreb: Learning from the Past?" *Global Europe,* April 18, 2012, http://www.global-europe.org/detail-articles.php?articles = 0000000025.

87. Anthony H. Cordesman, Arleigh A. Burke, and Aram Nerguizian, *The North African Military Balance: Force Developments & Regional Challenges,* Center for International and Strategic Studies, December 7, 2010, 28, http://csis.org/files/publication/101203_North_African_Military_Balance_final.pdf.

88. A. Barnett, "MoD Targets Libya and Iraq as 'Priority' Arms Sales Targets," *The Observer,* September 26, 2006, http://www.guardian.co.uk/uk/2006/sep/24/politics.military.

89. Des Carney, "Arming the Maghreb," *ISN Security Watch,* November 17, 2009, http://www.isn.ethz.ch/isn/layout/set/print/content/view/full/73?id=109644&lng=en.

90. Africa Europe Faith and Justice Network—*AEFJN,* "Arms Exports and Transfers: Europe to Africa by Country," December 2010, 27, http://www.aefjn.org/index.php/arms-361/articles/aefjn-report-arms-exports-and-transfers-europe-to-africa-2107.html.

91. See "Libya," in Amnesty International, "Arms Transfers to the Middle East and North Africa: Lessons for an Effective Arms Trade Treaty," 2011, 37–53, http://www.amnesty.org/en/library/asset/ACT30/117/2011/en/049fdeee-66fe-4b13-a90e-6d7773d6a546/act301172011en.pdf.

92. Des Carney, "Arming the Maghreb," http://www.isn.ethz.ch/isn/layout/set/print/content/view/full/73?id=109644&lng=en.

93. "Second of Three Sigma Frigates Transferred to Royal Moroccan Navy," *Defense Web,* March 14, 2012, http://www.defenceweb.co.za/index.php?option = com_content&view = art icle&id=24360&catid=74&Itemid=30.

94. Des Carney, "Arming the Maghreb," http://www.isn.ethz.ch/isn/layout/set/print/content/view/full/73?id=109644&lng=en.Africa Europe Faith and Justice Network—*AEFJN,* "Arms Exports and Transfers: Europe to Africa by Country," December 2010, 27, http://www.aefjn.org/index.php/arms-361/articles/aefjn-report-arms-exports-and-transfers-europe-to-africa-2107.html.

95. Africa Europe Faith and Justice Network—*AEFJN,* "Arms Exports and Transfers: Europe to Africa by Country," December 2010, 26, http://www.aefjn.org/index.php/arms-361/articles/aefjn-report-arms-exports-and-transfers-europe-to-africa-2107.html.

96. "Dépenses Militaires Algériennes: en Hausse de 44% en 2011," *El Watan,* May 24, 2012.

97. *AEFJN,* "Arms Exports and Transfers: Europe to Africa by Country," December 2010, 26, http://www.aefjn.org/index.php/arms-361/articles/aefjn-report-arms-exports-and-transfers-europe-to-africa-2107.html

98. "The oil and gas producing countries of North Africa and the Middle East," IFP Energies Nouvelles, Panorama Technical Report 2012, http://www.ifpenergiesnouvelles.com/publications/notes-de-synthese-panorama/panorama-2012, 6. See also *BP Statistical Review of World Energy 2012,* http://www.bp.com/sectionbodycopy.do?categoryId=7500&contentId=7068481.

99. EUROSTAT Statistical Books, *European Business: Facts and Figures,* 2009, 78, http://epp.eurostat.ec.europa.eu/cache/ITY_OFFPUB/KS-BW-09-001/EN/KS-BW-09-001-EN.PDF.

100. Franz Eder, "The European Union's Counter-Terrorism Policy toward the Maghreb: Trapped between Democratization, Economic Interests, and the Fear of Destabilization," *European Security,* 20, 3 (September 2011): 442.

101. For a comprehensive study on the 5+5 Dialogue, see Jean-François Coustillière, ed., *Le 5+5 Face aux Défis du Réveil Arabe* (Paris, L'Harmattan, 2012).

102. Eugenia Pecoraro, "China's Strategy in North Africa: New Economic Challenges for the Mediterranean Region," *EUGOV, Working Paper No. 26/2010,* http://www.iuee.eu/pdf-publicacio/186/If6YcJztGdNXbHibFVLF.PDF.

103. Daniel Volman, "AFRICOM: What is it and What will it Do?" *Review of African Political Economy,* 34, 114 (December 2007): 737–44.

104. Gaïdi Mohamed Faouzi, "Des Hélicoptères AH-64 Américains et MI- 28 Russes pour l'Algérie," *El Watan,* May 24, 2012, http://www.russia-algeria.ru/5/Elwatan/052012/20120524.pdf.

105. Zoubir's interviews with Chinese scholars in Beijing and in Shanghai, 2010, 2011, 2012.

106. SIPRI Arms Transfers Database, http://www.sipri.org/databases/armstransfers.

107. SIPRI Arms Transfers Database, http://www.sipri.org/databases/armstransfers; *AEFJN,* "Arms Exports and Transfers: Europe to Africa by Country," December 2010, 26, http://www.aefjn.org/index.php/arms-361/articles/aefjn-report-arms-exports-and-transfers-europe-to-africa-2107.html, 21, (no longer accessible online); Paul Holtom, "Russian Arms Transfers to North Africa: Fuelling an Arms Race?" *RIA Novosti,* March 15, 2010, http://en.rian.ru/analysis/20100315/158200374.html.

108. Mark N. Katz, "The Russian-Libyan Rapprochement: What Has Moscow Gained?" *Middle East Policy,* 15, 3 (September 2008), http://www.mcpc.org/journal/middle-east-policy-archives/russian-libyan-rapprochement-what-has-moscow-gained.

109. Mark N. Katz, "The Russian-Libyan Rapprochement: What Has Moscow Gained?" *Middle East Policy,* 15, 3 (September 2008), http://www.mepc.org/journal/middle-east-policy-archives/russian-libyan-rapprochement-what-has-moscow-gained.

110. Keri Wagstaff-Smith, "Russia prepares to sell weapons worth $2.5 billion to Libya," *Jane's Defense,* April 16, 2008, http://www.janes.com/products/janes/defence-security-report.aspx?id=1065927845. The account was based on reports from Russian sources.

111. "Russia Loses $4 Billion in Libya Because of Gaddafi," *Pravda,* February 2, 2012, http://english.pravda.ru/russia/economics/02-02-2012/120401-russia_libya_gaddafi-0/.

112. Nicole Grimaud, *La Politique Extérieure de l'Algérie* (Paris: Karthala, 1984), 147.

113. For detailed analysis, see Yahia H. Zoubir, "Algeria and Russia: Reconciling Contrasting Interests," *The Maghreb Review,* 36, 3 (September 2011): 99–126.

114. Daniel Volman, "The Role of Foreign Military in the Western Sahara War," in *International Dimensions of the Western Sahara Conflict,* ed. Yahia H. Zoubir and Daniel Volman (Westport, CT, 1993), 159.

115. Nicole Grimaud, "La Diplomatie sous Chadli ou la Politique du Possible," *Annuaire de l'Afrique du Nord*, tome 30 (Paris, Editions du CNRS, 1994), 428.

116. Antonio Sánchez Andrés, "Political-Economic Relations between Russia and North Africa," *Real Instituto Elcano, Working Paper 22/2006,* November 7, 2006, 5.

117. Oksana Antonenko, "Russia's Military Involvement in the Middle East," Middle East Review of International Affairs (MERIA), Vol. 5, no. 1 (March 2001), http://www.gloria-center.org/meria/2001/03/cover.pdf.

118. Oksana Antonenko, "Russia's Military Involvement in the Middle East," *Middle East Review of International Affairs* (MERIA), Vol. 5, no. 1 (March 2001), http://www.gloria-center.org/meria/2001/03/cover.pdf.

119. These figures have been calculated from SIPRI reports by Derek Lutterbeck and Georgij Engelbrecht, "The West and Russia in the Mediterranean: Towards a Renewed Rivalry?" *Mediterranean Politics,* 14, 3 (2009): 385.

120. Yahia H. Zoubir, "The United States and Maghreb-Sahel Security," *International Affairs,* 85, 5, (September 2009), 977–95.

121. *Le Jeune Indépendant,* April 7, 2001.

122. Mouloud Aït-Chaâlal, "Algérie—Russie—Un Contrat Militaire pour 2,5 Milliards de Dollars," *Le Jeune Indépendant,* April 5, 2001, reprinted in http://www.algeria-watch.org/farticle/russie.htm. "Algeria and Russia to Develop Bilateral Cooperation in all Spheres," *Alexander's Oil and Gas Connections,* May 27, 2001, http://www.gasandoil.com/news/2001/07/ntr12717.

123. Site of the Algerian Air Force, http://www.mdn.dz/site_cfa/index.php?L=fr.

124. Les moyens que nous acquerrons auprès de la Russie n'entraîneront aucun déséquilibre stratégique dans la région (. . .); les moyens que nous avons et que nous moderniserons, et (ceux) que nous acquerrons sont destinés à la défense de l'intégrité de notre territoire . . . *Algeria Interface,* May 28, 2002. This publication no longer exists.

125. "Russian Arms Score Big in North Africa," *UPI,* March 16, 2010, http://www.upi.com/Business_News/Security-Industry/2010/03/16/Russian-arms-score-big-in-North-Africa/UPI-53521268771381.

126. Stephanie Torres, "General F-16 News: Morocco Receives first F16s," *F-16.Net,* August 5, 2011, http://www.f-16.net/news_article4403.html.

127. For a thorough, extensive assessment of the Maghreb Armed Forces and their equipment, see Anthony H. Cordesman, Arleigh A. Burke, and Aram Nerguizian, *The North African Military Balance: Force Developments & Regional Challenges,* Center for International and Strategic Studies, December 7, 2010, 28, http://csis.org/files/publication/101203_North_African_Military_Balance_final.pdf.

128. N. Ryad, "Après L'Effacement des Créances Militaires Russes: Le Grand Flou sur le Nouveau Volume de la Dette Extérieure Algérienne," *Liberté,* March 12, 2006, http://www.liberte-algerie.com/edit.php?id = 54022.

129. Zahir Benmostepha "Aucune Déclaration Algéro-Russe sur les Tractations Militaires-Mutisme sur les Contrats des Mig," *Liberté,* February 21, 2008, http://www.liberte-algerie.com/edit.php?id = 90743&titre = Mutisme sur les contrats des Mig.

130. Rafik Benkaci, "Remboursement de la Dette et Achat d'Armes Alger-Moscou: Le Compromis," *Liberté,* March 11, 2006, http://www.liberte-algerie.com/edit.php?id = 53969&titre = Alger-Moscou: Le compromis; "Algeria Could Become Russia's Main Military Partner," *RIA Novosti* (Moscow), March 29, 2007, http://en.rian.ru/russia/20070329/62781987.html.

131. "Germany Okays 10 bln Euro Defence Deal with Algeria," *Reuters,* July 3, 2011, http://www.reuters.com/article/2011/07/03/germany-algeria-arms-idUSLDE76209K20110703; see also, "L'Algérie Muscle sa Défense," *Zone Militaire Opex360,* July 5, 2011, http://www.opex360.com/2011/07/05/lalgerie-muscle-sa-defense/.

132. Guy Martin, "Algerian Navy Purchases Two Tiger Corvettes from Russia," July 1 2011, http://www.defenceweb.co.za/index.php?view=article&catid=51%3ASea&id=16804%3Aalgerian-navy-purchases-two-tiger-corvettes-from-russia&format=pdf&option=com_content&Itemid=106.

133. "Russia to Build Two Tiger Corvettes for Algerian Navy," *RIA Novosti* (St. Petersburg), June 30, 2011, http://en.rian.ru/russia/20110630/164924783.html.

134. "Algerian Navy Orders Vessel from Italy," UPI, August 2, 2011, http://www.upi.com/Business_News/Security-Industry/2011/08/02/Algerian-navy-orders-vessel-from-Italy/UPI-34201312308517/.

Conclusion

In raising the national security problem in the Maghreb, the question as to why the Maghreb countries do not follow the logic of collective security policy is worth asking. It needs to be investigated whether there is awareness of the need to move from national security to collective Maghreb security. Another question worth looking at is to know if the construction of Maghreb security can be conceivable without the construction of a Maghreb market as a precondition. In this book, we have provided a general perspective on the different facets of security in the Maghreb. We have reviewed the challenges, issues, levels, and dimensions of security. We uncovered the structural and cyclical vulnerabilities of the Maghreb, which appear as the source of threats for its own members but also for the non–North African players.

Although security cooperation in the Maghreb is limited and partial, it is nonetheless real. For instance, the Maghreb countries cooperate against terrorism in the Sahel, in the TSCTP, and on various issues within the 5 + 5 Dialogue. If this cooperation undoubtedly exists, it is however more sectorial (intelligence, border control, and combating terrorism) than comprehensive. This cooperation addresses short-term challenges; that is, it occurs in reaction to immediate imperatives and emergencies; a long-term perspective is thus absent in the conception of national security developed by the Maghreb security establishments. Because of the suspicions that characterize their relations, cooperation among the Maghreb states is articulated in a variable geometry depending on the stakeholders (bilateral or with states outside the Maghreb); policy makers do not think in terms of a collective Pan-Maghreb security perspective.

These shortcomings are due to the historical conditions of the construction of the Maghreb states. In most cases, the emergence of the national state in the Maghreb has been the product of a long, arduous process punctuated by repetitive cycles of violence. These cycles of violence have put forth a group of actors who hold some kind of legitimacy on which they rely for claiming the right to control and manage the state. The nation-state in the Maghreb is shaped essentially by violence, which has turned into a mechanism of political regulation. Indeed, violence has become one of the regulatory mechanisms underlying the authoritarian character of the nation-state. If in Morocco the monarchical nature of the system underlies the monopolization of power by the *Makhzen*, in the other Maghreb countries, the desire to preserve national unity has resulted in the ongoing imposition of political and ideological unanimity. However, whether liberal, like Morocco and Tunisia, or socialist, as was the case in Algeria and Libya, authoritarianism has been the common denominator in the four countries that make up the Maghreb. One might conclude that some sort of historical determinism justifies the authoritarian nature of the Maghreb countries, but it remains true that the elites who took power after independence have favored the centralizing and authoritarian nature of the state. However, this multifaceted and evolving authoritarianism gained an important source of legitimacy, namely, the need for security, which is linked to genuine insecurity, perceived or exaggerated. We can consider that bilateral tensions between Morocco and Algeria, between Algeria and Libya, and between Morocco and Mauritania, for example, have fueled the sense of insecurity among the ruling elites. The other insecurity causes are linked to internal tensions symbolized by the rise of armed Islamism, social movements, and sometimes violent insurgencies, which contributed greatly to keep, rightly or wrongly, a climate of insecurity. Almost six decades after the independence of the Maghreb countries, the authoritarian nature of their regimes is still under debate. Beyond this, the question of the nature of the state or more precisely the kind of social contract that binds the ruling elites to civil societies has still to be fully elucidated. Undoubtedly, the revolts that have shaken the countries in the region in 2011, either radically (Tunisia and Libya) or less dramatically (Algeria and Morocco), have accelerated this challenge. That said, the political changes do not suggest, at the time of this writing, a sweeping transformation of the security design. The precarious situation in the post–civil war in Libya, in particular, as well as the direct connections with security instability in the Sahel, have suddenly moved the debate of security to the level of hard security, when in fact political changes, democratic transition, and representative legitimacy are supposed to place the cursor on the soft dimension of security. The economic and political aspects are, of course very important, but are not considered a priority owing to the immediate security and the short-term risks.

Since independence, the Maghreb regimes have become managers of violence; they imposed a political order in which the regime's survival has been equated with that of the state. The most significant example is the Libyan case, where the institutions themselves had been personalized. Hence, a chaos resulted from the fall of Muammar Qaddafi, who had created a security order in which the regular army was marginalized in favor of paramilitary structures (*kataib*) and proved totally incapable of managing a popular uprising, having to also face foreign military intervention. Less symptomatic, but no less real, is the confusion between regime security and that of the state in Morocco, Tunisia, and Algeria. In the first case, the survival of the monarchy predetermines the reality of the state. The two attempted military coups against the king in the 1970s sustain this hypothesis. In Tunisia, the military had been marginalized by one of its own, Ben Ali, in favor of the police, a security structure that ensured the systematic control of society, in order to protect the Ben Ali regime against any popular uprising. Also, it is precisely this marginalization that proved to be the Achilles' heel of the regime, leading to its downfall. In Algeria, the creation of the armed forces preceded the construction of the state; the military proclaimed itself the guarantor of the state's existence. The official depoliticization of the military after 1989 did not, however, deprive the regime of its backbone: the military, or more precisely, the intelligence services. The conflict in the 1990s confirmed this postulate. The fundamental question of course is whether this means that popular democratic transitions would succeed in civilianizing the regimes and reduce the de facto security obsession of the Maghreb states. In order to address this question, we may envisage two scenarios.

The first scenario may be imagined as one where the initiation of the democratic transition results in the civilianization of security management. In post–Ben Ali Tunisia, the transition has occasioned the demobilization of the security establishment and the quasi civilianization of the regime. This may foreshadow the emergence of a peaceful adjudication of political and social conflicts. Logically, repression will cease to be the means of regulating sociopolitical conflicts. The completion of this process might augur the birth of a sequence through which the security of the state takes precedence over the security of the regime. Therefore, the security of the regime will be decided at the polls.

In Libya, the almost total dismantling of the authoritarian security apparatus marked the beginning of the civilianization of the regime. This trend might be reinforced by a combination of factors: the victory in July 2012 of the liberal movement in the first multiparty post-Qaddafi elections; the political support of many influential actors (Western countries and the Gulf monarchies); and the economic prospects in terms of modernization of the oil industry, increased production, and new oil discoveries. Libya has a small population and considerable wealth. Theoretically, it has the opportunity of building everything anew since few modern institutions existed under the Qaddafi regime. Therefore, the collapse of the regime has provided the new authorities with the possibility of erecting a modern state endowed with democratic institutions. Under such scenario, civilian control of the security services can be envisaged.

As to Morocco, the heart of the security problem lies mainly in occupied Western Sahara and the protracted irresolution of the dispute. While it is reasonable to foresee the transformation of Morocco from a constitutional monarchy to a parliamentary monarchy, the acceptance of a referendum in Western Sahara as a definitive solution remains implausible. Indeed, the idea that Western Sahara belongs to Morocco has garnered national consensus domestically, no matter the ideological differences among the political parties. Besides, the Sahrawi question is no longer managed exclusively through security means. The strategy of King Mohammed VI has been to pursue a political-administrative project to incorporate the disputed territory into the kingdom; the security strategy consisting of annexing the territory through force having failed, thus compelling the regime to use other means.

In Algeria, the election of a civilian president has not completely excluded from power the security services, even if their role in the decision-making process has declined compared to what it was before 1999 when Bouteflika took office. Indubitably, the democratic transformation will change the nature of military-civilian relations in such a way that the management of security affairs would no longer be the sole responsibility of the security services and be submitted to scrutiny in an elected, legitimate parliament. Furthermore, the promotion of a younger generation of personnel to the military command has already resulted in the nomination of highly qualified senior officers, less politicized and capable of maintaining a dispassionate relationship with the legitimacy gained by their elders through the war of liberation. This trend could be greatly enhanced if the current project of professionalization of the army continues and succeeds.

The second scenario is one where the transition to democracy does not lead to the civilianization of the management of the security sector. In Tunisia, the fragility of the institutional order and the fragility of the new social contract have already underscored the vulnerabilities that may potentially constitute sources of insecurity. Thus, the secular nature of the republic is now facing politico-religious forces that represent a challenge to the future of the secular state and the management of security. The ability of the new ruling elite to keep the debate on the ideological terrain and prevent any drift toward the security sphere depends on the ability of the authorities to meet adequately the socioeconomic needs of the population: requirements, which remain dependent on overseas sources (FDI, tourism, and growth).

In Libya, the first optimistic scenario must be tempered by elements of structural instability. First, the fall of Qaddafi's repressive machinery has led to the de-monopolization of the legitimate use of violence because of the emergence of new actors claiming revolutionary legitimacy. Second, like in Tunisia, radical Islamist movements justify their right to resort to violence in the name of their historic opposition to the old regime. The multiplicity of actors, notably the armed militias, claiming the legitimate use of violence has transformed Libya into a de facto platform used to fuel violence in other regions (Sahel, Syria). Third, the fragility of the old political structure had kept the national feeling in an embryonic state, which explains the emergence today of secessionist tendencies of the federalists in Cyrenaica and Fezzan. These three factors of insecurity may be reduced if the new ruling elite manage to disarm the militias who believe in violence as a means of political arbitration. The challenge is not, as in Tunisia to prevent the emergence of violence in the political debate, but appease political tensions. Furthermore, in Libya the tribal and regional rivalries make sociopolitical consensus difficult. The intertribal tensions resulting from the violence during the civil war and the acquisition of weapons by the tribes (and the militias) will be difficult to overcome. Thus, the ability of the new authorities to mediate between the tribes and achieve national consensus will certainly be constrained by the countries' sociological realities.

With regard to Morocco, the decision of the Alaouite monarchy to adhere to the GCC reveals the conservative tendencies of the monarchy rather than any genuine radical reformist initiatives. However, even assuming that the shift of status from that of a constitutional monarchy to a parliamentary monarchy is possible, the abandonment of the obsession with security, especially in the handling of Western Sahara, is not certain. First, the army whose task has been to pacify the region could refuse marginalization and demand a greater role in the management of the state. The commercial benefits that many high-ranking officers are drawing from their presence in Western Sahara makes a resolution of the conflict even more uncertain. Therefore, the civilianization of the Moroccan government will not automatically ease relations with Algeria. Finally, Morocco is faced with other sources of insecurity, such as social deprivation, trafficking of all kinds, and illegal migration. The security establishment will be reluctant to devolve old security prerogatives to civilians.

Regarding Algeria, even if civilianization of power occurs, it is not certain that the traditional obsession with security will recede. Several reasons account for this. First, the civilianization, which began in 1999 with the election of a civilian president seems to have remained a mere façade as decision-making in the security realm continues to be the prerogative of the army and intelligence services. Second, as long as terrorism continues to threaten national security, the status of the security services will be strengthened at the expense of civilians. Third, due to geopolitical imperatives (multiple, long, difficult borders to control; passageways of drugs, illicit trafficking; the junction between sub-Saharan Africa and Europe) handling of these issues requires security measures, and it is debatable whether the managers of violence view the treatment of the threats from another prism than that of security.

If the transition to democracy in the Maghreb countries is highly likely to streamline the management of security in those countries, one can raise the question whether this will necessarily translate into the creation of common Maghreb security.

In the first scenario, we can imagine a democratic Maghreb becoming the foundation of Maghreb security. With the emergence of democratic regimes, we might assume that bilateral and multilateral relations will obviously be less tense because of the presence of the following: renewed political elite; less passionate relations; elite less attached to the glorification of the past; and, more importantly, a condition, which has never been posited hitherto, authorities being held accountable to their respective public opinion about the decisions they make. On another level, this democratization could lead to the emergence of entrepreneurs inclined to promote market values and free trade, especially as the current political and legal constraints would be removed if a successful transition takes place. This would necessarily produce a different logic: the construction of an integrated economic region that would defuse tensions and be based on new common interests. These are precisely the elements of the founding of Maghreb security. To these factors one should also consider the threats that these countries face, namely, illegal migration, environmental predicament, trafficking of all kinds, integration to extra-regional security arrangements (NATO Mediterranean Dialogue, 5 +5), which will compel the Maghreb countries to foster cooperation upstream, thus minimizing their contentious visions.

In the second scenario, we can visualize a democratic Maghreb, which fails to deliver collective security to the Maghreb. The prospect of the emergence of a democratic Maghreb may be unable to give birth to Maghreb security. First, the conditions for the emergence of new elites may prevent them from getting rid of the old demons. Co-optation through financial enticements, the return of former apparatchiks to power through democratic elections, or the election of a radical religious party to office would result in regime change without however any concomitant transformation of the values of the new regime compared to those of the old with respect to the management of security. The integration of the Maghreb in extra-regional security arrangements does not guarantee the reduction of tensions either—the case of Turkey and Greece being the best illustration. The economic aspects should not be neglected either. Indeed, a democratic Maghreb must also be a region where economic development among countries is more or less equivalent and complementary. Otherwise, tensions related to unemployment, smuggling, financial crime, and petty crime may be factors dissuading or complicating extensive security cooperation. Under these conditions, the countries of the region will certainly be more tempted to withdraw into themselves rather than open up to their neighbors. Today, intra-trade in the Maghreb remains one of the lowest of any region in the world (less than three percent). Development issues continue to be treated from a national perspective. Furthermore, the Maghreb countries are still primary commodities/energy producers and are thus dependent on Europe in their commercial relations. The complementarity between the economies of the Maghreb has been established; however, beyond rhetoric, the Maghreb regimes have shown little inclination to implement genuine integration, which could help accelerate their growth. Again, even in the area of trade, suspicions and lack of trust are one of the major characteristics in Maghreb relations despite cognizance that increased intra-regional trade can result in better standards of living and higher GDP growth. Experts have calculated that the lack of Maghreb integration has cost a loss of two percent of their GDP annually. There is consensus that an integrated Maghreb would attract more FDI. Greater cooperation in the form of joint Maghreb companies could alleviate some of the problems of unemployment and other challenges that the Maghreb states face. This scenario is yet to happen.

The uprisings in the Middle East and North Africa have compelled the Maghreb states to revive the Arab Maghreb Union that has been dormant since 1994. The pattern observed in the Maghreb is that whenever the regimes were confronted with serious opposition, such as the rise of radical Islamism in the 1980s, they tend to cooperate in order to meet those challenges. However, once the dangers have passed, they revert to the old balance of power game and compete with one another or make alliances to weaken one grouping against another. As already seen, the policies of the incumbent regimes have created realities that are hard to alter. Thus, the monarchy played so much on the "Moroccan-ness" or Western Sahara that social consensus has formed around this issue preventing the monarchy from moderating its position without risking major opposition to its legitimacy. The same applies to Algeria; can the security establishment accept annexation of Western Sahara by Morocco without retaliating against Morocco one way or the other? Undoubtedly, unless the question of Western Sahara is resolved in a fair manner, animosity between Algeria and Morocco will not abate as has been the case in the last two decades. No matter the reasons (modernization of the armed forces, the threat of Al Qaeda in the Islamic Maghreb, or regional rivalry) for armament programs in the Maghreb, the security dilemma will persist and so will the suspicions that exist between the neighbors, even if one assumes that a democratic Maghreb might be more cooperative. Furthermore, democratic processes take a long time and related questions can be raised: Will Islamist regimes continue to abide by the rules of democratic competition? Will they surrender power should they lose at the polls? Will Islamists regimes be more cooperative with each other or will national differences supersede ideological affinities? Will

Islamist states in the Maghreb represent a threat to more secular neighbors and vice versa? One cannot predict what the future security outlook of the Maghreb will be; however, one can wager that generational change, genuine integration, and political resolve based on trust will alter the perceptions prevailing in the region and may augur a democratic Maghreb and Maghreb collective security.

Biographies

ALGERIA

Abdelaziz Bouteflika

Born on March 2, 1937, he joined the National Army of Liberation (ALN) immediately after secondary school at the age of 19. He was general inspector of Wilaya V in 1957–1958. He joined as the chief of staff of the ALN based in western Algeria and later the general chief of staff. In 1960 he was based in the "Malian front; hence, his nickname "Abdelkader the Malian."

After Algeria's independence, Bouteflika was elected to the first Algerian parliament and then minister of sports and youth at the age of 25. In 1963, he became minister of foreign affairs. He took part in the coup d'état against President Ahmed Ben Bella in June 1965. He remained minister of foreign affairs until 1979.

As foreign minister, Bouteflika tried to apply the main principles of the country's foreign policy in terms of good neighborliness, a new international economic order, support for movements of liberation and the Palestinians, and the fight against apartheid. He played a key role in the summits of the Group of 77 in 1967 and 1968. In 1974 he was elected chairman of the ninth round of the United Nations General Assembly.

He left Algeria in 1980 and remained in self-imposed exile for several years. In 1994, he was asked to serve as chief of the state, but he declined the offer.

He returned to Algeria in April 1999 and was elected president. His strategic mission was to put the reconciliation process on track and improve the country's image on the international scene. He initiated vast economic projects, fulfilled the national reconciliation, concluded the Association Agreement with the European Union, participated in the NATO Dialogue, and played a key role in the NEPAD, the new economic project of African development. Bouteflika has been reelected twice, in 2004, and in 2009 after revising the 1996 Constitution in 2008; the 1996 Constitution had limited to two the number of the presidential mandates.

Mohammed Mediène aka General Tewfik

Unlike most senior members of the intelligence services, Tewfik is not from the wartime Ministry of Armament and General Liaisons (MALG). He belongs to the Red officers who received training at the KGB in the USSR.

He started his career as lieutenant in the second military region under the authority of Colonel Chadli Benjedid, who became the third president of Algeria in 1979. Tewfik worked as intelligence officer in a very sensitive region—the one that borders Morocco. During his stay in the second military region, he met Major Larbi Belkheir, the "the maker of presidents" who served then as chief of staff in that region. In 1983, he was sent to Tripoli, where he served in the staff of the Algerian Embassy. In 1986 he was appointed chief of the department of defense and security at the presidency when Larbi Belkheir served Chadli's chief of staff. When the General Department of Protection and Security (DGPS) was created in May 1987, Mohammed Mediène became the director of military security (the political police of the national army). The structure was dissolved after the October 1988 uprising; subsequently, the Security and Intelligence Department (DRS) replaced the military security. He has headed the DRS ever since.

His role became central after President Chadli's forced resignation in 1992 and more so during the violent confrontation with terrorist groups throughout the decade. He was the chief of the security forces, the external intelligence, and the army's security.

Not much is known about General Tewfik. His face is not known to the public.

Ahmed Ouyahia

He was born on July 2, 1952 in Tizi Ouzou, capital of the Kabylie, 60 miles east of Algiers. He graduated from the Institute of Political Science and from the prestigious National School of Administration in the 1970s. He served in the Ministry of Foreign Affairs as well as many embassies, namely, Cote d'Ivoire and Mali, where he served as ambassador in 1992–1995. From 1995 to 1998 he served as head of government. He occupied many high-level positions, as minister of justice between 1999 and 2002, and state minister, special representative of the president until 2003. He has been prime minister from 2008 to 2012.

Ahmed Ouyahia was the official mediator in the conflict between the Tuareg and the government in Mali in 1992 and in the Ethiopian-Eritrean conflict in 1999. Ouyahia also presided over the RND Party for 15 years; he stepped down in 2012.

Nourredine "Yazid" Zerhouni

He was born in 1937 in Tunis. He studied in secondary school in Morocco and obtained a bachelor's degree in law and a graduate degree in international relations. He joined the FLN in Morocco in 1955 and the Wilaya V of the ALN two years later. He contributed to the creation of the first military and political leadership school. In 1958, he created the Direction of Documentation and Research, a branch of the intelligence services. One year later, he was in charge of intelligence in the ALN.

Soon after independence, he was put in charge of developing the intelligence services in addition to the direction of international relations inside the Defense Ministry. In 1979, he was appointed head of the security direction of the state. In 1982, he started a diplomatic career and served as ambassador in Mexico, Japan, and the United States.

From 1999 to 2010, he was the all-powerful minister of the interior. Since then, he has been vice prime minister with no real power.

Abdelmalek Guenaizia

He was born on November 20, 1936 in Souk Ahras in eastern Algeria. He joined the national movement and the ALN in April 1958 as a training officer. Shortly after independence, he enrolled in military schools in the USRR and France. He became chief of staff, commander of division, and central director of supply and logistics in the Ministry of Defense. In 1973 he took part in the war against Israel as a chief of division.

In 1984, he was promoted to the rank of brigadier general and was appointed as the commander of the air force. General Guenaizia also occupied the position of deputy chief of staff of the ANP until 1990. In 1993, he retired and started a diplomatic career; he served as Algeria's ambassador to Switzerland, a position he held for seven years. In 2005, he was appointed minister-delegate for defense.

Daho Ould Kablia

Daho Ould Kablia was born on May 4, 1933 in Tangier, Morocco. Having passed his Baccalaureate in 1955, Ould Kablia undertook a law degree in Toulouse, France.

After Algeria's independence, he held many responsibilities in local administrations as a Wali (head of region) in Mostaghanem, Tiaret, Oran, Skikda, and Algiers.

In addition to these local government responsibilities, Ould Kablia occupied the function of general secretary of the Interior Ministry from 1980 to 1983.

Before being appointed as delegate minister to local collectivities Ould Kablia was a member of the senate. He was in charge of local collectivities for nine years until he succeeded Yazid Zerhouni as interior minister. Ould Kablia is the president of the powerful Association of Veterans of the MALG—the forerunner of the Algerian secret services.

Mourad Medelci

Mourad Medelci was born on April 30, 1943. He holds a graduate degree in economics from the University of Algiers. Before joining the government, Medelci held many managerial positions in Algerian companies. He worked as general secretary of the Ministry of Trade from 1980 to 1988. In 1988, he entered the government as trade minister and in 1990 as delegate minister for the budget. In 2001, he became finance minister. From 2002 to 2005, he served as adviser to President Bouteflika until 2005 before returning to the Finance Ministry. In June 2007, Medelci became minister of foreign affairs, a post he has occupied until now.

Ahmed Gaïd Salah

He was born on January 13, 1940 in Batna, eastern Algeria. He joined the national liberation movement at the age of 17. Shortly after independence, he undertook training in the USRR—training which allowed him to serve in the air force. He specialized in air defense, but also served as commander of intelligence services in the third military region. He then went on to become the commander of the southern intelligence sector (third military region), vice commander of the fifth military region, and the commander of the third and the second military regions. Gaid Salah was promoted to the rank of general in July 1993 and commander of the air force in 1994. He was nominated as chief of staff of the ANP in 2004, rising to the rank of lieutenant general in 2005—the highest rank in the Algerian Armed Forces. Unlike many of the senior generals, such as the late Mohamed Lamari, the elderly Gaïd has the reputation of being apolitical which explains the good rapport he has held with Bouteflika.

LIBYA

Muammar Qaddafi

Muhammad Mohammed Abdeslam Abu Meniar Qaddafi was born on July 7, 1942 in Syrte and died in the same city on October 20, 2011. He had the longest reign in Libya since 1951.

He was educated in Sabha in southern Libya. He joined the University of Benghazi in eastern Libya, but did not finish his studies and joined the military instead.

He was a big admirer of Egyptian President Gamal Abdel Nasser and his qawmiya Arabia (Arab nationalism). On September 1, 1969, Muammar Qaddafi was only 27 years old when he seized power through a coup d'etat against King Idriss el Sanusi. He replaced a pro-Western monarchy with the Jamahiriya (republic of the masses).

In the 1970s, Qaddafi published his Green Book in which he outlined his political philosophy. Initially focused on the unity of the Arab world, he turned his attention toward Africa. He tried in vain to become the king of African kings. His hostility toward the West and his links with terrorist groups and their violent actions resulted in his isolation for a long period. Because of his anti-Western policies and his support for various groups opposed to U.S. interests, the United States sought unsuccessfully to eliminate him.

Fouzi Taher Ahmed abdel Ali

He was born on July 1, 1971 in Misrata. He obtained a graduate degree in law from Qaryounes University in 1993. He was member of the High Security Commission, the National Council of Transition (NCT) in Misrata, the Local Council of Misrata, and the Military Commission of the NCT. He is also the president of the Security Commission of Misrata, the Investigation Commission of Misrata, and president of the Security Commission in the NCT. In addition to these numerous functions, he is also the director of the Commission against Drugs, Economic Crimes, and Illegal Immigration.

Mustapha Abdul Jalil

Mustapha Abdul Jalil is head of the National Transitional Council and former attorney general in the Qaddafi regime (2007–2011). He was born in 1952 in Al Beida. He graduated in Shari' a studies and law from the University of Libya (1975). He became prominent before the outbreak of the civil war on February 2011 when, as head of the justice department, he sentenced to death three of the Bulgarian nurses that had been accused of inoculating HIV viruses to Libyan children. Later, however, he publicly criticized the security agencies for continuing to detain prisoners despite the fact that they had been acquitted by the courts. When the violence broke out in February 2011, Qaddafi sent Mustpha Abdul Jalil to Benghazi to negotiate the release of hostages taken by Islamists. He was the first high-ranking official to announce his resignation from his position in the government to express his solidarity with the protesters. His resignation enhanced his credibility which helped him lead the National Transitional Council.

Abdul Fatah Younis

Born in 1940 in Jalu; he was a close associate of Muammar Qaddafi. His mother was Chadian and his father Libyan from the Mjabra tribe in central Libya. He was member of the Council of the Revolution in 1969 and became defense minister of the Jamahiriya, a position designated as Secretary of the Temporary General Commission of Defense. He was appointed chief of staff in 1970 and was promoted to the rank of colonel six years later. General Younis was not known to interfere in political affairs. When the revolt in February 2011 broke out, General Younis distanced himself from Colonel Qaddafi by refusing to repress the protesters. He was assassinated in mysterious circumstances on July 24, 2011.

Ossama Al Jouili

Ossama Al Jouili was born in 1961 in Zantan. He studied military science, specializing in electronic logistics. At the start of the revolt in February 2011, he played a leading role in creating the military council of Zantan. He led the military operations in Jebel el Gharbi and in the seaside cities of Zaouia, Serman, Ajilet, Sebrata, and Zwawa. Al Jouili led the operations that resulted in the capture of the airport and Qasr Ibn Ghashir. He resigned from his post as minister of defense in March 2012.

Achour Ben Khial

Achour Ben Khial was born in 1939 in Derna. After completing his studies in economics at the Libyan university in 1963, Ben Khial joined an accounting firm. He joined the Ministry of Foreign Affairs where he moved up through various positions. He was appointed to several diplomatic representations, such as Rome, New York, and Seoul. In 1984, Ben Khial resigned from his position in protest against the crimes committed by Qaddafi's regime and the repression of Libyan students in London. He joined the opposition and took a leading role in the creation of the National Congress of the Libyan Opposition over which he presided between 2005 and 2008.

Abdullah al-Megrahi al-Senussi (Former head of Libyan Intelligence Services)

Abdullah al-Senussi was born on December 5, 1949 in Barak Achatii. He belongs to the Megraha tribe to which Abdessalam Jalloud, one of the masterminds of the military coup of 1969, belongs. The Megraha tribe was one of most sympathetic to Qaddafi's regime even during the revolt of February 2011. However, the defection of Colonel Abdessalam Jalloud forced this tribe to distance themselves from the Al Qaddafi clan.

Senussi, after many years with the organization, became the head of the intelligence services. He was in charge of military intelligence and, later on, of foreign intelligence. He was the type of man that Colonel Qaddafi relied upon to assure the security of the regime. He is accused of eliminating many leading opposition figures, both inside Libya and abroad. Many accuse him of being responsible for the massive repression in Abu Salim prison in Tripoli in 1996 which caused the death of 1,200 prisoners.

As head of Libyan intelligence services, Senussi was wanted by the French authorities for his involvement in the bombing of the UTA flight over Niger in 1989 which caused the death of 170 air passengers. After the fall of the Qaddafi regime in August 2011, Senussi fled to Morocco, where he kept low profile. He was arrested in Mauritania, which extradited him in September 2012 to Libya, where he faces trial and possible execution.

MOROCCO

Hassan II

Born in Rabat on July 9, 1929, King Hassan II received religious and cultural education. He joined the royal Quranic School in 1934 and attended Bordeaux University, from which he graduated with a law degree in 1951.

He was present with his father Mohammed V during the historical meeting between Roosevelt and Churchill in Casablanca in 1943. He played an influential part in the independence document presented to the French authorities in 1944. Soon after independence, Hassan II became the general chief of the Royal Armed Forces and defense minister in 1960. The year after, his father died, and Hassan II became the 22nd king of the Alaouite state.

Hassan II established a constitutional monarchy and introduced several amendments to the constitution. He initiated negotiations with France, Spain, and the United States, enabling these foreign powers to have military bases on Moroccan territory. His most notable act was the invasion of Western Sahara in 1975.

He tried to modernize the national economy and increase the profitability of the agricultural sector which represents one of the most important pillars of the Moroccan economy. Hassan II, an openly pro-Western ruler, took part in the creation of several regional organizations, such as the African Union Organization (OAU), the Islamic Conference Organization, the Arab Maghreb Union, and the Commission of El Quds. As the "commander of the faithful," he sought to serve as a link between the West and the Muslim world. Because he wanted to promote a moderate, tolerant Islam, he financed the building of many mosques in Africa. This spiritual diplomacy had religious and political goals because Hassan II wanted to obtain support among African countries on the Western Sahara issue. He withdrew from the OAU in 1984 following the admission of the Sahrawi Arab Democratic Republic as a full member of the organization. Hassan II died on July 23, 1999.

Mohammed VI

Mohammed VI was born on August 21, 1963 in Rabat. He became the 23rd king of the Alaouite state. The Alaouites claim to be the descendants of Prophet Mohammed. Mohammed VI became king on July 30, 1999.

Mohammed VI studied at a Quranic School at an early age and later gained a law degree and doctorate from the University of Nice in 1993. He wrote his thesis on Morocco's relations with the European Union. As heir to the throne, Mohammed participated in many international conferences and events. His first official mission took place in April 1974, when he represented his father at French President Pompidou's funeral. In 1980, he undertook an African tour that led him to Senegal, Nigeria, and Cameroun. He was the head of the Moroccan delegation in several regional and international summits between 1983 and 1997. As amir el mouminin (commander of the faithful) he received the baiaa (allegiance) and led his first weekly prayer on July 30, 1999 the first day of his reign.

Driss Basri

Driss Basri was King Hassan II's all-powerful interior and information minister for more than 25 years. He died in exile in Paris at the age of 69 in 2007. Before his appointment as minister in 1974, Driss Basri was head of the department in charge of the surveillance of the Moroccan territory (intelligence services). As interior minister, Basri built up a large political network. In 1992, he was appointed state minister, a position that gave him more leverage to the extent that many in Morocco considered him to be as powerful as King Hassan II. When he succeeded his father, Mohammed VI fired Basri, thus putting an end to his 25-year career. Mohammed VI feared that Basri would overshadow his rule, and he brought on board his own trusted associates.

Saad-Eddine El Othmani

He was born on January 16, 1956 in Inzekan. He graduated with a doctorate in medicine in 1986 as well as in psychology in 1994 and Islamic studies in 1999. He practiced medicine and psychology in Barchid and Casablanca. He has several publications in fiqh (Islamic Jurisprudence). El Othmani was vice president of the parliament in 2010–2011 and has been president of the national council of the Justice and Development Party since 2008. He is a member of the General Congress of the Arab Parties and a member of the parliamentary commission which investigates developments in Al 'Ayoun, the capital of Western Sahara. He also served as vice president of the Parliamentary Commission for Foreign Affairs. He was appointed foreign minister following the November 2011 legislative election in which his party won the majority.

Abdelillah Benkirane

Prime minister since the victory of his party at the polls in November 2011, Abdelillah Benkirane was born in 1954 in Rabat. He is a physicist who taught in higher education. When he was a student, Benkirane joined the Islamic youth movement. He was editor in chief of several newspapers, such as Al Islah (reforms), Al Raya (flag), and Atadjdid (renewal). Abdelilah Benkirane was the leader of the Al Islah or Atadjidid movement, and he also serves as the general secretary of the Party for Justice and Development—a moderate, domesticated Islamist party.

Hosni Benslimane

Lieutenant General Hosni Benslimane was born on December 14, 1935 in El Jadida. He has been the commander of the Royal Moroccan Gendarmerie since 1974. In the aftermath of the independence of Morocco, Benslimane joined the Royal Armed Forces. He was appointed commander of the mobile intervention company (ICJ) in 1965. In 1967, he was appointed director general of national security. Between 1971 and 1972, Hosni Benslimane held the position of governor of Tangier and Kenitra. In the aftermath of the failed military coup against King Hassan II in 1972, he was promoted to commander of the Royal Moroccan Gendarmerie.

Abdelaziz Benani

The general inspector of the Moroccan Royal Armed Forces, Lieutenant General Abdelaziz Benani was born on December 3, 1939 in Taza. He is known as one of the principal architects of the desert war against the Polisario Front; this earned him the nickname "the fox of the desert" because he has waged the war against the Sahrawiis since its outbreak in 1976.

From 1976 to 1983, Colonel Benani was field commander of the royal forces located in occupied Western Sahara. After the assassination of General Dlimi in 1983, King Hassan II elevated Benani to the rank of general and appointed him as the commander of the southern military zone (Western Sahara).

Mohamed Yacine Mansouri

Born on April 2, 1962 in Rabat, Mohamed Yassine Mansouri completed his secondary education at the Collège Royal de Rabat. He holds a degree in law and two advanced diplomas in public law. Between 1987 and 1999, Mansouri worked at the Ministry of Information and the Interior Ministry. In 1992, King Hassan II sent him for a special training at the FBI in the United States.

In November 1999, he was appointed director of the official press agency Maghreb Arab Press (MAP), a function he held until his appointment in 2003 as Wali (governor), director general of internal affairs in the Interior Ministry. In 2005, King Mohammed VI appointed him director general of intelligence services.

TUNISIA

Zine el Abidin Ben Ali

He was born on September 3, 1936 at Hamam Sousse. He was president of Tunisia from November 7, 1987 to January 14, 2011. He became the second president of Tunisia after he overthrew Habib Bourguiba through a medical coup, while serving as prime minister. Ben Ali established a police, authoritarian state, one of the most repressive in the Arab world. Violations of human rights and censorship of the media were the main characteristics of Tunisia under his iron-fist rule.

Ben Ali was trained in the French military school of Saint Cyr, in the military school of intelligence and security in Baltimore, and in defense operations in the United States. This background allowed him to take control of the Tunisian intelligence services from 1977.

After a brief period of openness he cracked down on the popular Islamist party Ennahda, which he banned in 1989. Ben Ali instituted neoliberal policies; the system however was extremely corrupt and controlled by three families: the Trabelsis, Ben Iyads, and to a lesser extent the Ben Yeders. These families were interconnected and used state tools (violence, spying, nepotism, and clientelist networks) to increase and strengthen their business empires. All this came under the heavy-handed role of his second wife Leila Trabelsi.

In 2010–2011, protests and riots targeted the homes that belonged to the Trabelsi extended family. It was reported that Leila Ben Ali took 1.5 tons of gold bars (worth about $65 million) from the Central Bank of Tunisia (representing half of the Tunisian gold reserves) before fleeing the country when her husband abdicated on January 14, 2011. On June 20, 2011, Ben Ali and his wife were sentenced to 35 years in prison in absentia after being found guilty of theft and unlawful possession of cash and jewelry.

Moncef Marzouki

Moncef Ben Mohamed El Bedoui Marzouki was born on July 7, 1945. From 1981 to 2000, Marzouki taught medicine at the University of Sousse. In parallel, he was an active opponent of President Ben Ali before he was forced to exile in France. He returned to Tunisia on January 18, 2011. He published 16 books in Arabic and four in French, dealing with community medicine, medical ethics, human rights, and the problem of democratization in the Arab and Muslim countries. He began his struggle for human rights in 1980 in the Tunisian League for Human Rights (LTDH). In 1989 he was unanimously elected as president of the LTDH. However, on June 14, 1992, the corporation was dissolved under pressure of the regime which passed a restrictive law on associations. In 1994, he decided to run for the presidential election but failed to meet the required number of signatures to participate in the election. From 1989 to 1997, he was also a board member of the Arab Organization for Human Rights based in Cairo and an active member of the Tunisian section of Amnesty International. He was appointed chairman of the Committee of Arab Human Rights between 1996 and 2000 and spokesman for the National Council for Liberties in Tunisia, a position he held from 1998 to 2001. He was elected president in December 2011 by the members of the Constituent Assembly with 153 votes out of 217.

Kamel Morjane (also spelled Kemal Mourjan)

Born on May 9, 1948 in Hamam Sousse, Morjane was a politician and diplomat who served as Tunisia's defense minister from 2005 to 2010 and as minister of foreign affairs from 2010 to 2011. He holds a bachelor's degree in law and a diploma in public administration from the University of Tunis. He also studied international law at the Graduate Institute of International Studies in Geneva. He obtained a diploma in emergency management from the University of Wisconsin and a research certificate from The Hague Academy of International Law. He worked at the United Nations High Commission for Refugees (UNHCR) from 1977 to 1996; he served as director for South West Asia, North Africa, and the Middle East (1990–94), then as director for Africa (1994–96). He was appointed in October 1996 as permanent representative of Tunisia to the United Nations and International Organizations in Geneva. In November 1999 he was selected by the UN Secretary General as his special representative for the Congo (DRC); his main task was to build up the UN Peacekeeping Mission (MONUC).

He had to leave the DRC in September 2001 for family reasons and was offered the post of assistant high commissioner for refugees. Between August 17, 2005 and January 14, 2010 he served as defense minister of Tunisia. On January 14, 2010, he was appointed as minister of foreign affairs. After the ousting of Tunisian President Ben Ali, Morjane resigned from the coalition government on January 27, 2011. He created a new political party, Al Moubadara (The Initiative), on April 1, 2011.

Hamadi el Jebali

Born in October 1949 in Sousse, he graduated in renewable energies from a French university. Hamadi Jebali was appointed as head of the energy division in a consulting office in Tunis. After the trial that sentenced the main Ennahda leaders to jail, Jebali was elected as the new leader of the Islamist movement. In 1984, when Rashed Al Ghanouchi and other leaders were set free, Jebali became a member of the political office and played a leading role in the management of the crisis that led to the arrest of more than 7,000 members of the Ennahda movement. In 1991, a military court sentenced him to 17 years along with 30,000 Ennahda sympathizers who had been arrested by Ben Ali's police. In 2006, he was set free, but remained under house arrest. In March 2011, the militants of Ennahda chose him as secretary general of their movement. Six months later, President Moncef al Marzouki appointed him as the prime minister of Tunisia. He resigned in February 2013 due to disagreements with his own party.

Abdelkrim Zoubeidi

Zoubeidi was born in June 1950 in Mahdia. He is professor of medicine and held various positions, such as dean of the department of medicine, minister of health in 2001, and minister of technology and scientific research in 2002. Between 2002 and 2010, Zoubeidi was appointed to many positions, including dean of the faculty of medicine (2005–2008); he was also the CEO of the Errazi hospital and president of the scientific council of the technological center in Sousse. In January, 2011, Zoubeidi was appointed defense minister in the Tunisian government.

Defense and Security in the Maghreb Constitutions

(EXTRACTS FROM THE MAGHREB COUNTRIES' CONSTITUTIONS)

Morocco: 2011 Constitution

Article 53

The king is the supreme head of the Royal Armed Forces. He appoints to the military offices (*emplois*) and can delegate this right.

Article 54

A *Conseil supérieur de sécurité* (Higher Security Council) is created as the instance of *consulation* concerning the strategies of internal and external security of the country, and of management of crisis situations, which also ensures the institutionalization of the norms of a good security governance.

The king presides over this council and can delegate to the head of government the presidency of a meeting of the council, on the basis of a specific agenda.

The Higher Security Council is composed of, other than the head of government, the president of the Chamber of Representatives, of the president of the Chamber of Councilors, the president-delegate of the Superior Council of the Judicial Power, the ministers responsible for (*chargés*) the interior, of foreign affairs, of justice, and the administration of national defense, as well as those responsible (persons) of the administrations competent in security matters, of the superior officers of the Royal Armed Forces and any other prominent person whose presence is useful to the work of the said Council.

The internal regulations of the council establish the rules of its organization and of its functioning.

Algeria: 1996 Constitution (Amended in 2008)

Article 77

In addition to the powers bestowed, explicitly, upon him by other provisions of the Constitution, the president of the republic has the following powers and prerogatives:

- He is Commander-in-Chief of all the Armed Forces of the Republic;
- He is responsible for National Defense;
- He has power to define and conduct the foreign policy of the Nation;
- He has power to grant pardons, remission or commutation of sentence;
- He may, on any matter of national importance, refer to the people by referendum;
- He has power to conclude and ratify international treaties;

Article 78

—The president of the republic appoints: to posts and mandates provided by the Constitution:

- to state civil and military posts;
- to nominations decided in the cabinet;
- the magistrates;
- high officials of security bodies;
- the "walis" (heads of regions).

Tunisia: 1959 Constitution (under Revision in 2012)

Article 44

The president of the republic is the Commander-in-Chief of the Armed Forces.

Article 46

Should imminent peril menace the institutions of the Republic, threaten the security and independence of the country and obstruct the proper functioning of the public powers, the President of the Republic may take the exceptional measures necessitated by the circumstances, after consulting the Prime Minister, the President of the Chamber of Deputies and the President of the Chamber of Advisors.

He addresses, to that effect, a message to the people.

During this period, the President of the Republic may not dissolve the Chamber of Deputies, and no motion of censure may be presented against the Government.

These measures cease to bear effect as soon as the circumstances that produced them come to an end.

Article 47

The president of the republic may submit to a referendum any bill that is of national importance and any questions that concern the country's vital interests, provided these bills and questions do not go against the Constitution.

Article 48

The president of the republic concludes treaties.
He declares war and concludes peace, with the approval of the Chamber of Deputies.
He has the power to exercise the right of pardon.

Article 49

The president of the republic directs the general policy of the state, defines its basic options and informs the Chamber of Deputies accordingly.

Article 55

The president of the republic appoints high civilian and military officials, on the recommendation of the government.

The president of the republic may delegate to the prime minister the power of appointment for some of these positions.

Libya

The Libyan Republic does not have a constitution yet. The 1951 Constitution had been annulled and replaced in 1969 with a provisional constitution when Qaddafi seized power. In 2007, the liberals within the regime under the leadership of Saif el Islam Qaddafi signaled that they were about to elaborate a new constitution, but this was shelved in 2009 due to domestic disputes between liberals and conservatives. The constitutional assembly elected in July 2012 has the task of crafting one.

1969 Constitution

Article 18 (Revolutionary Command Council)

The Revolutionary Command Council constitutes the supreme authority in the Libyan Arab Republic. It will exercise the powers attached to national sovereignty, promulgate laws and decrees, decide in the name of the people the general policy of the state, and make all decisions it deems necessary for the protection of the Revolution and the regime.

Article 23 (War)

The Revolutionary Command Council shall declare war, conclude, and ratify treaties and agreements, unless it authorizes the Council of Ministers to do so.

Article 24 (Martial Law)

The Revolutionary Command Council shall make decisions concerning martial law or the state of emergency whenever there is a threat to the internal or external security of the state and whenever the Revolutionary Command Council deems it necessary for the protection and defense of the Revolution.

Article 25 (Emergency)

The Revolutionary Command Council shall make decisions concerning martial law or the state of emergency whenever there is a threat to the internal or external security of the state and whenever the Revolutionary Command Council deems it necessary for the protection and defense of the Revolution.

Article 26 (Armed Forces)

The state alone is empowered to establish the armed forces who shall protect the people and insure the security of the country, its republican system, and national unity.

APPENDIX C

Maghreb Armed Forces: Military Balance (2010)

Total Manpower in North African Military Forces

	Morocco	Algeria	Libya	Tunisia
Total Active Regular	195,800	147,000	76,000	35,800
Paramilitary	50,000	187,200	0	12,000
Reserve	150,000	150,000	40,000	0

Source: Anthony H. Cordesman, Arleigh A. Burke, Aram Nerguizian, "The North African Military Balance. Force Developments & Regional Challenges," *Center For Strategic and International Studies,* 2010, 52.

Total Regular Military Manpower in North African Forces by Service

	Morocco	Algeria	Libya	Tunisia
Active Army	175,000	127,000	50,000	27,000
Paramilitary	50,000	187,200	0	12,000
Navy	7,800	6,000	8,000	4,800
Air Force	13,000	14,000	18,000	4,000

Source: Anthony H. Cordesman, Arleigh A. Burke, Aram Nerguizian, "The North African Military Balance. Force Developments & Regional Challenges", *Center For Strategic and International Studies,* 2010, 53.

Comparative Naval Strength

	Morocco	Algeria	Libya	Tunisia
Mine			4	
Other Ocean and Coastal Patrol	23	11	4	13
Missile Patrol	4	9	14	12
Other Corvettes				
Guided Missile Corvettes		6	1	
Other Frigates				
Guided Missile Frigates	3	3	2	
Destroyers				
Submarines		2	2	

Source: Anthony H. Cordesman, Arleigh A. Burke, Aram Nerguizian, "The North African Military Balance. Force Developments & Regional Challenges," *Center For Strategic and International Studies*, 2010, 79.

APPENDIX D

Defense Budgets

Military and Defense Statistics

	Expenditures Billion $			% Governmental Expenditures			% GDP	
	2010	2011	2012	2010	2011	2012	2010	2011
Algeria	5.6	8.6	8.8	14	15	15	3.6	3.9
Morocco	3.1	3.3	5.5	12.3	12.8	13.3	3.5	3.55
Libya	1.1 (2008)	1.5		1.2 (2008)			1.17	1.2
Tunisia	0.5	0.6		4.3	4.2		1.4	1.1

Sources: Sipri: http://milexdata.sipri.org/
Perspective Monde, University of Sherbrook: http://perspective.usherbrooke.ca/bilan/BMEncyclopedie/
BMEncycloListePays.jsp.
Law of finance (Algeria and Morocco):
http://www.globalfirepower.com/country-military-strength-detail.asp?country_id=Libya.
http://www.globalfirepower.com/countries-listing.asp.

APPENDIX E

Demographics

Algeria Demographic Profile, 1950–2050

Indicator	1950	1955	1960	1965	1970	1975	1980	1985	1990	1995	2000	2005	2010	2015	2020	2025	2030	2035	2040	2045	2050
Rural population (thousands)	6,809	7,175	7,505	7,435	8,316	9,558	10,620	11,498	12,114	12,437	12,260	12,050	11,868	11,679	11,436	11,104	10,630	10,067	9,459	8,833	8,185
Urban population (thousands)	1,944	2,540	3,295	4,488	5,430	6,460	8,191	10,600	13,168	15,828	18,246	20,804	23,555	26,409	29,194	31,779	34,097	36,189	38,111	39,888	41,425
Percentage urban (%)	22.2	26.1	30.5	37.6	39.5	40.3	43.5	48.0	52.1	56.0	59.8	63.3	66.5	69.3	71.9	74.1	76.2	78.2	80.1	81.9	83.5

Indicator	1950–1955	1955–1960	1960–1965	1965–1970	1970–1975	1975–1980	1980–1985	1985–1990	1990–1995	1995–2000	2000–2005	2005–2010	2010–2015	2015–2020	2020–2025	2025–2030	2030–2035	2035–2040	2040–2045	2045–2050
Rural annual growth rate (%)	1.05	0.90	-0.19	2.24	2.78	2.11	1.59	1.04	0.53	-0.29	-0.35	-0.31	-0.32	-0.42	-0.59	-0.87	-1.09	-1.25	-1.37	-1.52
Urban annual growth rate (%)	5.35	5.20	6.18	3.81	3.48	4.75	5.16	4.34	3.68	2.84	2.62	2.48	2.29	2.01	1.70	1.41	1.19	1.03	0.91	0.76

Libya Demographic Profile, 1950–2050

Indicator	1950	1955	1960	1965	1970	1975	1980	1985	1990	1995	2000	2005	2010	2015	2020	2025	2030	2035	2040	2045	2050
Rural population (thousands)	828	865	980	1,077	1,004	918	916	945	1,060	1,160	1,263	1,362	1,447	1,504	1,517	1,497	1,459	1,414	1,367	1,315	1,254
Urban population (thousands)	201	261	369	546	990	1,548	2,147	2,905	3,305	3,674	4,083	4,561	5,098	5,654	6,181	6,647	7,060	7,458	7,860	8,240	8,565
Percentage urban (%)	19.5	23.2	27.3	33.7	49.7	62.8	70.1	75.5	75.7	76.0	76.4	77.0	77.9	79.0	80.3	81.6	82.9	84.1	85.2	86.2	87.2

Morocco Demographic Profile, 1950–2050

Indicator	1950–1955	1955–1960	1960–1965	1965–1970	1970–1975	1975–1980	1980–1985	1985–1990	1990–1995	1995–2000	2000–2005	2005–2010	2010–2015	2015–2020	2020–2025	2025–2030	2030–2035	2035–2040	2040–2045	2045–2050
Rural annual growth rate (%)	0.87	2.51	1.87	-1.40	-1.79	-0.04	0.63	2.29	1.82	1.70	1.50	1.22	0.76	0.18	-0.27	-0.52	-0.62	-0.67	-0.78	-0.95
Urban annual growth rate (%)	5.24	6.88	7.87	11.90	8.94	6.54	6.05	2.58	2.12	2.11	2.21	2.23	2.07	1.78	1.45	1.21	1.10	1.05	0.94	0.77

Indicator	1950	1955	1960	1965	1970	1975	1980	1985	1990	1995	2000	2005	2010	2015	2020	2025	2030	2035	2040	2045	2050
Rural population (thousands)	6,609	7,322	8,213	9,078	10,032	10,779	11,503	12,314	12,803	13,019	13,452	13,660	13,523	13,332	13,042	12,630	12,102	11,484	10,802	10,087	9,348
Urban population (thousands)	2,344	2,811	3,413	4,245	5,278	6,526	8,064	9,985	12,005	13,931	15,375	16,835	18,859	20,999	23,158	25,235	27,157	28,913	30,512	31,965	33,234
Percentage urban (%)	26.2	27.7	29.4	31.9	34.5	37.7	41.2	44.8	48.4	51.7	53.3	55.2	58.2	61.2	64.0	66.6	69.2	71.6	73.9	76.0	78.0

Indicator	1950–1955	1955–1960	1960–1965	1965–1970	1970–1975	1975–1980	1980–1985	1985–1990	1990–1995	1995–2000	2000–2005	2005–2010	2010–2015	2015–2020	2020–2025	2025–2030	2030–2035	2035–2040	2040–2045	2045–2050
Rural annual growth rate (%)	2.05	2.30	2.00	2.00	1.44	1.30	1.36	0.78	0.33	0.65	0.31	-0.20	-0.28	-0.44	-0.64	-0.85	-1.05	-1.22	-1.37	-1.52
Urban annual growth rate (%)	3.63	3.88	4.36	4.36	4.24	4.23	4.28	3.68	2.98	1.97	1.81	2.27	2.15	1.96	1.72	1.47	1.25	1.08	0.93	0.78

Tunisia Demographic Profile, 1950–2050

Indicator	1950	1955	1960	1965	1970	1975	1980	1985	1990	1995	2000	2005	2010	2015	2020	2025	2030	2035	2040	2045	2050
Rural population (thousands)	2,390	2,500	2,637	2,791	2,898	2,970	3,192	3,384	3,455	3,442	3,456	3,423	3,394	3,347	3,270	3,161	3,012	2,840	2,657	2,472	2,284
Urban population (thousands)	1,140	1,360	1,583	1,839	2,229	2,697	3,265	3,947	4,760	5,493	5,996	6,455	6,980	7,537	8,096	8,636	9,115	9,524	9,877	10,181	10,427
Percentage urban (%)	32.3	35.2	37.5	39.7	43.5	47.6	50.6	53.8	57.9	61.5	63.4	65.3	67.3	69.2	71.2	73.2	75.2	77.0	78.8	80.5	82.0

Indicator	1950–1955	1955–1960	1960–1965	1965–1970	1970–1975	1975–1980	1980–1985	1985–1990	1990–1995	1995–2000	2000–2005	2005–2010	2010–2015	2015–2020	2020–2025	2025–2030	2030–2035	2035–2040	2040–2045	2045–2050
Rural annual growth rate (%)	0.90	1.07	1.13	0.75	0.50	1.44	1.17	0.42	-0.07	0.08	-0.19	-0.17	-0.28	-0.46	-0.68	-0.97	-1.18	-1.33	-1.45	-1.58
Urban annual growth rate (%)	3.54	3.03	3.00	3.85	3.81	3.82	3.79	3.75	2.86	1.75	1.48	1.56	1.54	1.43	1.29	1.08	0.88	0.73	0.61	0.48

Source: United Nations, Department of Economic and Social Affairs, Population Division, Population Estimates and Projections Section, http://esa.un.org/unpd/wup/unup/index_panel3.html.

APPENDIX F

Treaty Instituting the Arab Maghreb Union

No. 26844

Morocco, Algeria, Libyan Arab Jamahiriya, Mauritania and Tunisia

Treaty instituting the Arab Maghreb Union (with declaration). Concluded at Marrakesh on 17 February 1989.

Authentic text: Arabic. Registered by Morocco on 29 September 1989.

Maroc, Algérie, Jamahiriya Arabe Libyenne, Mauritanie et Tunisie

Traité instituant l'Union du Maghreb arabe (avec déclara tion). Conclu à Marrakech le 17 février 1989.

Texte authentique: arabe. Enregistré par le Maroc le 29 septembre 1989.

Vol. 1546, 1-26844 1989_____United Nations — Treaty Series » Nations Unies — Recueil des Traités_____161 (Translation 1 Traduction 2)

In the name of God, the Clement, the Merciful

Treaty instituting the Arab Maghreb Union

His Majesty Hassan II, King of the Kingdom of Morocco,

His Excellency Zein El Abidin Ben Ali, President of the Republic of Tunisia,

His Excellency Shadli Ben Jedid, President of the People's Democratic Republic of Algeria,

The leader of the Great first of September Revolution,

Colonel Muammar Kaddafi, the Great Arab People's Socialist Libyan Jamahiriya, and His Excellency Colonel Muawiya Uld Sidi Ahmed Tayea, Chairman of the Military Committee for National Salvation and Head of State of the Islamic Republic of Mauritania, having faith in the strong ties based on common history, religion and language that unite the peoples of the Arab Maghreb, in response to the deep and firm aspirations of these peoples and their leaders to establish a Union that would reinforce the existing relations and provide them with the appropriate ways and means to gradually proceed toward achieving a more comprehensive integration among themselves, conscious that this integration will have effects that will enable the Arab Maghreb Union to acquire a specific weight allowing it to make an effective contribution to world balance, to the consolidation of peaceful relations within the international community, and to the establishment of security and stability in the world, aware that the institution of the Arab Maghreb Union requires tangible achievements and the setting up of common rules embodying the effective solidarity among its components and ensuring their economic and social development, expressing their sincere determination to make the Arab Maghreb Union a means for the construction of total Arab unity and a starting point for a wider union comprising other Arab and African countries, have agreed on the following:

ARTICLE ONE

By virtue of this treaty, a Union, to be called the "Arab Maghreb Union," is hereby instituted.

1   Translation supplied by the Government of Morocco.

2   Traduction fournie par le Gouvernement marocain.

3   Came into force on 1 July 1989, the date agreed upon by the Parties at a meeting held at Rabat on 30 June 1989 at which was recorded the completion of the ratification procedures provided for in article 19:

   State

   Algeria

   Libyan Arab Jamahiriya

   Mauritania

   Morocco

   Tunisia

ARTICLE TWO

The Union aims at:

Strengthening the ties of brotherhood which link the member states and their peoples to one another; Achieving progress and prosperity of their societies and defending their rights; Contributing to the preservation of peace based on justice and equity; Pursuing a common policy in different domains; and Working gradually towards achieving free movement of persons and transfer of services, goods and capital among them.

ARTICLE THREE

The common policy referred to in the previous article aims at reaching the following goals: In the international field: to achieve concord among the member states and establish between them a close diplomatic cooperation based on dialogue;

In the field of defence: to preserve the independence of each of the member states;

In the economic field: to achieve industrial, agricultural, commercial and social development of member states and take the necessary measures for this purpose particularly by setting up joint ventures and working out general and specific programmes in this respect;

In the cultural field: to establish a cooperation aimed at promoting education on its various levels, at safeguarding the spiritual and moral values emanating from the tolerant teachings of Islam, and at preserving the Arab national identity, and to take the necessary measures to attain these goals, particularly by exchanging teachers and students and creating joint university and cultural institutions as well as joint institutions specialized in research.

ARTICLE FOUR

The Union shall have a Presidential Council composed of the heads of state of the member states and constituting the supreme authority of the Union. The chairmanship of the Council shall be for a period of six months in rotation among the heads of state of the member states.

ARTICLE FIVE

The Presidential Council of the Union shall hold its ordinary sessions every six months; it may hold extraordinary sessions whenever deemed necessary.

ARTICLE SIX

Only the Presidential Council shall have the authority to take decisions, and its decisions shall be taken unanimously.

ARTICLE SEVEN

The prime ministers of the member states, or their homologues, may meet whenever deemed necessary.

ARTICLE EIGHT

The Union shall have a Council of Foreign Ministers which shall prepare the sessions of the Presidential Council and look into the points submitted by the follow-up committee and the specialized ministerial committees.

Vol. 1546, 1-26844 1989_____United Nations — Treaty Series » Nations Unies — Recueil des Traités_____163

ARTICLE NINE

Each state shall appoint a member of its ministerial Council, or general popular committee, to be in charge of union affairs; these appointees shall form a committee for the follow-up of the affairs of the Union and shall submit the results of their proceedings to the Council of Foreign Ministers.

ARTICLE TEN

The Union shall have specialized ministerial committees set up by the Presidential Council which shall determine their tasks.

ARTICLE ELEVEN

The Union shall have a general secretariat composed of one representative for each member state; the general secretariat shall exercise its functions in the country presiding over the session of the Presidential Council under the supervision of the chairman of the session whose country shall cover the expenses involved.

ARTICLE TWELVE

The Union shall have a consultative Council comprising ten members for each state, to be chosen by the legislative bodies of the member states or according to the internal system of each State.

The consultative Council shall hold an ordinary session every year as well as extraordinary sessions at the request of the Presidential Council.

The consultative Council shall advise on all draft decisions handed over to it by the Presidential Council, as it may submit to the Presidential Council any recommendations it might consider likely to strengthen the action of the Union and achieve its goals.

The consultative Council shall elaborate its rules of procedure and submit them to the Presidential Council for approval.

ARTICLE THIRTEEN

The Union shall have a Judicial Organ, composed of two judges for each state to be appointed by the state concerned for a six-year period, and renewed by half every three years. The Judicial Organ shall elect a chairman from its members for a one-year period.

The Judicial Organ shall specialize in examining conflicts related to the interpretation and implementation of the treaty and the agreements concluded within the framework of the Union and submitted by the Presidential Council or any of the States parties to the conflict or as provided for by the Statutes of the Judicial Organ, the verdicts of which shall be binding and final.

Likewise, the Judicial Organ shall give advisory opinions on legal questions laid before it by the Presidential Council.

The Judicial Organ shall elaborate its statutes and submit them to the Presidential Council for ratification. The statutes shall constitute an integral part of the treaty.

The Presidential Council shall determine the seat of the Judicial Organ and its budget.

Vol. 1546, 1-26844 164 United Nations—Treaty Series » Nations Unies—Recueil des Traités 1989

ARTICLE FOURTEEN

Any aggression directed against one of the member states shall be considered as an aggression against the other member states.

ARTICLE FIFTEEN

Member states pledge not to permit on their territory any activity or organization liable to threaten the security, the territorial integrity, or the political system of any of them.

They also pledge to abstain from joining any alliance or military or political bloc directed against the political independence or territorial integrity of the other member states.

ARTICLE SIXTEEN

Member states are free to conclude any agreements between them or with other states or groups provided these agreements do not run counter to the provisions of this treaty.

ARTICLE SEVENTEEN

Other states belonging to the Arab Nation or the African community may join this treaty if member states give their approval.

ARTICLE EIGHTEEN

Provisions of this treaty may be amended upon the proposal of one of the member states, and such amendment becomes effective after its ratification by all member states.

ARTICLE NINETEEN

This treaty goes into effect after its ratification by the member states according to procedures in force in each member state. Member states are committed to take the necessary measures to this end within a maximum period of six months from the date of signature of this treaty. Done in the city of Marrakesh on the blessed day of Friday the tenth of Rajab1409 of the Hegira (1398 of the Death of the Prophet), corresponding to 17 February (Nuar) 1989.

DONE in the city of Marrakesh on the blessed day of Friday, the tenth of Rajab 1409 of the Hegira, corresponding to 17 February 1989.

For the Kingdom For the Republic of Morocco: of Tunisia: HASSAN II ZEIN EL ABIDIN BEN ALI

For the Popular Democratic For the Great Arab People's Republic of Algeria: Socialist Libyan Jamahiriya:

CHADLI BEN JEDID MUAMMAR KADDAFI

The President of the Islamic Republic of Mauritania: MUAWIYA ULD SIDI AHMED TAYEA

http://www.oapi.wipo.net/wipolex/fr/treaties/text.jsp?file_id=201318

Index

About the Authors

YAHIA H. ZOUBIR is professor of international studies and international management and director of research in geopolitics at Euromed Management, Marseille School of Management, France. He is the editor and main contributor of *North Africa in Transition-State, Society & Economic Transformation in the 1990s* (University Press of Florida, 1999). He is coeditor of *L'Islamisme Politique dans les Rapports entre l'Europe et le Maghreb* (Lisbon, Friedrich Ebert Stiftung, 1996). Also, he is coeditor and main contributor of *International Dimensions of the Western Sahara Conflict* (Praeger Publisher, 1993). His latest works include the following: *North Africa: Politics, Region, and the Limits of Transformation*, co-edited with Haizam Amirah-Fernández (2008); "The End of the Libya Dictatorship: The Uncertain Transition" *Third World Quarterly* (2012); "Algeria's Path to Political Reforms: Authentic Change?" *Middle East Policy* (2012); "Algeria and Russia: Reconciling Contrasting Interests," *The Maghreb Review* (Sept. 2011); "The United States and Libya: The Limits of Coercive Diplomacy," *Journal of North African Studies* (2011); "The Sahara-Sahel Quagmire: Regional and International Implications," *Mediterranean Politics*, Vol. 17, No. 3, (2012); and "Tilting the Balance toward Intra-Maghreb Unity in Light of the Arab Spring," *International Spectator* (2012).

LOUISA DRIS-AÏT-HAMADOUCHE is senior lecturer at the University of Political and Information Sciences, Algiers 3. She has published numerous articles about the Maghreb and western Mediterranean security in various international academic journals. Her publications include the following: "The Maghreb: Social, Political, and Economic Developments," *Perspectives on Global Development and Technology* (2007); "The 2007 Legislative Elections in Algeria: Political Reckonings," *Mediterranean Politics* (2007). Her other publications on political Islam, U.S. policy, and European security issues have appeared in *Confluences Méditerranée* (2012), *Maghreb Review* (2006), *Maghreb-Machrek* (2010), *L'Année du Maghreb* (2010), *Cahiers du Cread* (2009), *Journal of Contemporary European Studies* (2009), as well as numerous chapters in edited volumes.